SOLVING YOUR FINANCIAL PUZZLE

Making Ends Meet
Plus More

by John M. Orth

**Financial
Solutions
Ltd.**

Cover by Joshua Koza, Claudia Previn, and John Orth
Illustrations by Joshua Koza
Edited by Gloria Frender

Library of Congress Catalog Card Number:
96-92828

ISBN 0-9655379-0-0

PRINTED BY JOHNSON PRINTING, INC.
Boulder, Colorado

Acknowledgements and formal notices of copyright for all material under copyright appear on page 371, which is hereby made an extension of the copyright page.

Dedicated to My Father
Milton J. Orth, deceased
And
My Mother,
Helen D. Orth, residing
in Iowa City, Iowa

ACKNOWLEDGMENTS

As author of this book, I want to acknowledge the following individuals for contributing in their own unique ways to its content, organization, and publication:

My parents, Milton and Helen Orth of Iowa City, Iowa, for instilling within me the philosophy of managing my financial resources wisely and effectively.

Gloria Frender, of Boulder, Colorado, educational consultant and author for her consistent and persuasive encouragement for the writing of this book, as well as for her dedication in helping me throughout the writing with refreshing ideas, timely comments, and countless editing recommendations.

Joshua A. Koza, of Iowa City, Iowa, for his appropriate graphics throughout the book and his skill in co-designing the cover.

Mark Eads, Founder and President of CFS, Center of Financial Services, a consumer credit counseling center of Cedar Rapids, Iowa. I appreciate his valuable time helping me learn and thoroughly understand what I believe is the most innovative and effective eight-step program taken in helping people to become debt free.

Michael Cavitt, President of Cavitt Asset Management, Inc. of Iowa City, Iowa, for writing the foreword for this book.

James C. Nemmers, Copyright Attorney with Shuttleworth & Ingersoll, of Cedar Rapids, Iowa, for his timely advice and assistance in obtaining the documents necessary for publishing this book.

Walter B. Kehn, Division Manager of Waddell & Reed, Inc., of Boulder, Colorado, for his unlimited hours, extended efforts, and constant encouragement. He assisted me greatly during my many years as a registered representative of this firm.

My loyal clients and personal friends for providing me with continued encouragement, ideas, and valuable insights while I was taking on a project of such magnitude and intensity.

I am grateful for all of your assistance and advice in completing this book.

FOREWORD

I have learned many things in seventeen years in the financial field. One aspect is that each person looks at financial matters a little differently than the next. This situation is the reason for so many different types of books on financial planning, investments, cash management, etc.

John Orth has, with this book and its worksheets, created a sound resource of working materials to help individuals take better control of their financial futures. It will meet the needs of a diverse group of individuals because of the many different tools available.

Think about this book as a tool box. Choose the job you need to do or the problem you need to solve. Browse through the book and the worksheets to find a tool which will help you move ahead with the job or solve your particular problem.

This is not to say that you shouldn't take an organized approach to your finances. If you haven't done any financial planning, start at the beginning of the book and work your way through using the worksheet(s) which best fit you.

Remember, you only have three choices with your money: (1) you can make a part time job or hobby of managing it, (2) you can hire a professional to manage it, or (3) you can lose it. Most financially successful people do a combination of the first two.

J. Michael Cavitt, CFP
President, Cavitt Asset Management, Inc.
Iowa City, Iowa

PREFACE

Each of us has the desire to become financially successful in our lifetime. We learn about the importance of having money at a very early age. Teenagers earn money to buy or support a car, pay for college, or for extra cash. Most of our educational experience has been geared to learning ways and opportunities for earning money. This is especially true in vocational schools, high schools, junior colleges and universities today. In graduate school, we learn specialties in various professions to enhance our earning capabilities. On the other hand, in the educational process, from junior high school through graduate school and beyond, we are taught very little about wisely and efficiently managing the resources we earn from our professions and employment. Is it any wonder why so many of us don't know where to begin with the financial planning basics? If we don't learn it at home, the chances of not learning it at all are fairly high.

It was from the need to increase financial awareness, set priorities, and make wise financial decisions that led to writing this book. An organized financial program will enable you to become better prepared to make knowledgeable monetary decisions. For persons satisfied with their current financial situation, this book provides ideas that will:

- reinforce and reassure your positive aspects of personal money management.
- streamline and better organize what you're already doing.
- enhance your current system to be more efficient and effective.

Many people constantly get caught in the dilemma of attempting to finance specific needs and find ways to pay for their desires and dreams as well. If you find yourself in this predicament, it may become necessary to carefully assess your current indebtedness. Obviously, the money supply is not sufficient to fund each of these areas. Somewhere along the line it is necessary to make some choices and priorities. To be financially successful, it is critical that you examine your current life style along with your present financial situation.

By applying some of the techniques and principals presented in this book, you will find that you really do have sufficient money to accelerate a credit card or automobile loan payment. You will also be able to:

- organize monthly bills and important documents.
- track your income and expenses in an easier and more effective way.
- monitor your monthly cash flow that could easily save you between 5 - 15% of your net income.

- accumulate funds for your retirement income, a child's education fund, or a luxurious vacation.

- review your current status and know how to begin an effective money management plan.

- recognize and set your own priorities for spending and saving money.

READ ME FIRST
TIPS FOR USING THIS BOOK

There are several ways to effectively use this book. You can start at the beginning and do each of the exercises in chronological order or you may decide to work on two chapters at the same time. Two or three chapters might demand your immediate attention. This book is designed as an active hands-on workbook approach to the planning and management of your financial resources. Vital methods of filing credit card statements, collecting cash receipts, charting investments, and balancing a checkbook are just a few of the strategies thoroughly covered in **Solving Your Financial Puzzle**.

All chapters are organized the same. A general table of contents at the beginning of the book, as well as individual chapter tables of contents are included to help you locate materials quickly and easily. The third page of each chapter focuses on ten specific points or concepts that are emphasized in that chapter. Whenever an example or illustration is presented, the appropriate worksheet(s) and/or table(s) will be referenced in Appendices C and D located in the back of the book. This allows you to complete your individual application while following a step-by-step procedure. Summaries of the material discussed, called Action Steps, close each section. It is recommended that you complete each of the steps by placing a "✔" in each "❏" before going on to the next unit or chapter.

Each chapter ends with a list of tasks or objectives that you will have accomplished in the "You Should Now Be Able To" section. You may even want to create a "to do" list of your own. A brief "Concluding Remarks" section closes each chapter.

Each worksheet in Appendix C, provided on pages 227 - 348, is meant to be duplicated when used. You may want to compile your own financial planning notebook by making copies of necessary worksheets and arranging them in a three ring binder with dividers to separate different sections of your notebook. In this way, it will be a simple task to insert additional worksheets as they are needed.

| General Formulas | are highlighted throughout the book in this manner. They will help you to readily identify calculations to be performed. |

An *italic font* will be used throughout the book to denote either the name of a row or the heading of a column when referring to a chart, table, or worksheet. The name of the individual chart, table, or worksheet will have the first letter of each word capitalized. An example would be ". . . the *Current Budget (Dollars)* column of the Budget Planning Worksheet . . ." as illustrated in the second paragraph on page 74.

OVERVIEW

You begin the financial planning process evaluation in Chapter 1 by first determining your life values; then prioritize and confirm those that are most important to you. Are any of them related to money or your current financial status? Setting realistic monetary goals that match your life values and priorities is a critical step in achieving financial objectives. Practical applications illustrate the importance of the goal setting process.

It has been said that those who accumulate considerable wealth during their lifetime have also been excellent record keepers. Chapter 2 offers numerous ideas for creating a personal system to effectively manage your financial assets and liabilities, as well as to efficiently organize records and documents. The system can be readily implemented and takes little time to maintain. A Records and Documents Chart gives guidelines regarding appropriate locations to place various types of information, together with the length of time this information should be kept. Examples are given to illustrate how the variety of forms can be useful to accomplish your specific objectives and tasks so that you, too, can become an outstanding "record keeper."

Chapter 3 introduces key documents essential to the effective management of your financial resources: the Networth Statement and the Cash-Flow Statement. The first document is necessary to evaluate your financial wellness; the second, more commonly known as a household budget, is vital to the management of your monthly income. Suggestions are provided for preparing a simple budget, along with ideas for selecting basic categories. Step-by-step procedures guide you through the various stages that ultimately lead to the desired goal: implementation of a realistic and workable spending plan.

Once a budget has been committed to writing, it needs to be kept as simple as possible, yet realistic, otherwise the chances of it being implemented are very low. Chapter 4 suggests ways to organize your financial notebook from the check book register to each of the appropriate account summaries used in your budget. Posting procedures for each of the forms are clearly explained, as well as illustrated with examples. The chapter concludes with suggested ways to avoid the most common financial stumbling blocks and those unforeseen expenses that will literally destroy even the best of budgets.

The use of credit is as common to the American way of life as ice cream and apple pie. Every day people apply for and receive credit cards; yet, what guidelines if any, are used to select them? Do people choose the credit card that best meets their needs? What are a cardholder's responsibilities? What is revolving credit? Is there a way to know when to quit using a credit card before it's too late? Chapter 5 addresses these very issues and concerns and many others as well. It is imperative that individuals and families understand their limits when using credit. Persons who "just get by" each month using revolving credit will greatly diminish their chances for achieving financial independence during their lifetime.

Occasionally a family will find that they are over their heads in debt. How do they "dig" themselves out? It is almost certain that they didn't get into financial bondage over night, or possibly, even in a year. The only realistic way to become financially free is through a total elimination of debt. Warning signs such as bouncing checks or running out of money before pay day may catch most peoples' attention. Chapter 6 illustrates ways to identify financial problems, then suggests practical ways to solve them. Valuable ideas for contacting creditors, overcoming obstacles, and revising payment schedules are included in this chapter.

Chapter 7 is a case study involving a young married couple whose lack of restraint in the management of their finances eventually causes severe marital problems. When this couple realizes they are not equipped to handle the situation themselves, they seek the immediate help of a financial counselor. Under the counselor's perceptive guidance and wisdom, the couple is finally able to acquire the self discipline necessary to adapt to the budget of their existing income, rather than living without any plan. The ideas and strategies used by their financial counselor are many that successful consumer credit counselors apply today for individuals and couples of all ages in an effort to get them back on their feet financially.

APPENDICES

The Needs Analysis Appendix is inserted to allow you a way to plan for future events, all of which are crucial to nearly everyone's life. Three such events are planning for adequate life insurance protection, funding a child's education, and having sufficient income or assets on which to retire within your means. The needs analyses in Appendix A presents a realistic method to calculate the required amounts for each of these situations. It is necessary, however, that accurate data be used to achieve reasonable results.

Frequently, people possessing several credit cards may wonder which card, or cards, is a "better deal" for them. It is entirely possible in comparing two credit cards, that the card with a slightly higher interest rate, may have a significantly lower monthly finance charge. The reason for the difference can be found in the way each card issuer computes the average daily balance, commonly known as the ADB method. Appendix B is provided for anyone who is curious, in addition to having time and patience, to learn how various finance charges are computed. It is not necessary to comprehend this material to appreciate or understand the appropriate use of credit cards. It is important, however, to know what method of calculating the average daily balance is used by each of your card issuers to determine your finance charges, especially if you carry a large monthly balance. See Figure 144 on page 221. The purpose of this material is to compare four common ways used by major bank card issuers for arriving at monthly balances by illustrating how calculations are made over a three month period of making regular purchases and timely payments.

Appendices C and D of this book are extremely useful, containing in excess of 100 perforated, ready-to-use forms and three tables to assist you with your financial planning and record keeping endeavors. The majority of the forms are used in various applications and/or examples presented in the first seven chapters. It is not intended, nor suggested, that you use every form in this section; simply copy and use only those which meet the specific needs and objectives of your current individual or family situation. You may even want to modify or completely revise some forms to meet your particular situation. In any event, it is my hope that you greatly profit from their use.

The glossary in Appendix F contains approximately 150 useful financial and estate planning words and phrases. Understanding these terms will enable you to become more informed with planning and preparing your own financial affairs.

TABLE OF CONTENTS

★ Chapter 3 - Preparing Financial Documents

★ Chapter 6 - Overcoming Financial Bondage

★ Chapter 7 - A Real Life Situation

★ Appendix A

★ Appendix B

★ Appendix C

★ Appendix D

★ Appendix E

★ Appendix F

★ Appendix G

★ Acknowledgements

★ Order Forms

A

POINT

"There is no dignity quite so impressive, and no independence quite so important as living within your means."

Calvin Coolidge

TO

PONDER!

CHAPTER 1

ESTABLISHING BASIC FINANCIAL PRINCIPLES

GO FOR YOUR GOAL

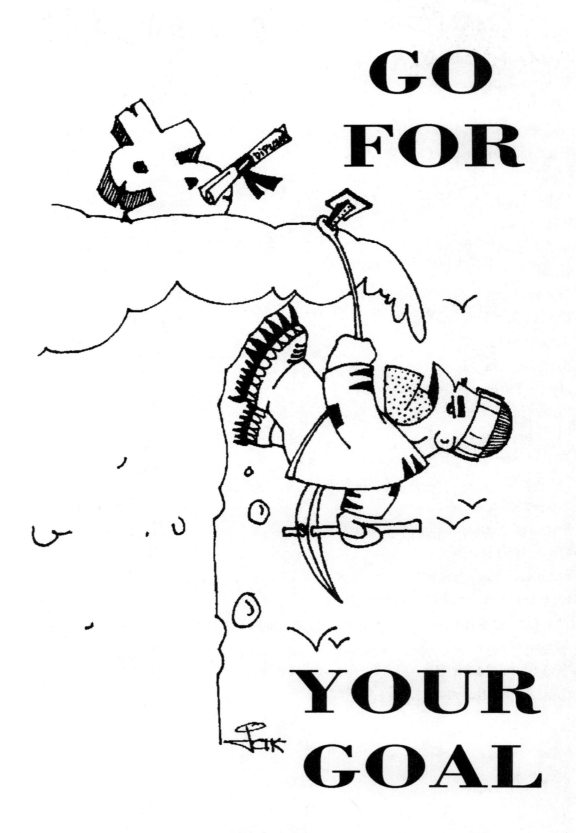

FOCUS ON:

ACHIEVING FINANCIAL GOALS

1. Realize your strengths and weaknesses in the area of financial responsibility.

2. Review your attitude towards money.

3. Establish and prioritize your life values.

4. Set realistic and attainable financial goals.

5. List financial obligations.

6. Determine financial priorities.

7. Write an action plan to insure goal achievement.

8. Implement your action plan immediately.

9. Monitor your plan at regular intervals.

10. Reward yourself for successfully achieving your financial goal.

ESTABLISHING BASIC FINANCIAL PRINCIPLES

"In philosophy, it is not the attainment of the goal that matters, it is the things that are met with by the way."

Havelock Ellis

IDENTIFY LIFE VALUES

The way we handle money is reflected by our values. We acquire these values at a very early age from family members, peers, and outside groups such as church, school, and community. Values are extremely personal and inspire decisions, choices, beliefs, and feelings. Today, we are constantly bombarded with a variety of life styles and belief systems. Is it any wonder then, that we experience a great deal of confusion and frustration, along with a general conflict of individual and family values? It is essential that we identify the values inherent with ideals we prize and cherish. This is especially true in the area of personal finances.

This chapter is divided into sections that requires you to perform specific tasks. It is of utmost importance that each task be completed in the given sequence since your answers to these tasks will be used as part of the material, information, illustrations, examples, and applications in later sections of this chapter and following chapters. The first prerequisite in the planning process of a successful financial program is to examine the fundamental values that determine your current life style.

Begin determining your life values by completing steps 1 - 4 of the Values Clarification Worksheet on page 5.

LIFE VALUES

- ❑ Adventure/Excitement
- ❑ Authority/Power
- ❑ Close Family Relationships
  (Spouse/Children/Parents)
- ❑ Freedom
- ❑ Friendships
- ❑ Good Health
- ❑ Happiness
- ❑ Independence
- ❑ Inner Peace
- ❑ Integrity
- ❑ _____
- ❑ _____

- ❑ Intimacy/Mature Love
- ❑ Knowledge/Education
- ❑ Pleasure
- ❑ Recognition/Fame
- ❑ Respect (Self/From Others)
- ❑ Security (Family/Financial)
- ❑ Sense of Achievement
- ❑ Spiritual Growth/Salvation
- ❑ Wealth
- ❑ Wisdom
- ❑ _____
- ❑ _____
- ❑ _____

VALUES CLARIFICATION WORKSHEET

1. Select - ☑ - up to five fundamental values from the above list that determine your current life style. Add any that do not appear on the list provided.

2. Rank the items in order, 1 being the most important and 5 being of least importance. (Read the "/" symbol as "or;" that is, Adventure or Excitement.)

○ 1. _____

○ 2. _____

○ 3. _____

○ 4. _____

○ 5. _____

3. Place a "$" in the "○" by the value(s) you selected that either require money or affect the use of money.

4. Set the remaining values aside for possible future use.

Figure 1 - Worksheet page 227

ESTABLISH FINANCIAL GOALS

You have now defined and ordered the fundamental values that determine your present life style. Your next objective will be to set realistic and attainable financial goals that correlate with these selected values. Goals that do not match important life values are likely to be in conflict with one or more of your important values and can create a feeling of emptiness or even frustration. For example, if your most important value is financial security, the number one goal might be to eliminate current financial obligations and indebtedness. The examples given in this chapter provide a step-by-step procedure to guide you through the goal setting process; similar to the principles presented in Figure 2 on page 7. A written statement of financial goals creates your own personal "Financial Road Map" that assists in fulfilling your basic needs, desires, and dreams. Equally important, you have set specific priorities with commitments for their achievement.

Listing your goals or priorities does not necessarily guarantee that they will be begun, let alone achieved. The completion of each specific activity carries a price tag in the form of time, energy, or money. The question now becomes, "Am I willing to pay the price necessary for accomplishment," and then begin by taking immediate action? It is essential to take action if you intend to accomplish anything, from a task required at work to a mundane chore of cleaning the garage or kitchen. The number one reason why people fail to achieve their goal or task is procrastination. Many financial planners have said, "People don't plan to fail, they just fail to plan." Therefore, take immediate action, whatever the goal or task might be. If the goal seems overwhelming or you have trouble beginning, break down the task into small(er) units. Remember, the "Action Step" is a commitment that will take both discipline and persistence on your part.

Finally, when you have accomplished a goal, regardless of its magnitude, take time to reward yourself and enjoy the benefits for having achieved the task. You might begin by completing a small or immediate size goal to keep motivation and commitment high. Such a task might be resolving to live with your income by writing out a family budget or paying off a very low credit card balance. Celebrating the successful fulfillment of each goal builds confidence and self esteem. This will also encourage you to realize your potential by attempting future goals of even greater significance.

                                    Solving Your Financial Puzzle

GOAL SETTING PRINCIPLES

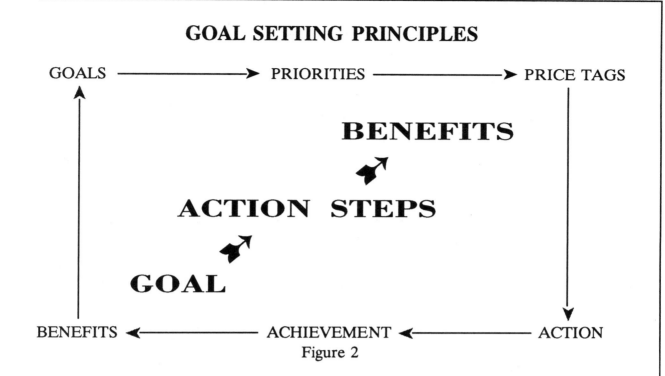

Figure 2

FAILURE TO SET FINANCIAL GOALS

Even though the benefits of setting goals are obvious, a commitment to setting a goal is seldom a priority. Often, it's the result of a crisis that compels a person to set goals. None the less, there are times when people become goal setters in order to enhance their personal, professional, or family life.

Although we can set goals for any area of our life by using the action steps outlined on pages 9 - 10 of this chapter, this book is primarily concerned with defining and achieving financial goals. These goals are the primary key to motivate us to accumulate wealth, become financially independent, and have financial freedom at retirement. Goals also provide the direction and purpose needed to reach future objectives-- whether it is to fund a college education or finance that once-in-a-lifetime trip.

Why then, do most of us neglect to set financial goals? One reason may be that if a goal is not set, there will be no fear about not meeting it. Worrying about the approaching commitment of a goal or task, such as organizing a credit card file, frequently creates an enormous amount of anxiety. We feel overwhelmed by sudden pressure, the tension experienced when we wait until April 14th to begin preparing our Federal Income Tax return. Where do we begin? This stress often appears out-wardly in the form of procrastination, possibly, even total lack of interest, while our inner feelings are one of confusion and hopelessness. Whatever our original goal had been, we find abundant excuses for not beginning the task.

On the other hand, we may not know what specific financial goals to set. Certainly, setting improper financial goals can easily lead to disastrous consequences. Perhaps we just don't know (or have not been taught) how to set realistic and attainable goals. It is of critical importance to be able to set financial goals; if you don't have a financial target (goal), you'll miss the bull's-eye every time. Goals will serve as your personal road map to financial success. They are intended to make your journey as efficient and productive as possible without unwanted detours. You probably have learned from driving around an unfamiliar city without a road map that you can drive around for hours and not arrive at the destination. This proves the fact "that if you don't know where you're going, just about any road will get you there."

> "We must walk consciously only part way toward our goal, and then leap in the dark to our success."
>
> Author Unknown
> Attributed to
> H. D. Thoreau

☑ ACTION STEPS ☑

- ❑ Write down your goal(s)
- ❑ Set deadlines
- ❑ Take action

SET REALISTIC AND ATTAINABLE GOALS
THE FORMULA FOR FINANCIAL SUCCESS

There are several excellent books and articles, along with a number of audio and video tapes on the market today relating to the goal setting process. To receive the greatest benefit from your goals, they need to match or correlate with the life values you consider to be most important. Goals need to be both realistic and attainable. The eight basic action steps outlined on pages 9 and 10 have proven to yield excellent results. Even though you may not use all of the basic action steps in writing your goal, it is essential to make use of each characteristic in the process of carrying out your financial goals.

GOALS NEED TO BE:

1. A "Positive" Written Statement

Goals need to be written down on paper. It has been said that "if the item is in writing, it is a goal; if the item is in your head, it is a dream or a wish." Having goals in writing allow you to visually focus on them. If the goal is to increase your income over the next twelve month period, you might write: I will increase my income one and one-half times over the next twelve month period.

2. Specific And Well Defined

Your goal has to be defined using specific locations, models, colors, etc. If your goal is to have a new home, where is located? If it is an automobile, describe the make, model, color, etc. If it is an occupation, name the specific profession.

3. Measurable

Your goal needs to be defined using dollars, numbers, etc. This will hold you accountable for achieving the goal. If it is to acquire a home or an automobile, specify the amount of down payment. If it is an extensive trip or vacation, give the total cost.

4. Stated With Specific Starting And Completion Dates

Write down the date you plan to begin the goal along with the date you expect to have the task completed. Setting deadlines have a way of producing desired results.

Short-term goals are usually twelve months or less.

Medium-term goals are one to five years in length.

Long-term goals are considered five years and longer.

5. A Plan Of Action

Your plan of action indicates how the goal will be achieved. It should give the strategy required to complete the goal. The plan might include the organization(s) or people that need to be contacted, as well as possible obstacles that you must overcome to realize the goal. Be sure to include the amount of money that is to be set aside on a regular monthly or annual basis, as well as how it is to be saved or invested.

6. Stated With Results Or Benefits

In what way does accomplishing the particular goal improve your life? Does it increase your feeling of self-worth? Are you able to make better financial decisions? Be sure to list each of the benefits received from the accomplishment of your goal.

7. Prioritized

Priorities are a key to achieving goals. Setting priorities will identify financial goals that have the greatest impact on your current situation. When you list goals in the order of their importance, it greatly increases motivation to take action. In this way, what you truly value becomes readily apparent.

8. Periodically reviewed

Once you have implemented the goals, review them regularly to assess interim progress. By periodically evaluating your goals, you will be able to modify or take corrective action when appropriate in an effort to attain the desired outcome. A good rule to follow is to review goals of one year or less on a monthly basis with medium-term and long-range goals reviewed annually.

Last, and most important of all to achieve the desired goals, you need to have:

Self discipline
Persistence
A commitment to act now!

The following Goals Clarification Worksheet will guide you through the goal setting process so that you can achieve any realistic goal desired:

GOALS CLARIFICATION WORKSHEET

Goal: _____

1. Positive Statement: _____

2. Specific and Well Defined:

Location _____   Make _____

_____   _____

Model _____   Color _____

_____   _____

3. Measurable:

Dollars _____   Amount _____

_____   _____

4. Stated With Specific Starting and Completion Dates:

Starting Date _____   Completion Date _____

5. A Plan of Action:

Strategy _____

_____

_____

People or Organizations _____

_____

Potential Obstacles _____

_____

Financing _____

_____

6. Stated With Results or Benefits:

_____

_____

_____

_____

7. Prioritized:

_____

_____

_____

8. Periodically Reviewed:

_____

_____

_____

Figure 3 - Worksheet page 228

FAMILY - INDIVIDUAL GOALS

You are now ready to analyze your own current goal situation by completing the Family - Individual Goals Worksheet on page 229. Completing this form will greatly assist you with calculating an appropriate amount of money to be saved on an annual or monthly basis in order to accomplish a desired goal. Consider each goal in the first column of Figure 4 below. If the goal is not important, or has already been completed, place "NA" for not applicable, in the second column. If the goal is important, enter "Yes" or "Essential," depending upon the degree of urgency. For each goal which you feel is important, state whether the time period needed to complete the goal is short-term, medium-term, or long-term. In the fourth column, state the date that you intend to begin your goal. Finally, place the estimated completion date in the last column. By placing both a beginning and completion date on the goals worksheet, you have made a written commitment toward the completion of the goal. Remember, setting deadlines has a way of producing results.

FAMILY - INDIVIDUAL GOALS WORKSHEET

Goal	Importance	Length Of Time	Beginning Date	Completion Date
Prepare Budget	Yes	Short	January 9, 1995	January 16, 1995
Organize Credit Card File	Essential	Short	January 6, 1995	February 3, 1995
Eliminate Debt	Essential	Medium	February 1, 1995	February 1, 1999
Home Down Payment (See first example, pages 13 - 15)	Yes	Medium	February 1, 1995	February 1, 2000

Figure 4 - Worksheet page 229

 **ACTION STEP**

❏ Apply the Goals Clarification Worksheet on pages 10 - 11 for individual or family goals, using each of the steps indicated on the worksheet.

 Solving Your Financial Puzzle

SET FINANCIAL GOALS

The three examples that follow will give you a variety of ideas for using the Family - Individual Goals Worksheet and the Monthly Savings Worksheet. In addition, practical application problems are provided on page 19 to illustrate the affect of inflation when setting short-term, as well as long-term financial goals.

★ HOME PURCHASE ★

A POSITIVE WRITTEN STATEMENT - Specific and well defined.

We plan to save enough money each month to have a down payment of $8,000 in five years or by March 1, 2000 for the purchase of our first home. We estimate that our investments will earn an annual rate of return of 6% after taxes and that the annual rate of inflation will be 5%.

MEASURABLE in terms of numbers, dollars, etc.

Considering today's housing costs, we estimate that $8,000 will be needed.

STATED WITH STARTING AND COMPLETION DATES

We will begin a monthly savings program this month and have it completed by March 1, 2000, or 60 months from today.

A PLAN OF ACTION

❶ **Monthly Savings Worksheet**
Complete columns 1, 2, 3, 4, and 7 of the Monthly Savings Worksheet (Figure 5, page 14) using information under "A Positive Written Statement" above.

❷ **Cost of Living Adjustment Table**
Use the Cost Of Living Adjustment Table shown on page 14 and provided on page 351 to calculate the <u>future</u> inflated cost of the down payment in column 6. Go down the *Years* column to 5; from that point go right three places to the

5% column and locate the number 1.276. Enter the number 1.276 in column 5; then multiply $8,000 x 1.276 = $10,208 to obtain the desired result in column 6.

MONTHLY SAVINGS WORKSHEET

1	2	3	4	5	6	7	8	9	10
Goal	Present Cost or Value	When Needed (In Years)	Inflation Rate	Cost of Living Adjustment Factor	Future Cost or Value (Cols. 2 x 5)	Annual Savings Investment Earnings	Annual Savings Factor	Annual Savings Needed (Cols. 6 x 8)	Monthly Savings Required (Col. 9) ÷ 12
Purchase New Home	$8,000 ❶	5 Years ❶	5% ❶	1.276 ❷	$10,208 ❷	6% ❶	0.177 ❸	$1,807 ❸	$151 ❹

Figure 5 - Worksheet page 230

COST OF LIVING ADJUSTMENT (COLA) TABLE

Years	3%	4%	5%
2	1.061	1.082	1.103
3	1.093	1.125	1.158
4	1.126	1.170	1.216
5	1.159	1.217	★1.276
6	1.194	1.265	1.340
7	1.230	1.316	1.407

Figure 6 - Table page 351

❸ Annual Savings Accumulation Table

We determine the annual savings necessary to reach the desired goal from the Annual Savings Accumulation Table in Figure 7 and on page 352. Go down the *Years* column to 5; from that point, go right two places to the *6%* column and locate the number 0.177. Enter the number 0.177 in column 8; then multiply $10,208 x 0.177 = $1,806.82, the required annual amount shown in column 9 of Figure 5.

❹ Monthly Savings Required

Divide: $1,807 ÷ 12 = $150.58. Therefore, by investing $151 each month, at the annual rate of 6%, our goal of $8,000 will be achieved.

                    Solving Your Financial Puzzle

ANNUAL SAVINGS ACCUMULATION TABLE

Years	5%	6%	7%
2	0.488	0.485	0.483
3	0.317	0.314	0.311
4	0.232	0.229	0.225
5	0.181	★0.177	0.174
6	0.147	0.143	0.140
7	0.123	0.119	0.116

Figure 7 - Table page 352

Notice from Figure 5 on page 14, that we will not have to save the entire $10,208. This fact is evident by multiplying $151 x 60 months = $9,060. The remaining $1,148 needed for the down payment is the interest accumulated during the course of the five years. The point that this example stresses is that by paying ourselves on a monthly (or annual) basis in advance, we will save considerable money over the time taken in achieving our goal.

STATED WITH RESULTS OR BENEFITS

We will achieve our long time dream of owning a home after ten years of living in an apartment.

★ ★ LUXURIOUS TRIP ★ ★

A POSITIVE WRITTEN STATEMENT - Specific and well defined.

I plan to take a six week trip to Australia and New Zealand in two years. The cost of the trip would be $6,000. I estimate that there will be no inflation and that I can earn 6% on my investments after taxes.

MEASURABLE in terms of numbers, dollars, etc.

Today's cost of the trip is $6,000. Since I am not anticipating any inflation, I expect that the price of the trip will remain $6,000.

STATED WITH STARTING AND COMPLETION DATES

I will begin a monthly investment program on October 1, 1995 and have it completed by October 1, 1997.

A PLAN OF ACTION

❶ **Monthly Savings Worksheet**

Complete columns 1, 2, 3, 4, and 7 of the Monthly Savings Worksheet shown in Figure 8 and using information under "A Positive Written Statement" provided on page 15.

MONTHLY SAVINGS WORKSHEET

1	2	3	4	5	6	7	8	9	10
Goal	Present Cost or Value	When Needed (In Years)	Inflation Rate	Cost of Living Adjustment Factor	Future Cost or Value (Cols. 2 x 5)	Annual Savings Investment Earnings	Annual Savings Factor	Annual Savings Needed (Cols. 6 x 8)	Monthly Savings Required (Col. 9) ÷ 12
Australia & New Zealand	$6,000 ❶	2 Years ❶	None ❶	1.000 ❷	$6,000 ❷	6% ❶	0.485 ❸	$2,910 ❸	$243 ❹

Figure 8 - Worksheet page 230

❷ **Cost of Living Adjustment Table**

Since I am not anticipating any inflation for the next two years, the Cost of Living Adjustment Factor in column 5 will be one. Multiplying $6,000 x 1.000 = $6,000 is the amount that I will need to accumulate and is placed in column 6.

❸ **Annual Savings Accumulation Table**

To determine the annual savings necessary to reach the desired goal, go two places to the right of the "2" in the *Years* column to the number 0.485 (*6%* column). Enter the number 0.485 in column 8; then multiply $6,000 x 0.485 = $2,910, the required annual amount shown in column 9 of Figure 8.

❹ **Monthly Savings Required**

Divide: $2,910 ÷ 12 = $242.50. Therefore, by investing $243 each month, at the annual rate of 6%, my goal of $6,000 will be achieved.

  Solving Your Financial Puzzle

STATED WITH RESULTS OR BENEFITS

I will enjoy six weeks of relaxation to fulfill a long time dream of traveling to this area of the world.

★ ★ ★ COLLEGE FUNDS ★ ★ ★

A POSITIVE WRITTEN STATEMENT - Specific and well defined.

We plan to pay $40,000 (in today's dollars) towards the college education of our three-year-old daughter. I estimate that the inflation rate of college costs will be 6% and that we can earn 10% on investments after taxes.

MEASURABLE in terms of numbers, dollars, etc.

Today's cost for her four year college education would be approximately $40,000. With inflation and increased school costs, the price in fifteen years or September 1, 2010 will be about $96,000.

STATED WITH STARTING AND COMPLETION DATES

I will begin a monthly investment program for this specific purpose on September 1, 1995 and have it completed by September 1, 2010.

A PLAN OF ACTION

My plan of action requires that I save $250 a month for 15 years to have the necessary education funds available when our daughter enters college. We will also investigate scholarships, government grants, and work study programs during her last two high school years if we should have insufficient college funding or that in the event she would be better served at a private university. My calculations are based on the data obtained from the tables used in the two previous examples.

❶ **Monthly Savings Worksheet**
Complete columns 1, 2, 3, 4, and 7 of the Monthly Savings Worksheet (Figure 9, page 18) using information under "A Positive Written Statement" above.

MONTHLY SAVINGS WORKSHEET

1	2	3	4	5	6	7	8	9	10
Goal	Present Cost or Value	When Needed (In Years)	Inflation Rate	Cost of Living Adjustment Factor	Future Cost or Value (Cols. 2 x 5)	Annual Savings Investment Earnings	Annual Savings Factor	Annual Savings Needed (Cols. 6 x 8)	Monthly Savings Required (Col. 9) ÷ 12
College Education Fund	$40,000 ❶	15 Years ❶	6% ❶	2.397 ❷	$96,000 ❷	10% ❶	0.031 ❸	$2,972 ❸	$250 ❹

Figure 9 - Worksheet page 230

❷ **Cost of Living Adjustment Table**

Go down the *Years* column to 15; then right four columns to the number 2.397 (*6% column*). Enter this value in fifth column, multiply $40,000 x 2.397 = $95,880 to obtain the future inflated cost for college funding located in column 6.

❸ **Annual Savings Accumulation Table**

To determine the annual savings necessary to reach the desired goal, go down the *Years* column to 15; then right six columns to the number 0.031 (*10% column*). Enter the number 0.031 in column 8; then multiply $95,880 x 0.031 = $2,972.28 (column 9). This will be the amount of annual savings required to reach our desired goal of college funding for our daughter.

❹ **Monthly Savings Required**

Divide: $2,972 ÷ 12 = $247.67. Therefore, by investing $250 each month (column 10) for 180 months in a variety of investments, we have excellent potential for accumulating the necessary college funds by the time they are needed.

STATED WITH RESULTS OR BENEFITS

I believe that this will fulfill our responsibility as parents to contribute "within our means" towards our child's future education costs.

☑ **ACTION STEPS** ☑

❑ Complete the appropriate columns of the Monthly Savings Worksheet.
❑ Calculate the **future** inflated cost of your goal.
❑ Determine the annual savings amount required to finance your desired goal.
❑ Calculate the amount to be set aside on a **monthly** basis.

   Solving Your Financial Puzzle

SETTING FINANCIAL GOALS
APPLICATIONS

To appreciate the usefulness and value of the Monthly Savings Worksheet, some typical examples would seem most appropriate. Use the Cost of Living Adjustment Table and Annual Savings Accumulation Table on pages 351 - 352 to find out how much a family would need to save on a monthly basis to make each of the following financial commitments. Answers, along with a detailed solution to each of the problems, are provided on the following two pages.

Give your answers:

    A. Without inflation cost consideration, then

    B. With inflation cost being a consideration

1. A family would like to replace a stove in two years. If the present cost of the stove is $550, the annual inflation rate = 4%, and their annual investment earnings = 7%, how much will they need to save each month to pay cash for the stove in two years?

2. The Smith family is thinking about replacing their refrigerator in five years. The current cost of a refrigerator they like is $850. If their current investments are earning 9% per year and the annual inflation rate = 3%, how much will they need to save each month to pay cash for this purchase?

3. A young married couple with well-paying professions wish to begin a college education fund for their two-year-old daughter. If the present cost for a four year college education at a state supported university is $28,500, how much money will they need to set aside each month to have the money available when it is needed 16 years from now? The annual inflation rate is 6% and they feel that their investments will earn an average annual return of 13%.

4. A family is currently thinking about taking a European trip in six years when their son completes his high school education. If the cost of a current tour is $6,000, the annual inflation rate = 3%, and their investments currently earning an annual rate of 10%, how much money will this family need to save each month to have the necessary funds available for the trip when it is needed?

ANSWERS TO APPLICATION PROBLEMS

The charts in Figure 10 below are used to solve each of the four application problems on page 19. A detailed explanation for the solution of problem one is provided on page 21. Follow these five steps to determine the monthly dollar amount required, with and without inflation, for meeting each of the goals in application problems 2 - 4. Since the savings amounts are required **with** and **without** inflation, note that some of the Monthly Savings Worksheet columns in Figure 10 below are rearrange (in this example only) to simplify the necessary calculations.

	1	2	3	4	5	6	7
MONTHLY SAVINGS WORKSHEET							
Goal	Present Cost or Value	When Needed (In Yrs)	Annual Savings Investment Earnings	Annual Savings Factor	Annual Savings Needed (Cols. 2 x 5)	Monthly Savings Required (Col. 6) ÷ 12
Stove	$ 550	2 Years	7%	0.483	$265.65	$22.14
Refrigerator	$ 850	5 Years	9%	0.167	$141.95	$11.83
Education Funds	$28,500	16 Years	13%	0.021	$598.50	$49.88
European Trip	$ 6,000	6 Years	10%	0.130	$780.00	$65.00

1	8	9	10
GOAL	Annual Inflation Rate	Cost of Living Adjustment Factor	Monthly Savings Required After Inflation (Cols. 7 x 9)
Stove	4%	1.082	$ 23.95
Refrigerator	3%	1.159	$ 13.71
Education Funds	6%	2.540	$126.70
European Trip	3%	1.194	$ 77.61

Figure 10

 Solving Your Financial Puzzle

DETAILED SOLUTION FOR PROBLEM 1

1. Complete the first five columns of the table as shown on page 20.

2. Calculate the Annual Savings needed (Columns 2 x 5) in column 6 by multiplying: $550 x 0.483 = $265.65.

3. Divide: $265.65 ÷ 12 = $22.14 to obtain the monthly savings amount required without inflation. Place this result in column 7.

4. Calculate the amount needed each month after adjusting for inflation.

    A. Refer to the Cost Of Living Adjustment Table.

    B. Go down the *Years* column to 2.

    C. From that location, go right two columns to the *4%* column and enter the number 1.082 in column 9.

    D. Multiply the value of 1.082 in column 9 by the result of $22.14 in column 7; $22.14 x 1.082 = $23.95 to obtain the monthly savings adjusted for inflation.

5. Continue with items 1 - 4D for problems 2 - 4.

Answers To Application Problems 2 - 4

Number	Column 7	Column 9	Column 10
2	$ 11.83	1.159	$ 13.71
3	49.88	2.540	126.70
4	65.00	1.194	77.61

Figure 11

FINANCIAL PRIORITIES

Now that you have carefully assessed your financial goals, focus on financial priorities. List your goals in the order of their importance using the Financial Priorities Worksheet on page 231. After each goal, complete the remaining six columns with the information requested. To illustrate, a couple who have the ability to save on a monthly basis, would like to purchase a new automobile in the next few years. Notice from the example in Figure 12 that a commitment of $300 a month for each of the next 36 months (36 x $300 = $10,800) will leave this family just $200 short of the $11,000 cash price necessary to purchase the automobile.

FINANCIAL PRIORITIES WORKSHEET

Financial Goals Ranked By Priority	Number Years To Accomplish Goal	Dollar Amount Needed	Amount Accumulated To Date	Current Savings Per Month	Remaining Amount Needed	Willing To Commit Dollars/Month
New Automobile	3	$12,500	$1,500	$300	$11,000	-0-

Figure 12 - Worksheet page 231

Upon the completion of the Financial Priorities Worksheet, it may become readily apparent that one of your financial priorities will be to eliminate financial obligations that are preventing you from reaching current and future financial goals. Examples of such debt might be: credit cards, automobile payments, and student and bank loans. The Current Financial Obligations Worksheet on page 232 will assist in the elimination of your financial obligations by organizing the information necessary to eliminate the debt.

Suppose that you signed a purchase agreement for a Baby Grand Piano in the amount of $9,500. The terms of the agreement were for five years at 9.5% interest with no down payment. You have already made twenty-four payments of $197.95 each when you suddenly realize that the "total paid-off price" of the piano will be $11,877, of which $2,377 is interest. Being very alarmed by the amount of interest being charged, you quickly decide to accelerate the payments by committing an additional $102.05 of principal each month. The increased payment will enable you to pay for the piano in forty-five months instead of sixty months with previous monthly payments of $197.95.

Figure 13 on the following page illustrates how information for this loan can be organized in a simple and meaningful way. This makes you instantly aware of the "price tag" for not taking immediate action on paying off the loan, especially if dollars are available

            Solving Your Financial Puzzle

in your budget for doing so. The money you save from achieving this goal can then be applied to reaching future goals.

CURRENT FINANCIAL OBLIGATIONS WORKSHEET

Financial Obligation	Total Years To Pay Off Obligation	Total Payment Amount	Amount Paid To Date	Current Monthly Payment	Remaining Dollar Amount Needed	Commit Extra Dollars/ Month
Baby Grand Piano	5 Years	$11,877	$4,751	$197.95	$7,126	$102.05

Figure 13 - Worksheet page 232

We have now focused on four major areas of the planning process:

1. Examine the fundamental values that determine your current life style.
2. Set realistic and attainable family/individual financial goals.
3. Determine priorities based on your value system and goals you wish to achieve.
4. Eliminate all potential financial obligations which prevent you from achieving current and future financial goals.

Your next task is to focus on specific financial responsibilities which occur throughout a lifetime.

FINANCIAL RESPONSIBILITIES

Lifetime Financial Responsibilities charts on pages 25 - 30 provide financial guidelines for various life stages. Each age-range chart lists several objectives and recommendations for their accomplishments. Objectives are given in **bold** print; suggested procedures for achieving the desired result(s) follow each objective. The symbol "☎", which appears to the left of several statements in this section, indicates that you may wish to phone or consult with the appropriate professional for assistance. These professions might include the following specialist: certificated public accountant, estate planning attorney, knowledgeable insurance agent, or certified financial planner. Again, this is only a "guideline," not a hard and fast rule to be followed in order to become financially independent by retirement time from a current profession.

Various living arrangements existing today have made it difficult to give specific financial guidelines at different ages. These new life styles have created problems for society and unfortunately, financial solutions for solving them have not kept up at the same pace. Many living arrangements that exist in our society today include the following:

1. Singles
2. Single parents
3. Living together
4. Dinks - dual income, no kids
5. Blended families - yours, mine, and ours
6. Married couples - two careers plus children
7. Traditional families - one family, one income
8. Sandwich families - families responsible for their children as well as their parents

Each of the life style groups identified above needs to be evaluated according to your family/individual situation. For example, consider the need for life insurance for a single adult at age twenty-seven and a married couple of the same age with two young children. It is readily apparent that there is a need for considerable life insurance in the case of the young family, while as a general rule, there seems to be less of a need for the single adult. Obviously, there are unique circumstances, such as a specific health problem or a large estate that might warrant a life insurance policy for the single individual.

Analyzing each of the financial objectives within your life style group allows you to determine both appropriate strategies and action steps to be completed for a successful financial program. Therefore, the challenge is to use the guideline chart, with any necessary modifications, to reach your ultimate goals and individual or family financial security.

"Nothing can stop the man with the right mental attitude from achieving his goal; nothing on earth can help the man with the wrong mental attitude."

W. W. Ziege

LIFETIME FINANCIAL RESPONSIBILITIES

AGES 18 - 24

1. **Develop career skills.**
   - Prepare for a trade or profession to provide adequate income for basic needs and wants.
   - Recognize and develop human potential.
2. **Establish a credit rating.**
   - Pay monthly credit obligations promptly.
3. **Develop a monthly budget.**
   - Establish a monthly spending plan (or budget) for living within your income.
   - Develop consumer skills that pertain to spending and become knowledgeable of debt management.
   - Avoid overcommitment of income.
4. **Develop the habit of regular saving.**
   - Open a checking and savings account at a local bank or credit union.
   - Provide "side" savings accounts for major repairs or replacements such as automobile(s) and appliances.
5. **Develop and maintain a filing system for all financial records.**
   - Establish a central filing location for your lists of assets and liabilities, checking and saving accounts, credit cards, monthly expenses, legal documents, taxes, warranties, and medical records, as well as all other records pertaining to your financial situation.
6. **Build a cash reserve fund for emergencies.**
   - Establish, then maintain, three - six months living expenses for a reserve emergency fund.
☎ 7. **Purchase adequate insurance (risk management) protection.**
   - Purchase health, homeowner's or renter's insurance, automobile, umbrella liability coverage, and disability income if appropriate.
   - Consider need for life insurance, and business insurance when/where it applies.
☎ 8. **Draw up a will.**
   - Designate guardians for minor children and make provisions for distribution of property; name executor (or personal representative) of your estate.
☎ 9. **Begin an investment program.**
   - Build an investment portfolio that meets your goals and objectives, as well as your tolerance for risk. (Don't be a "Follow-the-Herd-Investor" by simply taking advice from others.)

☎ Consider a formal consultation with the appropriate professional specialist before taking action.

Adapted from the American Council of Life Insurance & U.S. Department of Agriculture Extension Service, Washington, D.C., ☻ late 1970's. Used by permission.

LIFETIME FINANCIAL RESPONSIBILITIES

AGES 25 - 34

1. **Develop financial goals.**
   - Establish appropriate and realistic family/individual short-term, medium-term, and long-term financial goals.
2. **Keep household inventory records.**
   - Make a detailed inventory record of all household and personal possessions. Include video and photographs, especially of valuables.
   - Keep these in a safe deposit box or other secure location outside the home and update every five years or when you move to a different location.
☎ 3. **Review and update insurance coverage (if necessary).**
   - Review all insurance programs, including beneficiaries, with appropriate agent.
   - Update and increase coverage where necessary.
4. **Plan for increased family expenses.**
   - Watch for overcommitment of family income, along with increased use of credit.
   - Review budget, and revise if necessary, to keep income balanced with expenses and savings.
   - Develop "side" savings accounts for major repairs or replacements if not done previously.
5. **Educate family members, including children, in accepting financial responsibility.**
   - Educate children on the wise use of handling money.
   - Begin, or accelerate payment of loans and credit card debts.
   - Take advantage of seminars, workshops, and adult education classes on financial and retirement planning ideas.
☎ 6. **Purchase a home.**
   - Consider the purchase of a home to build an asset base as well as to reduce your tax liability. (Maximum borrowing capability to qualify for a loan is approximately two and one half times your annual gross income **and** not more than 8% of monthly consumer debt.)
7. **Plan for children's education expenses.**
   - Begin, or increase savings and investments for children's education funding.
☎ 8. **Review will or trust, and update if necessary.**
   - Review beneficiary designations of your insurance, investment, and retirement account programs. (Revision may be necessary, especially if you moved to a different state or have changed your marital status.)
☎ 9. **Begin, or continue, saving for retirement.**
   - Save as much as your financial situation will allow.
   - Take maximum advantage of employer retirement benefits.

☎ Consider a formal consultation with the appropriate professional specialist before taking action.

Adapted from the American Council of Life Insurance & U.S. Department of Agriculture Extension Service, Washington, D.C., ● late 1970's. Used by permission.

                                        Solving Your Financial Puzzle

LIFETIME FINANCIAL RESPONSIBILITIES

AGES 35 - 44

1. **Eliminate loan (except home mortgage) and credit card debt.**
   - Eliminate annual overspending; pay off all personal loans and credit card balances.
2. **Continue or step up children's education funding.**
   - Continue to add and diversify investments for children's education.
☎ 3. **Realign insurance coverage as family needs change.**
   - Review and update all insurance programs; prioritize and adjust coverage as necessary.
   - Maximize protection on the person(s) providing the majority of family income.
   - Give special attention to homeowners, replacement value, and liability insurance.
☎ 4. **Establish and work toward retirement goals.**
   - Estimate future retirement needs; do not rely totally on social security benefits.
   - Maintain regular, maximum investing to IRA's and qualified retirement plans.
   - Consider investing for long-term growth.
☎ 5. **Develop an estate plan.**
   - Consult with an attorney to decide how distribution of assets, insurance proceeds, and real estate will be made upon your death to minimize expenses and taxes. If appropriate, consider a trust.
☎ 6. **Invest for future "needs" and "wants."**
   - Consider investing in stocks, bonds, mutual funds, etc. that will provide for long-term growth.
   - Diversify to minimize the impact of investment risk.

☎ Consider a formal consultation with the appropriate professional specialist before taking action.

AGES 45 - 54

1. **Provide funding of higher education for children.**
   - Continue to save and invest for children's education as needed.
2. **Review and update household inventory records.**
   - Review, and update previous inventory records of household and personal possessions every five years or when major purchases are acquired.
   - Be sure to include recently acquired possessions and assets.
   - Place inventory in a secure location outside the home.

☎ Consider a formal consultation with the appropriate professional specialist before taking action.

Adapted from the American Council of Life Insurance & U.S. Department of Agriculture Extension Service, Washington, D.C., ● late 1970's. Used by permission.

LIFETIME FINANCIAL RESPONSIBILITIES

AGES 45 - 54 (Con't.)

☎ 3. **Evaluate investment portfolio, realign if necessary to meet current and future objectives.**
   - Adjust savings and investment programs to your changing family/individual situation.
   - Consider taking advantage of tax-deferred and tax-exempt investments when appropriate.

☎ 4. **Review and evaluate retirement program; update if needed.**
   - Continue to invest the maximum amount in your company retirement plan, or contribute as much as your financial situation will allow.

5. **Communicate with family members regarding estate planning.**
   - Analyze your estate plan and adjust as needed.
   - Discuss the estate plan provisions, as well as location of plan documents, with family members.

6. **Accelerate home mortgage payments.**
   - Accelerate your mortgage payoff time by including additional "principle payments" with each regular monthly payment.

☎ 7. **Assist parents and/or other dependents with the evaluation of their present and future financial needs.**
   - Encourage your parents to purchase (if needed) a private medicare supplement policy and/or a long-term care policy while they still qualify for a program.
   - Recommend that your parents provide for future needs by protecting their investments against inflation.
   - Advise your parents to consult with an attorney to insure that their wills (or trusts) avoid as much estate and inheritance taxes as possible.

☎ Consider a formal consultation with the appropriate professional specialist before taking action.

AGES 55 - 64

1. **Plan for retirement location.**
   - Investigate housing expenses in various locations that are of interest if you are planning to relocate for retirement.

2. **Make plans for reduced amount of income at retirement.**
   - Provide for additional income at retirement by increasing your investments and savings as your family expenses decline.

☎ Consider a formal consultation with the appropriate professional specialist before taking action.

Adapted from the American Council of Life Insurance & U.S. Department of Agriculture Extension Service, Washington, D.C., ● late 1970's. Used by permission.

Solving Your Financial Puzzle

LIFETIME FINANCIAL RESPONSIBILITIES

AGES 55 - 64 (Con't)

☎ 3. **Consolidate investment assets.**
  - Realign your investment portfolio strategy to have the following balance: income for living expenses, growth for inflation protection, and safety to reduce risk.
  - Consider selling tax-sheltered investments, placing the proceeds in investments that have more liquidity.

4. **Provide for future financial security by supplementing retirement income.**
  - Seek additional sources of income during retirement by investigating the possibility of part time employment.

☎ 5. **Continue with estate planning.**
  - Review your will or trust; update as necessary.
  - Write letter of last instruction.
  - Prepare the following documents: living will, organ donation, etc.

☎ 6. **Evaluate need for a private medicare supplement and/or long-term care insurance program(s).**
  - Consider the purchase of a private medicare supplement policy to help cover the costs of hospital and doctor deductibles.
  - Consider buying a private long-term care policy to cover coinsurance for skilled nursing home care.

7. **Meet responsibilities of aging parents or other dependents.**
  - Be knowledgeable of the retirement income needed at different age levels.
  - Be prepared to sacrifice income for purchasing your wants and desires in order to provide for the care and necessities of aging parents or dependents.

☎ Consider a formal consultation with the appropriate professional specialist before taking actions.

AGES 65 AND OLDER

☎ 1. **Provide for a satisfactory adjustment or change in retirement income.**
  - Reevaluate and adjust your living conditions and spending habits as they relate to your health and income.
  - Make maximum use of community resources as well as your consumer knowledge and skills.
  - Obtain reliable assistance in the management of your personal and economic affairs.

☎ Consider a formal consultation with the appropriate professional specialist before taking action.

Adapted from the American Council of Life Insurance & U.S. Department of Agriculture Extension Service, Washington, D.C., ● late 1970's. Used by permission.

LIFETIME FINANCIAL RESPONSIBILITIES[1]

AGES 65 AND OLDER (Con't)

2. **Seek a satisfying retirement life style.**
   - Provide for, and be able to finance recreational and leisure time activities.

☎ 3. **Provide for a reliable source of monthly income.**
   - Restructure investments to produce additional income as well as provide a cash reserve for emergencies.
   - Retain a portion of your growth investment as a hedge against inflation.

☎ 4. **Finalize insurance programs.**
   - Review your current need for life insurance; update coverage as necessary.
   - Secure appropriate medicare supplement and/or long-term care policies for your family/individual situation.

☎ 5. **Complete estate planning.**
   - Finalize letter of last instruction.
   - Provide an orderly plan for the transfer of property.

☎ 6. **Have durable power of attorney.**
   - Appoint someone to take care of your affairs, such as paying monthly expenses and medical bills, should you unexpectedly become incapacitated.

7. **Complete home mortgage payment.**
   - Have home mortgage paid off by retirement time.

☎ Consider a formal consultation with the appropriate professional specialist before taking action.

"Why did the Lord give us so much quickness of movement unless it was to avoid responsibility?"

Ogden Nash

---

[1] Tables on pages 25 - 30 were adapted with permission from a publication (no longer in print) produced by the American Council of Life Insurance and the U.S. Department of Agriculture Extension Service, Washington, D.C., in the late 1970's.

TAX LAW IMPACT

The tax law has its impact on each of our lives, from birth through death. Just as there are financial responsibilities from late teenage years to age 65 and older, there are specific milestones in our lives for which we, or our parents, are both responsible and accountable to the Internal Revenue Service. The "life markers" which may be among those considered to be the most significant are only listed below.

Since tax laws frequently change, as well as due to the complexity of the Internal Revenue Code, it is strongly advised that each person seek professional consultation with a knowledgeable specialist for the most recent tax implication(s) as it applies to the individual or family involved **before** taking action on any of the following "life markers."

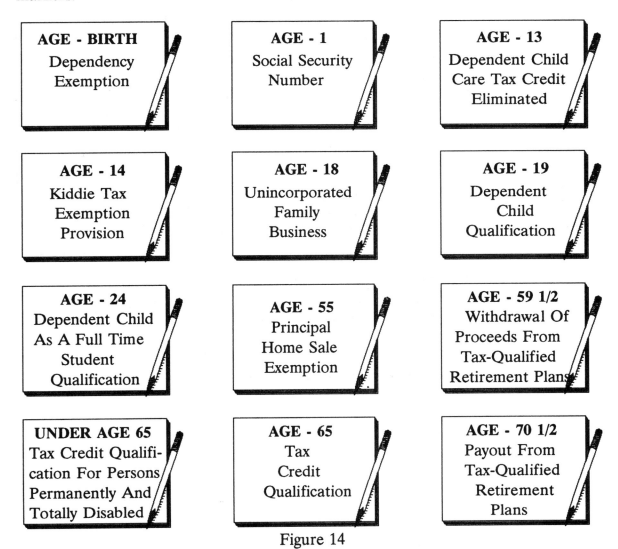

AGE - BIRTH Dependency Exemption	AGE - 1 Social Security Number	AGE - 13 Dependent Child Care Tax Credit Eliminated
AGE - 14 Kiddie Tax Exemption Provision	AGE - 18 Unincorporated Family Business	AGE - 19 Dependent Child Qualification
AGE - 24 Dependent Child As A Full Time Student Qualification	AGE - 55 Principal Home Sale Exemption	AGE - 59 1/2 Withdrawal Of Proceeds From Tax-Qualified Retirement Plans
UNDER AGE 65 Tax Credit Qualification For Persons Permanently And Totally Disabled	AGE - 65 Tax Credit Qualification	AGE - 70 1/2 Payout From Tax-Qualified Retirement Plans

Figure 14

☑ ACTION STEPS ☑

- ❑ Set realistic and attainable goals
- ❑ Determine your priorities
- ❑ Take immediate action
- ❑ Reward yourself for achieving success

YOU SHOULD NOW BE ABLE TO:

1. Identify your personal life values. Do they involve money in any way?
2. Set at least one realistic financial goal and be able to arrive at an annual or monthly commitment.
3. Develop a list of financial priorities for the next six months.
4. Determine a strategy for the payment of your financial obligations.
5. Decide on a practical payment schedule for at least one of your current debts.
6. Write a plan of action for achieving items 2 - 5 above.

CONCLUDING REMARKS

Setting realistic and attainable financial goals, together with knowing your current financial priorities, responsibilities, and obligations will serve as motivation for coming to grips with your present situation. The worksheets in the Forms section of the book provide the necessary tools to complete the various tasks to get your "Financial House" in order. Nevertheless, the task(s) will only be accomplished through **discipline**, **persistence**, and **action**.

"Nothing in the world can take the place of persistence. Talent will not; nothing is more common than unsuccessful men with talent. Genius will not; unrewarded genius is almost a proverb. Education will not; the world is full of educated derelicts. Persistence and determination alone are omnipotent. The slogan 'press on' has solved and always will solve the problems of the human race."

Calvin Coolidge

CHAPTER 2

ORGANIZING FINANCIAL RECORDS

ORDER IS POWER

FOCUS ON:

KEEPING ACCURATE FINANCIAL RECORDS

1. Develop a system for organizing materials that is simple, easily understood, and efficiently maintained.

2. Create a record keeping system that can be adjusted to your schedule and your life style.

3. Recognize what materials should be kept and what materials should be tossed immediately.

4. Decide how long to keep critical records.

5. Inform another person of your record keeping system.

6. Obtain a safe deposit box and keep it organized.

7. Maintain a home inventory list of all your possessions.

8. Develop the habit of asking for, and saving, your receipts.

9. Make your checkbook register the basis for your record keeping system.

10. Streamline your portfolio by keeping an investment log.

ORGANIZING FINANCIAL RECORDS

"Order means light and peace, inward liberty and free command over oneself; order is power . . . Order is man's greatest need, and his true well-being."

Henri Frederic Amiel
Journal Entry, January 27, 1860

GET ORGANIZED

No doubt you have often agonized over the thought of getting yourself organized. Even though you're sure where each financial account is located, your files are probably scattered in various places, from your office to throughout your home. If you are the only person who knows where important records and documents are located, you've got a major problem. Have you ever needed to obtain immediate answers to these questions:

1. What is my current networth?

2. Where are my income tax records for the previous two years?

3. Are each of my insurance programs current?

4. Do I need to change the beneficiaries on my life insurance policies (especially in the event of marriage or divorce)?

5. Is my will up to date?

6. When were my property taxes last paid, and what was the number of the check that I used to pay them?

7. When does my next Certificate of Deposit (CD) come due?

8. Do I thoroughly understand my pension plan and other employee benefits?

These are just a few of the myriads of questions that may demand a prompt response at any given moment of our lives. Perhaps there have been occasions you needed such relevant information, only to discover that you were not able to locate it. Being organized may well save you time, money, and frustration, in addition to simplifying the process for making decisions. More important, you have the peace of mind knowing that, in the event of an emergency, relevant information can be located on a moments notice.

> "Don't waste any time mourning - Organize."
>
> Joe Hill

The main purpose of this chapter is to assist you with the painful and laborious task of organizing your financial records. Besides taking control of your financial life, benefits for maintaining accurate records include:

1. Measuring your progress toward achieving financial goals and reducing stress.
2. Satisfying an IRS audit requirement.
3. Saving considerable money in tax preparation fees.
4. Satisfying a proof of loss requirement when filing insurance claims.
5. Simplifying your life, leaving you more time to pursue other interests.

CREATE A RECORDS SYSTEM

The first step in creating a records system is to identify a specific, central location for your permanent records and documents. A well organized filing system is essential for the keeping and maintaining of good records. Purchase a sturdy one or two drawer filing cabinet, along with a set of hanging file folders and the necessary adapter insert frame. You can buy hanging files of various colors, thereby creating your own individualized "color code" system, to identify major categories. Using multicolored files and/or tabs enables you to locate items quicker than the use of words only. Some of the most common categories are listed alphabetically below and on page 38:

★ Bank Records
★ Cash receipts
★ Children's File
★ Clothing
★ Contributions
★ Credit Records

- ★ Current Bills
- ★ Education Information
- ★ Employment Information
- ★ Entertainment/Vacation Expenses
- ★ Estate Planning Documents
- ★ Financial Planning Information
- ★ Home Residence Documents/Rental Information
- ★ Insurance Records
- ★ Investment Documents
- ★ Legal Documents and Records
- ★ Medical/Dental Records
- ★ Personal Growth and Development
- ★ Retirement Programs/Plans Information
- ★ Tax Information
- ★ Utility Records
- ★ Vehicle(s) Records
- ★ Warranties and Guarantees Information

The second step in the filing process is to place all statements, records, documents, and items of correspondence in the appropriate hanging file folder. To accomplish this task, purchase a box of 50 or 100 manila file folders to be inserted into the hanging files. Begin by using a different manila file folder for <u>each</u> expense item of a main category as shown in Figure 15. Suppose, for example, that you have credit cards from four financial institutions. Carefully, arrange all statements, receipts, and important information relating to each of the financial institutions in a separate manila

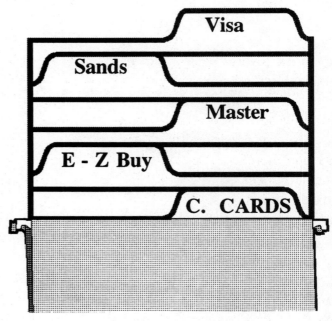

Figure 15

folder. Then, file the four folders alphabetically in the one hanging file folder titled "Credit Records" or "Credit Cards." Use this procedure for each of the hanging files.

     Solving Your Financial Puzzle

When organizing monthly budgeted expenses (credit card, gas and electric utilities, telephone bills, mortgage or rent payments, automobile payments), be sure your statements and records within each file folder are arranged in chronological order. By placing the most recent information in the <u>front</u> of the file folder, you will be able to consistently monitor the payment for each monthly statement. Always maintain accurate records regarding the status of outstanding loans or debts on your automobile(s), home, and any other major purchases. In this situation, you may want to create a section titled "Current Debts" in your file cabinet. Regardless of the method you choose in the keeping of your records and documents, be clear and concise with your system of filing; it is essential that any adult family member be familiar with its organization and contents.

ORGANIZE CANCELED CHECKS

Have you ever had this problem/concern? Did I pay my federal and state estimated taxes for the current quarter? If so, when were the checks written and what were their respective numbers? There will come a time, if it hasn't already, that it will be necessary to retrieve a check that you had written in the past. Perhaps it was a check written to the Internal Revenue Service within the past year; or it may have been a check written for a car or home mortgage payment several years ago.

If you are like many people, chances are that you have personal canceled checks that date back several years. No doubt you felt that there must have been a reason for keeping such checks, but you have no idea where they are located. What checks then, should one keep, and for how long? Actually, the majority of canceled checks can probably be tossed after a couple of years. Checks written for the usual everyday purchases of food, clothing, entertainment, and the like generally fall into that category and therefore need not clutter up your files for years on end. On the other hand, canceled checks that should be kept are those that provide proof for deductions you took on Schedule A, itemized deductions, of your income tax return. Included in this list are medical and dental expenses, taxes and interest you paid, charitable gifts and contributions, union dues, as well as any other deductions you noted on Schedule A.

The length of time that these checks should be kept depends upon your past, and probably more important, your future experiences with the IRS. It might be a good idea to place in your file folder all such checks with your annual tax returns. In that way, in the case of an audit, you will have the checks at your immediate disposal. It is highly recommended that you consult a professional accountant, tax planner, or an attorney who specializes in the area for which the check was written to determine what canceled checks should be kept and for how long in your individual situation. Checks written for major cash purchases such as a vehicle or boat, as well as for insurance claims may need to be kept indefinitely.

What should you do if you don't receive cancelled checks? Frequently, people choose accounts that don't return cancelled checks to avoid paying bank fees. There are also financial institutions (credit unions, banks, and mutual fund companies) that do not return cancelled checks to their customers, but shred them at regular intervals. However, every financial institution offering check writing privileges, whether it returns cancelled checks or not, is required to film each check, usually on microfilm, and to keep them for a time mandated by banking regulations. You can obtain a "copy" of any micro-filmed check(s) by contacting the financial institution involved. Some institutions may have a fixed charge for each microfilmed check copy, while others allow you to receive a minimum number of copies free. You can retrieve a copy of checks by request from your bank.

If you use credit cards to purchase goods and services, you may wish to create a separate file to store your itemized monthly billings. Be sure to identify on <u>each</u> <u>check</u> written to a credit card company, as well as in your check book register, the specific card used, along with either the place, item, or service purchased. This will provide you with complete records to return unsatisfactory items, as well as information to file complaints for any inadequate or unfulfilled services received. It is wise to write on the credit slip the item(s) purchased. Make a habit of this immediately after you sign your name and before placing it in your wallet. **Never** put credit card receipts in the bag with the item as the receipt can get lost or stolen too easily.

It might be advisable that you keep your personal check registers indefinitely. You may even want to use them as the basis of your record keeping system. Then, if you have a need or desire to know the price of an item purchased in the past, such as a piece of jewelry or an antique, it would be a simple task to retrieve your check registers to determine the exact price, date, and from whom the purchase was made. It would even be quite possible to obtain a copy of the check from the financial institution involved.

Saving your checks for even a few years can become a nightmare, especially if they are kept in envelopes. Store your checks and check registers together by purchasing a box approximately 4" x 6" x 18" in size. Many packaging stores will be able to provide you with such boxes for less than $2.00. Use labeled divider cards to organize checks by years. By having a system to organize your canceled checks, along with your check registers, you can save yourself needless worry, in addition to countless hours of frustration. Whatever way you choose to organize your canceled checks, consider keeping all check registers indefinitely, along with any checks written for taxes or

    Solving Your Financial Puzzle

payments on purchases for a home or a business venture. Be sure to note the location of your check registers and canceled checks in the Documents and Asset Location List which is explained on pages 41 - 47.

FAMILY FINANCIAL SUMMARY

It is absolutely necessary that each spouse have easy access to certain critical family financial information. In the case of a single individual, this information should be entrusted to a relative or close friend. The information forms provided on pages 233 - 234 represent a "snap shot" of your individual or family financial situation. It will direct your survivors to vital records and documents, as well as to important people you have selected to handle your financial affairs. Be sure to use a separate form for each child as well as one for you and your spouse. When completing this information, it is the responsibility of both you and your spouse to be involved in the planning process. In addition, the Family Financial Summary information should be reviewed on an annual basis, and updated when appropriate.

The Family Information chart illustrated in Figure 16 on page 42 is composed of three sections. The first section identifies your family's last name. The second component contains general information about each family member. Be sure to include the children's last name if it is different from the family name given in the Section I. The third section gives a detailed key (or guide) to the Documents and Asset Location List provided on pages 235 to 239. This location key identifies seven specific places (or locations) for a particular document or asset. Be sure to give complete and detailed information when completing Part III. Indicate the location in column 2, the address in column 3, and any necessary information in column 4. To illustrate, let A in the first row identify your safe deposit box at First Securities Bank. You would then write "Safe Deposit Box - First Securities Bank" in column 2. The address of the bank would be written in column 3, with the safe deposit box number in column 4. Rows B - G would be completed in a similar manner. The Advisors list shown in Figure 17 gives the titles of a variety of family consultants. Write the name of the individual or firm, together with the address in column 2. The telephone number(s) is then written in column 3.

The comprehensive Documents and Asset Location List is an essential financial planning tool that will assist your spouse, family member(s), and relatives in the event of your death. The list will also be of invaluable help to you in the organization of important documents. Notice that the seven columns labeled A - G in Figure 18 on page 43 correspond to rows A - G of Figure 16, Part III. You may wish to keep the Family Information and the Advisor pages in a place separate from the Documents and Asset Location List in an effort to protect the confidentiality of your possessions.

FAMILY INFORMATION

I.   Family Name: Barnes

II. Personal Information

Family Member	First Name	Social Security Number	Date of Birth	Birth Place (City, State)
Husband:	James	000 - 101 - 0101	01 - 22 - 60	Riverside, California
Wife:	Sandra	111 - 010 - 1010	07 - 04 - 58	Medford, Oregon
Children:	William	212 - 111 - 1001	12 - 24 - 84	Denver, Colorado

III. Key - Documents And Asset Location List

Column	Location	Address	Information
A	Safe Deposit Box - First Securities Bank	1605 E. Forest Dr. Boston, Mass.	Box #100
B	Home File - Local Residence	550 Cottage Grove Boston, Mass.	Attic Closet
C	Home Safe - Local Residence	550 Cottage Grove Boston, Mass.	Attic Closet
D	Office - File	400 Parker Building Boston, Mass.	Second File Drawer
G			

Figure 16 - Worksheet page 233

ADVISORS

Title	Individual Or Firm Name Address	Telephone Number(s)
Accountant	Ralph Birdsong 408 E. Market Street Boston, Mass.	(403) - 228 - 2503
Attorney	James G. Quick 2055 Green Forest Drive Boston, Mass.	(403) - 227 - 1860

Figure 17 - Worksheet page 234

    Solving Your Financial Puzzle

DOCUMENTS AND ASSET LOCATION LIST

BANK

		A	B	C	D	E	F	G
1.	Cancelled Checks	☐	☑	☐	☐	☐	☐	☐
2.	Certificates of Deposit	☑	☐	☐	☐	☐	☐	☐
3.	Checkbooks	☐	☐	☐	☐	☐	☐	☐
4.	Checkbook Register(s)	☐	☑	☐	☐	☐	☐	☐
5.	Checking/Savings Account Statements	☐	☑	☐	☐	☐	☐	☐
6.	Investment Securities	☑	☐	☐	☐	☐	☐	☐
7.	List of Checking/Savings Account Numbers	☐	☐	☑	☐	☐	☐	☐
8.	List of Contents in Safe Deposit Box	☐	☐	☐	☑	☐	☐	☐
9.	Money Market Accounts	☐	☑	☐	☐	☐	☐	☐

Figure 18 - Worksheet pages 235 - 239

IMPORTANT RECORDS AND DOCUMENTS

Besides knowing where your important records and documents are located, it is equally important to know the most practical or "safest" place in which to store your permanent records, as well as how long this information should be kept. Questions such as the following are frequently asked:

1. How many copies of my will should I have and where is the appropriate location to place each copy?

2. If I currently live in an apartment, what records are of critical importance that I keep?

3. Should I keep my warranties and instruction manuals? If so, where is the most practical place to store them?

4. Where is the most practical place to keep my automobile payment book?

5. When I purchase a home, what records and documents are important to keep and where is the best place to store them?

The Records and Documents Chart on pages 44 - 47 will be of assistance to you in this aspect of your record keeping process. There is no absolute answer to "how long" specific records should be kept; the information provided in the Length of Time column is to be used only as a guideline. You will need to consult with an accountant, financial planner, or an estate planning attorney to be sure what length of time is best for your individual or family situation.

RECORDS AND DOCUMENTS CHART

CATEGORY	SPECIFIC CONTENTS	WHERE TO KEEP	LENGTH OF TIME
Assets & Documents	Document and asset location list	Home file	Indefinitely
Automobile	Title	Safe deposit box	
	Owners manual & registration card	Either in home file or in car itself	Until vehicle is sold or traded
	Gasoline, oil, & lube records		
	Payment book	Home file	Until vehicle is paid in full
	Repair records, receipts for maintenance and parts, tires, other vehicle purchases		Until vehicle is sold or needed to prove tax-deductible business expenses
	Record of traffic violations or accidents		Three years after violation or accident, five years may be better
Bank	Passbook, savings records	Home file	Until account is closed
	Bank statements	Home file, move to dead storage annually	Ten years
	Cancelled checks		
Cash Receipts	Receipts for major purchases such as TV, VCR, appliances, cam corder, stereo, jewelry, etc.	Home file, move to dead storage annually	Three years, indefinitely if it's proof of purchase for an item on your personal inventory
Credit Records	List of credit card numbers with each creditor's name, address, pay off amount, payments left, monthly payment, due date if applicable	Home file	Until cards expire or are destroyed (after creditor has been paid in full, or following a bankruptcy)
	Installment contracts	Original in safe deposit box, one copy in file	Until debt is paid or until as needed

★ Consult with the appropriate professional specialist <u>before</u> destroying permanent records or documents.

44 © 1996 by John M. Orth, Iowa City, IA.   Solving Your Financial Puzzle

RECORDS AND DOCUMENTS CHART

Page 2

CATEGORY	SPECIFIC CONTENTS	WHERE TO KEEP	LENGTH OF TIME
Current Expenses	All unpaid bills and charge account slips	Home file, move to dead storage when paid in full or annually	Three years for general purposes Six years if needed to prove a tax deductible item Indefinitely if used to provide legal evidence as proof of purchase
Employment Information	Employee benefit and retirement information, handbook(s), and reports	Home file	As needed
	Employee pay stubs; current stub	Home file, most recent pay stub	Replace monthly with current pay stub
	Retirement records from previous employers	Home file	Indefinitely
Executor Will, Trust	Copy of will and/or trust documents	Original with attorney, one copy in home file, one copy in safe deposit box	Indefinitely, update as needed
	Letter of last instruction	Original in home file, copy in safe deposit box	Indefinitely, update as needed
Financial Planning Budget	Cash-flow statement, networth statement	Home file	As needed, update when major life changes occur
Insurance	List of policy numbers, name(s) of insured person(s), beneficiaries, issuing company, agent, type and amount of coverage, copies of all policies	Home file	Indefinite; update as necessary, especially when changes such as marriage, birth of children, or divorce occur

★ Consult with the appropriate professional specialist <u>before</u> destroying permanent records or documents.

RECORDS AND DOCUMENTS CHART
Page 3

CATEGORY	SPECIFIC CONTENTS	WHERE TO KEEP	LENGTH OF TIME
Financial Planning (continued) Investments	Bearer bonds	Safe deposit box	Until sold or maturity
	Certificates of deposit	Safe deposit box	Until maturity and redemption
	Records of stock, bond, mutual funds purchase & selling price	Home file	Indefinite; update as necessary for tax purposes
	Stock, mutual fund, & annuity certificates	Safe deposit box	Until sold
	Transaction slips (broker's purchase & sales statements)	Home file	Until sold, use for tax purposes
Taxes	Copies of old tax returns & supporting data	Dead storage	Ten years, you may want to keep them indefinitely
	Receipts for tax deductible items; e.g. mortgage interest paid, child care, medical & nursing home care, donations & charitable gifts, business related expenses, real estate taxes, property & casualty losses	Home file	Use annually, then store with old tax returns as supporting data
	Receipts for taxable items; e.g. interest & dividends, capital gains or losses, K-1's for partnership gains or losses	Home file	Use annually, then store with old tax returns as supporting data
	Paycheck stubs	Home file	Discard annually after checking W-2 totals
Housing	Home improvement receipts, record of land transfer taxes, purchase price, closing & selling costs, photographs of home contents	Home file	Keep all records of home improvements, buying & selling costs for tax purposes until home is sold

★ Consult with the appropriate professional specialist <u>before</u> destroying permanent records or documents.

     Solving Your Financial Puzzle

RECORDS AND DOCUMENTS CHART

Page 4

CATEGORY	SPECIFIC CONTENTS	WHERE TO KEEP	LENGTH OF TIME
Housing (continued) As Owners	Title insurance policy	Safe deposit box	Until property is sold
	Mortgage papers	Safe deposit box	Until property is sold, then keep a copy of sale agreement indefinitely
	Cemetery plot deed	Safe deposit box	Until needed
	Termite inspection policy, radon inspection papers	Home file	Until property is sold
As Renters	Copy of lease rental agreement, photographs showing the move-in condition of rental property	Home file	Until you move & claims are settled
Medical Records	Medical history, family members	Home file	Update as necessary
Property	Personal property inventory including original purchase price & photographs showing valuable or unusual possessions	One copy in safe deposit box & one in home file	Update as necessary
	Appraisals	Safe deposit box	Update as necessary
Social Security	Request for "Earnings and Benefit Estimate Statement," Form SSA - 7004 - SM	Home file	Keep indefinitely; update every 3 years ★ See comments provided on page 48
Warranties and Guarantees	All warranties	Home file, attach purchase receipt	Annually remove expired warranties or guarantees
	Instruction manuals	Home file	Until item is discarded or sold
Other Papers	Birth & death certificates, passport, marriage license, divorce papers, diplomas, military papers, social security number, driver's license number	Safe deposit box	Indefinitely

★ Consult with the appropriate professional specialist _before_ destroying permanent records or documents.

SOCIAL SECURITY CONSIDERATION

(Note From Page 47)

★ To receive an estimate of your post retirement income from Social Security, contact the Social Security Administration at 1-800-772-1213 and ask for the Request For Earnings And Benefit Estimate Statement. Completing this form will enable you to verify that your previous payments into the system have been properly recorded. Within a few weeks you will receive an accounting of your earnings record, along with estimated retirement benefits at ages 65 and 70. Survivor and disability benefit amounts are also provided. If the Social Security Administration has made an error in crediting payments to you, it may be much more difficult to correct the problem after the three year time period due to the necessary paperwork involved.

☑ ACTION STEPS ☑

❏ Purchase the necessary equipment and materials for your record keeping system: filing cabinet, hanging files with tabs, manila file folders, a box with dividers for cancelled checks, and calculator.

❏ Identify major categories, then label the hanging files using the tabs provided. Arrange the categories in alphabetical order.

❏ Place each **different** expense item in a separate manila folder, arrange the items in chronological order with the most recent statement or information in **front**. Place all related expense file folders in the appropriate hanging file.

❏ Develop a system for organizing your checks, bank statements, and check registers.

❏ Complete your personal or family information chart, together with your Documents and Asset Location List. (Update as needed)

❏ Complete your list of Advisors, include current addresses and telephone numbers. (Update as needed)

❏ Contact the Social Security Administration Office to update your Earnings and Benefit Estimate Statement.

                    Solving Your Financial Puzzle

PERSONAL INVENTORY

If you have not experienced the devastation caused by fire, hurricane, tornado, flood, or theft to your home, you will probably underestimate the need of having a Personal Inventory. However, few people today can afford the luxury of not knowing the value of their possessions. When filing a claim, you are required to provide the insurance company with a complete list of furnishings and contents that were taken or destroyed. In addition, you will need the value of each item you listed. Unfortunately, an educated guess will not satisfy the insurance company in this regard. The risks for not knowing the value of your personal belongings are just too great.

The inventory forms given on pages 240 - 245 will provide you with a detailed, yet simple strategy for arriving at a realistic value of your personal property. Since replacement costs continue to rise, it is necessary that you revise your inventory every year or two, especially if you have purchased valuable articles, updated your home, or discarded items of significant value. It is also an excellent idea to include appraisals of valuable possessions. Photographs or videos of every room, with closet or cabinet doors open, will substantiate an insurance claim, if it becomes necessary to file one. Be sure to write the date, general location, and the contents displayed, on the back of each photograph. Then, store a copy of your inventory, with any appraisals and the negatives of your photographs, in your safe deposit box. If a video is used, be sure to include an index on a sheet of paper placed inside the video cover denoting the rooms viewed, as well as the date they were taken.

The Inventory Summary on page 243 will give you an estimated value of your possessions. You may come to the realistic conclusion that you are seriously under insured. It is recommended that you have insurance of not less than 80% of the present, or replacement, value of your household goods. Be sure to consult with your insurance agent if you have any questions or concerns regarding your present coverage.

Your personal inventory consists of two main sections, Rooms and Special Inventory items. Begin by checking ☑ only those rooms and special inventory items listed on the next page that apply to your situation. Use a separate form, such as those provided on pages 241 and 242, for each of the category boxes you indicated on page 240. To illustrate this process, consider the living room as an example. On one of the Room forms, write the name of the room for which the inventory is taking place; in this case, the Living Room. List each item the room contains, along with the year the item was purchased, the original cost, and its estimated present value. Place the totals for columns 4 - 5 at the bottom of each form as shown in Figure 19 below. Remember that some of the categories you checked may require more than one form.

The Special Inventory section is completed in a similar manner, again using a separate form for each of the appropriate categories. When you have completed both sections of the inventory, transfer the final totals of each "individual" form to the Inventory Summary as illustrated by Figure 21 on page 51. Be sure to complete the calculations at the bottom of the page. You now have a clear estimate of your home furnishings, contents, and possessions. Even more important, you will also be able to determine at a glance, the amount of added insurance, if any, that will be needed to cover the loss of your belongings.

ROOMS

☑ Living Room   ☐ Recreation, Family Room
☐ Dining Room   ☐ Garage
☐ Kitchen, Breakfast, Pantry   ☐ Basement

ROOMS
LIVING ROOM

Number of Items	Item	Year Purchased	Original Cost	Estimated Present Value
2	Biffel Brass Lamps	1972	$ 320	$ 785
2	Modern Mahogany End Tables	1972	250	350
2	High Back Velvet Chairs	1972	380	575
1	Velvet 72 - inch Sofa	1972	460	620
1	48 - inch Glass Coffee Table	1972	170	385
1	Wahoo Baby Grand Piano	1975	4,600	12,000
		Totals	$ 6,180	$14,715

Figure 19 - Worksheet page 241

      Solving Your Financial Puzzle

SPECIAL INVENTORY

☐ Patio　　　　　　　　　　☐ Swimming Pool, Tennis Court
☐ Books　　　　　　　　　　☑ Musical Instruments

SPECIAL INVENTORY
MUSICAL INSTRUMENTS

Number of Articles	Article	Year Purchased	Original Cost	Estimated Present Value
1	Wahoo Baby Grand Piano	1983	$4,600	$ 12,000
1	Lablanc Clarinet	1953	330	2,400
1	Hines Flute	1958	445	3,800
		Totals	$5,375	$ 18,200

Figure 20 - Worksheet page 242

INVENTORY SUMMARY

Number of Items	Room or Special Inventory	Original Cost	Estimated Present or Replacement Value
7	Living Room (Exclude Piano)	$ 1,580	$ 2,715
9	Dining Room	3,350	4,750
3	Musical Instruments	5,375	18,200
	Final Group Totals (Not All Listed)	$14,950	$33,700
	Total Amount of Insurance Covering Personal Property		$25,000
	Additional Insurance, if Any, Required		$ 8,700

Figure 21 - Worksheet page 243

RISK MANAGEMENT PROGRAM
INSURANCE PROTECTION

Insurance can be thought of as a risk management program using rented dollars to cover expenses beyond either our willingness or financial ability to pay. Such expenses can range from a broken automobile windshield to replacing a home (including its contents), to paying for several months of intensive hospital care. A well thought out insurance program, along with sufficient cash reserves, are essential building blocks for developing a sound financial plan (see Figure 32 on page 66).

It is critical that insurance records are kept current, especially in view of the fact that we frequently buy, sell, and trade automobiles, purchase new homes, and continue to shop for the best life, health, and accident coverage available for the least cost. The three Insurance Record forms that are illustrated in Figures 22 - 24 below and on page 53 are provided on pages 275 - 277. Be sure to update each of these forms on a regular basis.

INSURANCE RECORDS

Property, Casualty, Automobile, Liability, Fire, Business Insurance Policies

Name of Insured	Name of Insurer	Policy Number	Policy Date	Coverage Amount	Coverage Deductible	Annual Premium	Item(s) Insured
J & D Smith	Midwest	AUTO4572	06-05-92	$250/$500	$100	$385.25	Auto
J & D Smith	Midwest	LIAB43-91	06-05-92	$1 million to $2 million	Underlying Liab. Limits + Retention Amount	$124.50	Auto/Home
J & D Smith	Midwest	HOME2640	06-05-92	$300,000 + Home Value	$250	$245.50	Home + Contents

Figure 22 - Worksheet page 275

Life Insurance Policies

Name of Insured	Name of Insurer	Policy Owner	Policy Number	Policy Date	Type of Policy	Face Amount	Annual Premium	Name of Beneficiary
J. Smith	Midwest	J. Smith	44-70-83	04-15-91	Level Term	$250,000	$245.78	Wife-Doris
D. Smith	Midwest	D. Smith	44-70-82	04-15-91	Level Term	$250,000	$224.98	Hus.-Jim

Figure 23 - Worksheet page 276

    Solving Your Financial Puzzle

INSURANCE RECORD

Health, Accident, Major Medical, Disability Insurance Policies

Name of Insured	Name of Insurer	Policy Number	Group Number	Policy Date	Coverage Amount	Deductible	Annual Premium	Name of Beneficiary
Health Insurance								
J. Smith	Western Mutual	M0045376	Gr. 2054	02-12-88	$1,000,000 limit	$500	$675.50	Wife-Doris
D. Smith	Western Mutual	M0045741	Gr. 2054	02-12-88	$1,000,000 limit	$500	$703.25	Hus.-Jim
Disability Insurance								
J. Smith	Western Mutual	DI4078	Gr. 1723	02-07-85	$500/ Month	No Waiting Period	$75.00	None
J. Smith	Midwest	782962	Individual Policy	06-19-87	$1,500/ Month	60 Day Wait Per.	$847.15	Wife-Doris
D. Smith	Midwest	965405	Individual Policy	11-23-87	$2,000/ Month	60 Day Wait Per.	$1,015.30	Hus.-Jim

Figure 24 - Worksheet page 277

CERTIFICATES OF DEPOSIT

While discussing the subject of record keeping, it would seem most appropriate to address the necessity of keeping reliable records for savings and investments. It is not only wise to keep such records for your personal networth statement; it is also essential for the planning of your future needs, goals, and desires. Certificates of Deposit, commonly referred to as CD's, are frequently used by persons who desire to take little or no investment risk to meet financial objectives that usually materialize within a few months or within one to two years. Keeping the term of the CD to six months or less, as well as staggering the maturity dates of the CD's as shown in Figure 25 on page 54, allows you to have available funds in a relatively short period of time without having to pay a penalty for redeeming the certificate before its maturity date. This method also allows you to shop for CD specials of three to nine months that are frequently advertised by various savings institutions.

CERTIFICATES OF DEPOSIT
AND SAVINGS BONDS

Date of Record: June 9, 1988

Certificate or ID Number	Owner	Amount of Investment	Issue Date	Length of Term	Maturity Date	Interest Rate or Value at Maturity	Name of Institution
23421669	Norman	$5,000	06-09-88	6 months	12-09-88	6.25%	First Bank
02-34287969	Diane	$2,500	03-12-88	6 months	09-12-88	6.75%	City Bank
23471138	Diane	$4,000	01-15-89	9 months	10-15-89	5.85%	First Bank

E Bonds M65475629E	Norman	$1,000	07-88	N A	N A	6.00%	N A

Figure 25 - Worksheet page 280

MUTUAL FUND INVESTMENTS

While savings accounts and Certificates of Deposit might be suitable investments for short term needs and objectives, another investment vehicle, known as a mutual fund, might be more appropriate for meeting objectives of four to five years or longer. According to the Investment Company Institute, nearly 25% of all households in the United States are currently shareholders in mutual fund investments.[2] By the end of 1992 assets of all mutual funds reached a record of $1.603 trillion[3] with an additional $342.8 billion of new sales generated after three quarters of 1993.[4] A reason for their popularity might be due to the fact that mutual funds offer investors a simple, affordable, and more convenient method of investing in the stock and bond markets,

---

[2]Investment Company Institute, <u>Mutual Fund News</u> (Washington, D.C.: December, 1989) Volume 11, No. 5.

The Investment Company Institute is the national association of the American investment company industry. Its membership now exceeds 4,350 open-end investment companies (or mutual funds), 350 closed-end investment companies, and 10 sponsors of unit investment trusts.

[3]Investment Company Institute, <u>Mutual Fund News</u> Washington, D.C.: March, 1993) Volume 15, No. 1.

[4]Investment Company Institute, <u>Mutual Fund News</u> (Washington, D.C.:November, 1993) Volume 15, No. 4.

thereby taking out much of the confusion and complexity of the financial market place. The excellent past performance of many funds, along with their ease in providing for regular investing, have made them a favorite choice of many investors as well. The Record of Mutual Fund Investments form on page 281 contains a list of all mutual fund purchases, together with significant information relating to each of the individual funds (Figure 26 below). Meticulously kept records are extremely necessary to identify the cost basis of acquired mutual fund shares. Reporting capital gains and losses (sold or transferred from one fund to another within any one fund family) is essential. Accurate records have been found to be invaluable when organizing annual tax return information or when preparing to answer questions for an IRS audit.

The purpose of this book is not to suggest ways to calculate gains or losses when you sell or transfer mutual fund shares; this activity is best left to a competent accountant or to a person suggested by the firm who sold you the investment(s). It might be an excellent idea to raise this question with the account executive or registered representative at the time of the initial purchase. You will also want to know if the company provides its clients with account histories. These records identify every account transaction made, whether it is a purchase, redemption, transfer or exchange, dividend, or capital gain. Such information is essential since fund shares, in the majority of cases, will eventually be redeemed or sold. The simplified Annual Account History shown in Figure 27 on page 56 illustrates the investment accumulation program presented below. The form can be completed quickly, is easy to keep current, and provides a systematic way to regularly monitor the performance for each individual mutual fund account.

George and Betty Smith began an accumulation program in March, 1983 with an original investment of $1,000 followed by regular monthly amounts of $100 each. They decide to have all dividends and capital gain shares reinvested instead of taking them in cash. In October, 1991 they decide to redeem $5,000, or 690 shares as a down payment on a new automobile, but continue with their regular monthly contributions of $100 each. The value of their account at the end of the ten-year period of time was $18,962.

RECORD OF MUTUAL FUND INVESTMENTS

Date of Record: March 10, 1983

Owner of Investment	Fund Group or Sponsor	Name of Fund	Listed Newspaper Symbol	Fund Objectives	Account & Fund Number	Date Account Opened or Purchase Date	Initial Dollar Amount Invested	Opening Share Balance	Initial Price per Share
G & B Smith	Poudre Cadre Funds	P - C Equity	PCEquity	Long Term Growth	71354662 4	03-10-83	$1,000.00	102.249	9.78

Figure 26 - Worksheet page 281

ANNUAL ACCOUNT HISTORY
INDIVIDUAL MUTUAL FUND INVESTMENTS

Date of Record: March 10, 1983

Owner of Investment: George & Betty Smith

Fund Group/Sponsor: Poudre Cadre Funds

Date Account Opened: March 10, 1983

Name of Fund: Poudre Cadre Equity Fund

Listed Newspaper Symbol: PCEquity

Account & Fund Number: 71354662 - 4

Investment Firm: Jones & Smith (P. Jackson)

Current Year	Dec. 31 Selling Price	Dollar Purchases Year To Date	Dollar Amount Sold/Redeemed Year To Date	Cumulative Dollars Invested	Cumulative Share Purchases	Cumulative Fund Shares	Dec. 31 Market Value	Cumulative Profit or Loss
1983	10.13	2,000		2,000	194.350	203.502	$ 2,061.48	$ 61.48
1984	7.64	1,200		3,200	344.565	409.601	3,129.35	-70.65
1985	8.73	1,200		4,400	481.446	579.185	5,056.29	656.29
1986	7.78	1,200		5,600	606.258	870.836	6,775.10	1,175.10
1987	5.75	1,200		6,800	743.045	1,506.328	8,661.39	1,861.39
1988	6.43	1,200		8,000	918.480	1,760.194	11,318.05	3,318.05
1989	7.12	1,200		9,200	1,068.010	2,232.465	15,895.15	6,695.15
1990	6.03	1,200		10,400	1,235.298	2,548.419	15,366.97	4,966.97
1991	7.15	1,200	-5,000	6,600	708.085	2,114.835	15,121.07	8,521.07
1992	7.50	1,200		7,800	857.292	2,480.418	18,603.14	10,803.14
1993	7.57	200		8,000	881.787	2,504.913	18,962.19	10,962.19

Figure 27[5] - Worksheet page 282

STOCKS, BONDS, AND ANNUITIES

If you are a person who has the expertise to make rational, instead of emotional decisions regarding your money, you might prefer to select and manage your own investments. Controlling your capital allows you the capability to hand pick individual stocks, bonds, and/or annuities from an unlimited number of choices. In addition, the flexibility to buy and sell as frequently as you desire creates the potential to achieve substantial rewards. On the other hand, to be successful in the trading of stocks and bonds, it is essential that you keep accurate records, as well as reliable information on each particular investment. The Investment Record of Stocks, Bonds and Annuities form in Figure 28 and provided on page 283 is designed to meet this need. Enter the

---

[5]The above Selling Price Data for the Account History was obtained from an assumed investment illustration provided me by an investment (mutual fund) company. The final balance, or market value, of the account on February 16, 1993 would have been the indicated value of $18,962.19 had any investor completed the above investment program.

          Solving Your Financial Puzzle

INVESTMENT RECORD OF STOCKS,
BONDS, AND ANNUITIES

Date of Record: June 17, 1988

Owner of Investment or Annuity	Name of Company	Type of Investment or Annuity	Account Number	Certificate Number	Date Account Opened or Purchase Date	Unit Price or Price Per Share	Number of Shares or Units Purchased	Dollar Amount Invested
G & B Smith	Science Technology	Stock	4785-207C	Cusip 4620d43	06-17-88	16.86	50 Shares	$843.00
G & B	Keo Widgets	Stock	MR5706-5	07-54776	12-02-89	6.78	75 Shares	$508.50
G & B	Lincoln Investments	Unit Invest-ment Trust MT-185-L	29432-64	185-546	02-12-90	1,015.40	10 Units	$10,154.00
G & B	Cedardale Utilities	Utility Revenue Bond	1746MC5	CS1485D	07-18-92	100.00	50 Units	$5,000.00
George Smith	City Investors Insur. Co.	Single Prem. Deferred Annuity	B0052174	15-462857	11-22-92	N A	N A	$15,000.00

Figure 28 - Worksheet page 283

ACCOUNT HISTORY OF INDIVIDUAL
STOCK, BOND, & ANNUITY INVESTMENTS

Date of Record: June 17, 1988
Owner of Investment: G & B Smith
Company: Science Technology, Inc.
Date Account Opened: June 17, 1988

Name of Investment: Stock - Science Technology
Account Number: 4785-207C
Certificate Number: Cusip 4620d43
Listed Newspaper Symbol: Scntch

Date of Transaction	Dollar Amount This Transaction	Purchase Price Per Share	Number of Shares Purchased or Sold	Dollar Amount Received Or Reinvested Dividends/ Cap Gains	Shares Obtained By Reinvested Dividends/ Cap Gains	Cumulative Dollars Invested To Date	Cumulative Shares Owned To Date	Selling Price Per Share	Market Value of Account
06-07-88	843.00	16.86	50.00	---	---	843.00	50.00	16.19	809.50
10-25-88	-185.00		-10.00	---	---	658.00	40.00	18.50	740.00
12-15-88	200.00	16.84	11.88	---	---	858.00	51.88	19.17	994.54
12-30-88	---	---	---	57.06	2.96	858.00	54.84	19.27	1,056.79

Figure 29 - Worksheet page 284

names of the specific investments, together with the necessary information relating to each investment, on a separate line of the chart. The Account History of Individual Stock, Bond, & Annuity Investments on page 284 and shown in Figure 29 provides a procedure to track the activity for each of your personal investments. By completing this chart on a regular basis, you will be able to monitor the progress for each of your investments.

TAX-FAVORED INVESTMENTS

Perhaps you are a person in a significantly high income tax bracket. In this case, you may find tax-favored investments to your liking as an alternative among your tax planning strategies. These investments will provide you additional diversification, as well as the possibility of tax-sheltered income or tax write-offs. On the other hand, since investments of this type can often incur greater risks, you are frequently required to meet certain "minimum salary and/or savings amounts" in order to qualify or participate in such programs. Therefore, it would be prudent for you to seek counsel from a qualified tax attorney, certified public accountant, or other individual knowledgeable with the appropriate IRS rules, together with your specific needs, goals, and objectives before investing your hard-earned dollars in such opportunities. Examples of such investments are shown in Figure 30 below.

TAX-FAVORED INVESTMENTS

Date of Record: August 23, 1987

Owner of Investment	Investment Description	Year Purchased	Dollar Amount Invested	Expected Annual Deductions or Depreciation	Present Value (if known)	Annual Income Expected
G & B Smith	Low Income Housing Ltd. Partnership	1987	7,500	500	~4,800	None
G & B	Equipment Leasing Ltd. Partnership	1988	5,000	0	~3,500	200
G & B	Oil & Gas Drilling Ltd. Partnership	1988	5,000	1,750 in 1989	~2,000	None
G & B	Real Estate Income Ltd. Partnership	1989	7,500	0	~6,250	400

Figure 30 - Worksheet page 285

✔️ ACTION STEPS ✔️

- ❏ Create a system for organizing your insurance records and policies.

- ❏ Complete information charts regarding your savings and investments: Certificates of Deposit (CD's), Stocks, Bonds, Annuities, Mutual Funds, Retirement Plans, Limited Partnerships, etc.

- ❏ Complete your Personal Inventory of household items, together with photographs and/or videos displaying each room and area of your home.

- ❏ Review records in the Forms section of the book which would be appropriate for your situation and begin them at this time; e.g. Automobile Records (pages 251 - 255).

YOU SHOULD NOW BE ABLE TO:

1. Create a filing system for yourself and/or your family.

2. Determine what should be done with your cancelled checks and how they should be organized.

3. Complete your Documents and Asset Location list.

4. Complete Insurance Record forms for each of your insurance programs.

5. Complete the appropriate investment record forms for your current investments.

6. Begin your Personal Inventory by taking pictures of each of the rooms and by completing the appropriate Room and Special Inventory forms.

"When you have got a thing where you want it, it is a good thing to leave it where it is."

Sir Winston Churchill

CONCLUDING REMARKS

Keeping excellent records need not be a laborious and painstaking task. The forms provided for this chapter at the end of the book are intended to lead you in the direction necessary to begin this essential process. Once the records are prepared, keeping them current will be relatively simple.

"If you delay till to-morrow what ought to be done to-day, you overcharge the morrow with a burden which belongs not to it. You load the wheels of time, and prevent it from carrying you along smoothly. He who every morning plans the transactions of the day, and follows out the plan, carries on a thread which will guide him through the labyrinth of the most busy life. The orderly arrangement of his time is like a ray of light which darts itself through all his affairs. But where no plan is laid, where the disposal of time is surrendered merely to the chance of incidents, all things lie huddled together in one chaos, which admits neither of distribution nor review."

Hugh Blair
Importance of Order in Conduct-1822

CHAPTER 3

PREPARING FINANCIAL DOCUMENTS

PUT A PLAN

IN YOUR LIFE

 　　　　　　　Solving Your Financial Puzzle

FOCUS ON:

DEVELOPING NECESSARY DOCUMENTS

1. Maintain (or begin) a record of your personal assets and liabilities.

2. Organize and regularly maintain a personal networth statement.

3. Develop a budget or cash-flow system and implement it immediately.

4. Be realistic in the provision of your family's basic needs.

5. Involve your spouse (or partner), along with children when appropriate, in the budget planning process.

6. Be committed to set money aside for future financial needs and goals.

7. Revise your budget when your needs, goals, or current life style changes.

8. Have a written plan for paying expenses on time.

9. Provide for a replacement account in your cash-flow system.

10. Use your cash-flow system as a financial planning tool to become debt free as soon as possible.

PREPARING FINANCIAL DOCUMENTS

"Making money is like bees making honey. You can make it, but they won't let you keep it."

Anonymous

THE FINANCIAL PLANNING PROCESS

Does the above quote sound familiar? Making money doesn't necessarily seem to be the problem for most of us; our concern is that we are not making enough or it doesn't go as far as we would like. Fortunately, there are simple procedures to track expenses. Careful planning often creates 5% to 15% more spendable income each month. The purpose of this chapter is to get you started on this "money making" concept by showing you easy techniques.

TWO KEY DOCUMENTS

Whether we are the owner of a small business or a shareholder in a major corporation, it is essential to know how the business or the company is doing. To locate this information, we consult both the Balance Sheet and the Cash-Flow Statement in the firm's annual report. In our personal situation, these two documents are commonly known as a Personal Networth Statement and a Budget. To remain in constant control of our money, and also to know whether or not we are making financial progress, it is necessary that we keep these two documents current.

PERSONAL NETWORTH STATEMENT

A company or business is required to maintain a financial statement, or balance sheet. This document shows, in dollar amounts on any given date, what the firm owns, what it owes, and its shareholders' ownership in the company. It is equally important that we keep a similar record of our own personal resources for which we are responsible. A Networth Statement, such as the one illustrated in Figure 31, gives us an immediate "snap shot" of our current assets and liabilities. Assets are the total value of those things we own; liabilities are the sum of all payments and debts we presently owe. The difference between our assets and liabilities; that is, assets minus liabilities is known as our networth. It is now readily apparent that an individual or family having more liabilities than assets, or a negative networth, is in very serious financial trouble.

Complete the Personal Networth Statement forms on pages 287 and 288 as it applies to your individual or family situation. This information is essential to evaluate your current networth. Regularly monitor the values of your assets and liabilities, in dollar amounts, to control any possible tendency to accumulate unnecessary debt. The proper use of this document as a planning tool allows you to assess your progress of financial wellness; without the Personal Networth Statement, it is next to impossible to measure your financial improvement.

PERSONAL NETWORTH STATEMENT

Liquid Assets	
Checking Accounts	$ 550
Savings Accounts	1,525
Total Liquid Assets	$ 2,075
Property Assets	
Home	$110,000
Vehicles	4,500
Personal Items	7,500
Total Property Assets	$122,000
Other Assets	
IRA	$ 6,300
Pension	14,500
Other	3,000
Total 'Other' Assets	$ 23,800
TOTAL ASSETS	$147,875
Liabilities	
Home Mortgage	$ 98,500
Credit Cards	7,500
Auto Loans	8,600
Student Loan	15,100
TOTAL LIABILITIES	$129,700
PERSONAL NETWORTH	$ 18,175
(Total Assets - Total Liabilities)	

Figure 31
Worksheet pages 287 - 288

Networth (What's Left) = Assets (Total Value) - Liabilities (Total Debts)

CASH - FLOW STATEMENT
A PERSONAL SPENDING PLAN

If someone asked you "How much money does it cost you to live each month?," what would be your response? We cannot underestimate the significance of this question. Rarely, do people today have even a clue of what they spend on a monthly or an annual basis. They don't know because they have not taken the necessary time to accurately account for their expenses. If you are a person who has a tendency to spend more than you earn, you are headed for serious financial problems. Personal financial planning requires that you keep reliable records, as well as have the necessary discipline to set reasonable spending guidelines for you and your family.

Companies are required to include a Statement of Cash-Flow in their investor reports to convey the activity of cash-flow throughout

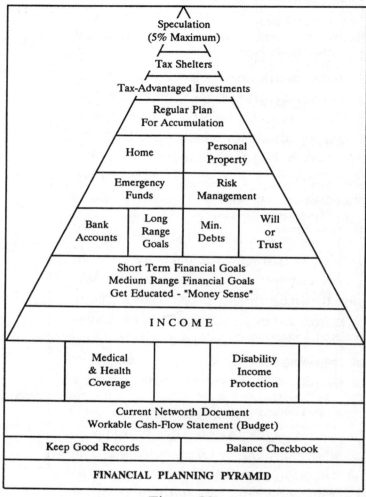

Figure 32

a particular time period. It is also essential that individuals and families develop a reliable plan to monitor the spending of their financial resources. A Cash-Flow Statement or Budget, such as the one illustrated in Figure 33 on page 67, might be considered the foundation of one's personal financial plan. Notice its location near the base of the Financial Planning Pyramid in Figure 32 above. A Cash-Flow Document offers structure for the way we manage money. The boundaries it provides are freeing; we then know where the limits are placed, giving us latitude to spend our money within them. A budget also provides the individual who maintains family records the choice of being as detailed as he or she desires within each of the general categories. A well-defined spending plan does not restrict the allocation of our financial resources, but provides us with flexible guidelines for the spending of money.

CASH-FLOW STATEMENT

TOTAL GROSS INCOME	$ 2,080
Less Deductions	
Federal Taxes	$ 320
State, Local Taxes	90
FICA	175
TOTAL DEDUCTIONS	$ 585
NET SPENDABLE INCOME	$ 1,495
(Gross Income - Deductions)	
	CURRENT BUDGET
Housing	
Mortgage Payments (PITI)	$ 570
Gas, Electricity	75
Water, Sanitation	10
Telephone	25
Maintenance, Repairs	20
Total Housing	$ 700
Food	$ 180
Transportation	
Automobile Loan	$ 115
Auto Insurance, License, Taxes	30
Gas, Lube, Oil	40
Total Transportation	$ 185
Installment Debt	$ 125
Insurance	
Medical, Health	$ 40
Life Insurance	25
Total Insurance	$ 65
Health Care	
Doctors, Dentists	$ 50
Prescriptions	10
Total Health Care	$ 60
Clothing	$ 30
Entertainment	
Family Activities	$ 30
Vacation, Travel	75
Total Entertainment	$ 105
Miscellaneous	$ 45
TOTAL EXPENSES	$ 1,495

Figure 33
Worksheet pages 289 - 293

The benefits of having a budget are frequently rewarding. It helps us to make future financial decisions such as affording: a vacation, a new car, or a larger home. It also assists us in making those decisions in accordance with our goals and priorities. Probably the greatest benefit of having a budget is that it provides us with peace of mind knowing that we will be able to meet our current monthly expenses. In addition, a budget (or Cash-Flow Statement) provides us two essential bits of information:

1. sources and the amount of our income, and

2. items and the amounts for which our income is spent.

"Annual income, twenty pounds; annual expenditure, nineteen six; result--happiness. Annual income, twenty pounds; annual expenditure, twenty pounds ought and six; result -- misery."

Charles Dickens
David Copperfield
Chap. 12, Mr. Micawber

Why then, do so many individuals and families fail to have a basic plan for the spending of their income? In many cases people feel that keeping a budget takes too much time and effort. On the other hand, they may have not been shown how to keep good records. A third reason might be that people just don't realize the importance for having a personal financial plan.

RECORDING EXPENSES

Before a realistic budget can be prepared, you must first determine where your money is being spent. This, of course, means keeping records. Keeping a record of your expenses is not an easy task. However, accurate records will prove to be a very valuable, as well as an eye opening experience. The process for recording your expenses is based on the "cash method of accounting." In using this method, income is recorded when it is received; expenses are recorded when they are paid, not when they come due. If you must defer a regularly scheduled monthly payment from one month to the following month, be sure to record the expense in the month it was actually paid. Possible examples might include car or student loans, as well as credit card payments, especially if you have the habit of using several credit cards. In the same manner, when paying on monthly installments or loan balances, be sure to record only that amount you paid for the month; allocating all charges listed on the statement to the appropriate categories of your budget.

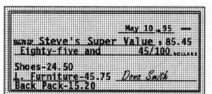

To get control of your cash "out-go" expenses, begin by writing checks only for the exact amount of the purchase, rather than the purchase amount plus additional cash. The extra cash will likely be spent with little or no idea where the money actually went. In addition, when writing out a check for several purchases, be sure to note the individual items and their respective cost on the check. To illustrate, when writing a check for $85.45, indicate shoes - $24.50, lawn furniture - 45.75, and back pack - $15.20 at the designated place on your check. In this way, you will be able to document the specific items in the appropriate budget category immediately. If you don't receive your cancelled checks from the bank, be sure that each item is recorded next to its amount on your receipt.

The ingredients of a workable and efficient cash-flow plan is to use a method that is simple, consumes very little time, and above all, proven to be successful. The method which follows has all three. In addition, this method has been known to provide those individuals and families who have stayed with it and were persistent with its application, a monthly excess cash-flow of between 5% and 15%. Furthermore, the only items you will need to complete this record-keeping task are (1) an envelope to keep each of your receipts for the given month and (2) a 3" x 5" spiral notebook for entering expenses for which <u>no</u> receipts are usually given.

COLLECTING RECEIPTS

The first item you will need is a plain 4" x 10" envelope. The envelope is used to collect <u>all</u> of your monthly (or weekly) receipts. Even if you are not usually given a receipt, be sure to ask for one. Such places that do not ordinarily give receipts, but will be glad to give you one upon request include: self-service gas stations, fast-food restaurants, and cafeterias. Place the receipts in your purse or billfold, not in a pocket (where they will go in with the laundry) until you arrive home; then label the receipt with the appropriate category (food, transportation, etc.), circle the amount spent, and place them in the envelope immediately.

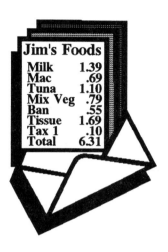

CASH EXPENDITURES

Have you ever thought how many checks you write on a regular basis that are made out to "cash"? Better yet, how many $25 and $50 cash withdrawals do you make during the month from automatic teller machines? Cash expenditures can be most difficult to estimate. It is vitally important that you track how cash is being spent.

The second and final item you will need to monitor your cash expenses is a 3" x 5" spiral notebook, one for <u>each</u> spouse. Use one sheet, front and back sides, for each of the categories that you intend to use in your spending plan or budget. The notebook will be used for items you seldom, if ever, get receipts. These include various vending machines such as pop and candy machines, stamp machines, self service car washes, cigarette machines, laundromats, and newspaper stands.

Be as specific as possible with recording information in your notebook by writing down the date, item purchased, category, and amount spent. Examples of two such expenses might appear as shown in Figure 34 on page 70.

PERSONAL CARE		
January, 1990		
10	Can Pop	.65
12	Hair Spray	6.45
18	World News Mag.	2.85

TRANSPORTATION		
January, 1990		
7	Gas	5.00
10	Car Wash	2.75
21	Lube, Oil	22.05

Figure 34

TABULATING EXPENSES

Tabulate your expenses at the end of the month by proceeding as follows:

- ❑ Sort each of your receipts according to the categories you have chosen.

- ❑ Staple all receipts of the same category together.

- ❑ Total the expenses of each category, placing the final total on the top (first) receipt.

- ❑ Tear out the pages in your spiral notebook that have expenses, staple each page to the same category as the receipts, and add to the receipt total.

By regularly recording your monthly expenses, you will now be forced to think about each of your purchases twice, not just once as before. This constant association involving a specific capital outlay with the actual recording of the item purchased will eventually build discipline in the way you think about money. Simply knowing what you spend in each category of your budget will sensitize you in the way you make buying decisions. You will soon learn to trim excess spending from various areas of your budget, thereby freeing up money for savings and investments. Before long, you will acquire a realistic, as well as a comfortable feeling, about the way you handle your finances.

"Living on a budget is the same as living beyond your means, except that you have a record of it."

Anonymous

☑ ACTION STEPS ☑

❏ Complete your Personal Networth Worksheet; calculate your current networth.

❏ Develop your Cash-Flow Worksheet; be sure to state all sources of income, and the amount of each.

❏ Save **each** of your receipts; request receipts if they are not offered.

❏ Purchase a 3" x 5" spiral notebook to record those expenses for which no receipt is available.

❏ Tabulate your expenses on a weekly, by-weekly, or monthly basis to determine your monthly spending pattern.

THE BUDGETING IDEA
KEEPING IT SIMPLE

The primary reason for taking the time and energy to put a spending plan together is to have a reliable tool to assist you in planning your expenditures and nothing more. A budget may also be used as a step-by-step guide for setting your spending and saving priorities. It can be an excellent way to involve the entire family in solving current or potential financial problems before they become too great to be discussed in a rational manner. A family discussion regarding finances can be a most valuable learning experience for children as well.

"Teach economy; that is one of the first virtues."

Abraham Lincoln

A Cash-Flow Statement or Budget, such as the one illustrated in Figure 33, is found on pages 289 - 293. Columns are provided for three months of income and expenses. Place the appropriate **months** in the spaces designated with a (_____). Basic categories are listed, along with some of their divisions; blank spaces are provided so that you may list additional items that best fit your particular individual or family situation. It is not intended that you use the entire list of categories, nor even all of the divisions of any particular category. They are only suggested as examples to give you ideas for arranging your expense items. Most of the time spent in preparing your plan will be in the selection of individual categories and corresponding divisions for keeping a record of your current and future expenses. You may even want to use some of the category headings as a division item; a possibility might be the category of *Gifts* or *Education Expenses*. Additional division ideas can be found in the Cash-Flow Supplement section on pages 294 - 296 of this book.

When you have your categories and corresponding divisions selected, you are ready to put your cash-flow statement to use. One idea would be to use "13-column" ledger sheets. They are ideal when placing the months across the top of the page with the categories placed down the left side. The thirteenth column can then be used to calculate your annual totals. Thirteen-column ledger pads usually have 40 lines on a page. They can be purchased at a local office supply store as well as many discount stores.

You might elect to use a home computer to personalize your own cash-flow statement as there are many excellent financial management and spread sheet programs, at very reasonable prices, available on the market today. If you decide on a spread sheet program, you may want to consider the 13-column ledger sheet idea; placing the *Months* and *Annual Total* across the top of the spread sheet with the selected categories again placed down the left side of the page. Whether you decide to use the 13-column ledger sheet approach or your own personally designed computer spread sheet program, be sure to add those expenses that are taken out of your checking account on a monthly basis as well as those expenses that you pay by check. These expenses could be insurance payments, mortgage and investment contracts, or utility bills.

The idea behind the budgeting process is to keep your plan as simple as possible and still stay within the guidelines that you and your family have set. For some individuals or families, the main categories are sufficient for their cash-flow statement. Other persons might prefer a highly detailed plan. Then, there will be those individuals or families who will have a cash-flow statement similar to the worksheets on pages 289 - 293. There is no right or wrong spending plan; the individual or family will need to choose the plan that best meets their needs.

In order to obtain a complete picture of your current spending pattern, it would be best to keep detailed records for a period of nine to twelve months before settling on a permanent budget. This will provide you with sufficient time to consider expenses for vacations and holiday seasons, as well as other special occasions that you and your family celebrate on an annual basis. On the other hand, it might be very likely that you can put together a spending plan that meets your needs in considerably less time. It is important you keep in mind that when changes do occur in your monthly income or in your life style, you will need to make the necessary changes in your spending habits.

Your cash-flow statement, if it does nothing else, will certainly make you aware of the amount of money which passes through your hands each month, but cannot be accounted. For families or individuals with high incomes, an unaccounted $200 or

 Solving Your Financial Puzzle

$300 a month may seem like a trifle amount; to others, it might mean keeping their home or losing an automobile. In any case, a mere $200 a month with daily compounding at just 6% a year for 20 years, would provide in excess of $92,800 for your retirement fund. The same $200 a month invested at 10% would grow to $455,865 over a 30 year period.

Since people are currently retiring from their professions at an earlier age, along with the increase in the average life span of people today, the fact remains that only a very small percent of people have the ability to retire financially independent. By gaining control of your spending habits, over a period of just a few years, you will be able to turn some of your unknown dollars into available money for future use. These might include a family vacation, a new automobile, children's education funds, a condominium at a ski or fishing resort, or to maintain a minimum style of living at retirement.

A cash-flow statement may not be as glamorous as investing in stocks, bonds, mutual funds, real estate, or commodity futures. However, coming to grips with building a household budget and a basic financial plan gives you a fighting chance to achieve your financial goals. You might find yourself sleeping better at night, living better, and perhaps, even living longer.

At this time it would be an excellent idea to carefully review the case study of A Real Life Situation on pages 164 - 173 before beginning the Analysis of Income and Expenses section which follows.

"If it were not for the holes in the pocket, we should all be rich. A pocket is like a cistern: a small leak at the bottom is worse than a large pump at the top."

Henry Ward Beecher

ANALYSIS OF INCOME AND EXPENSES

The simplest way to understand the progress that you have made over a period of time is to draw a pie chart. A pie chart, such as the one illustrated by Figure 36, shows the relative size of each expense category to the total expenses, as well as to each of the other monthly expenses. However, before expenses can be calculated, it is essential that we enter our sources of income as well as those fixed deductions (expenses) which are automatically withheld from each paycheck received. A pie chart to illustrate the amount of spendable income remaining after automatic deductions, as in Figure 35, can be used as an effective planning tool in the preparation of a final cash-flow statement.

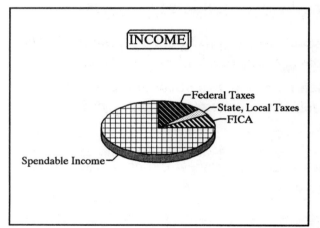

Figure 35

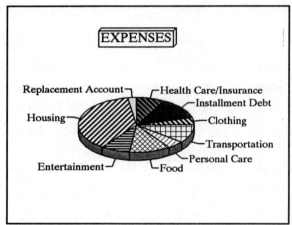

Figure 36

CURRENT BUDGET (DOLLARS)

Begin the analysis of your spending situation by completing the following six steps of the *Current Budget (Dollars)* column of the Budget Planning Worksheet on page 299. The result of this critical task will indicate your spending habits for the present month. The data for the calculations used in Figure 37 on page 76 was taken from the January, 1990 budget of Jane and Dean Smith given on pages 168 - 169.

Step 1.   Enter the gross monthly income amount from your Cash-Flow Statement Worksheet on line 1.

Step 2.   List your paycheck deductions and the amount of each deduction on lines 2 - 6; enter your total deductions on line 7.

                    Solving Your Financial Puzzle

Step 3. Enter your net spendable income (line 1 minus line 7) on line 8, and also on line 29.

The net spendable income (also known as NSI) is that portion of income available for living expenses after taxes, FICA, retirement (or pension), has been deducted from the gross monthly income.

Step 4. Enter the amount of money spent for each category of your Cash-Flow Statement on the appropriate line of column 2, *Current Budget (Dollars)*.

Do not feel that you must use all of the category items listed on lines 9 - 27. Use only those items that apply to your individual or family situation.

Step 5. Add your expense categories, lines 9 - 27; place this result on line 28, the *Total Expenses* line.

A. This number represents 100% of your expenses for the month.

B. The value on line 29, *Net Spendable Income*, will be used to calculate the percent for each of the categories in your Cash-Flow Statement.

Step 6. Subtract: *Net Spendable Income* amount minus *Total Expenses* amount; enter this value on the *Monthly Profit or Loss* line, line 30.

A. If the number on the *Monthly Profit or Loss* line is positive, then your task is to control your spending to maximize your savings and investment program.

B. If the number on the *Monthly Profit or Loss* line is negative, which indicates more spending than net spendable income available, your task is to correct the over spending and to restore balance to your budget.

CURRENT BUDGET (PERCENT)

Before a pie chart or circle graph can be created, it is necessary to determine the size of each piece, or individual expense category, by completing the *Current Budget (Percent)* column of the Budget Planning Worksheet. This brief, but important, task is easily accomplished by using the dollar amounts in column 2 of the worksheet with the seven-step procedure outlined below and on pages 77 - 78.

Step 1. Write down the general formula given below.

$$\textit{Current Budget (Percent)} = \frac{\textit{Current Budget (Dollars)}}{\textit{Net Spendable Income}}$$

BUDGET PLANNING WORKSHEET

1 Monthly Income	$ 2,750	
Monthly Payment Category	**Current Budget (Dollars)**	**Current Budget (Percent)**
Deductions		
2 Federal Taxes	$ 350	13 %
3 State/Local Taxes	110	4
4 FICA	215	8
5 Retirement/Pension	-----	-----
6 _____	-----	-----
7 **Total Deductions**	$ 675	25 %
8 **Net Spendable Income** (per month)	$ 2,075	100 %
9 Housing	$ 855	41 %
10 Food	285	14
11 Transportation	245	11
12 Installment Debt	295	14
13 Insurance	80	4
14 Health Care	70	3
15 Clothing	70	3
16 Entertainment	200	10
17 Children	-----	-----
18 Personal Care	100	5
19 Professional Services	-----	-----
20 Education Expenses	-----	-----
21 Gifts	-----	-----
22 Replacement Accounts	-----	-----
23 Miscellaneous	-----	-----
24 Savings	15	1
25 Investments	-----	-----
26 _____	-----	-----
27 _____	-----	-----
28 **Total Expenses**	$ 2,190	106 %
29 **Net Spendable Income**	$ 2,075	100 %
30 **Monthly Profit or Loss**	$ -115	-6 %

Figure 37 - Worksheet page 299

      Solving Your Financial Puzzle

A. The top number of your fraction, will be one of the numbers on lines 9 - 27 in the *Current Budget (Dollars)* column. This amount (or value) will usually change for each category.

B. The lower number of your fraction will be the value on line 29 (or line 8), *Net Spendable Income*, of the *Current Budget (Dollars)* column. This amount (or value) will <u>not</u> change with each category, but will remain the <u>same</u> for that particular month's calculations.

Step 2. Change the general formula in step 1 to a "specific" expense category.

For the purpose of this illustration, consider the *Housing* expense line in the January, 1990 Budget Planning Worksheet for Dean and Jane Smith, given on page 76.

A. Current *Housing* Percent $= \dfrac{\text{Current } \textit{Housing } \text{Expenses}}{\textit{Net Spendable Income}}$

B. Current *Housing* Percent $= \dfrac{\$\ 855}{\$2{,}075}$

Step 3. Calculate the Current *Housing* Percent:

A. Using a calculator, divide $855 by $2,075 ($855 ÷ $2,075) to obtain 0.412.

B. Change the decimal number, 0.412, in the above step to a percent.

   1. Move the decimal point exactly two places to the right. If necessary, add a zero or zeros to the "right" of the decimal point.

   2. Attach a percent sign (%) to the end of the number.

   3. The correct percent for A of step 3 above is 41.2%.

Step 4. Continue the procedure illustrated in step 2 and in step 3 for each of your category expense items.

Step 5. Enter each of the calculated percents on the appropriate line in the *Current Budget (Percent)* column.

Step 6. Calculate the total of the *Current Budget (Percent)* column by adding the percentages you have listed on lines 9 - 27. Enter this value on line 28, *Total Expenses*. The number should be very close to 100, the total of your expenditures during the month.

A. If the value on line 28 is greater than 100, you have spent more than your income is providing for you and your family. This is an instant signal that financial problems either have occurred or will occur very soon.

B. If the value on line 28 is less than 100, one of the following conditions exist:

1. You have money accumulating in a checking account (or another account), or

2. You have additional expenditures for which you have not yet accounted for during the current month.

Step 7. To determine the *Current Budget (Percent)* column for the *Deductions* portion of the Budget Planning Worksheet, follow the <u>exact</u> procedure in step 2 - step 5, and change:

A. *Net Spendable Income* (step 1 and step 2A, lines 8 and 29 of the worksheet) <u>to</u> *Monthly Income*, line 1, and

B. Current *Category Expenses* (step 2A, lines 9 - 27 of the worksheet) <u>to</u> current *Deductions*, lines 2 - 7.

CASH-FLOW ANALYSIS
GRAPHING YOUR RESULTS

Now that you have calculated the percentages for each of the expense categories, you may proceed to the placing of your income and expense items on a pie chart. The forms on pages 297 and 298 have been prepared for this specific purpose. The pie chart shown in Figure 38 on page 79 has 20 tick marks placed at 5% intervals on the circle, from 0% to 100%. Consider an initial line A from the center of the circle to the 3 o'clock position. If you draw a second line B from the center of the circle to the fifth tick mark, which is at the 12 o'clock position, you will have exactly one quarter, or 25% of the circle determined; the eighth tick mark will locate exactly 40% of the circle, and so on.

Begin your graphing process using a horizontal line in the 3 o'clock position as your base line. (line A in Figure 38.) Suppose that your first expense is housing, and it represents 30% of your net spendable income. You would then draw a line from the center of the circle to the sixth tick mark (5% times six tick marks equal 30%). Be sure to go in a counter-clockwise direction. The portion of the circle enclosed by the two lines represents the part of your net spendable income that is represented by your housing costs.

                    Solving Your Financial Puzzle

However, suppose that your housing expenses are 33% of your net spendable income. In this case you would go 3/5 of the distance from the sixth tick mark (30%) to the seventh tick mark (35%); place a small mark on the circle, then draw a line from that point to the center of the circle. The section between the two lines represents the portion of the circle that corresponds to your housing expenditures.

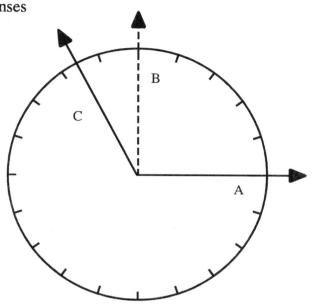

Figure 38
Worksheet - page 298

Now use the line you just completed, label it line C, as the first boundary line for your second category item. Count the number of tick marks, including any fractional parts, in a counter-clockwise direction to determine the next boundary line. Continue this process, going around the circle in a counter-clockwise direction, until you have completed all category expense items. If the amount of your total expenses is more than your net spendable income for the month, you will need to proceed to a second circle graph to complete your category items. Since you have spent in excess of 100% of your net spendable income, this excess is shown on a second pie chart.

When you have completed your last category item, you should be within 5% (or one tick mark) of having all items fit within your circle graph. This will give you an excellent idea regarding the relative size of each category when compared to the size of each of the remaining categories, as well as to the entire circle, which represents 100% of your net spendable income.

BUDGET ANALYSIS
THE CURRENT BUDGET

The circle graph you just completed portrays a "snap shot" of your current budget or spending habits. It clearly indicates the percent of your dollars you are presently spending in each of the selected categories. The areas where any overspending is taking place is readily visible by a larger than usual section of the circle graph. Any of the basic needs which are not currently met are also detected immediately.

The majority of people seldom, if ever, pay attention to their spending habits. Their reasons could range from "I don't have the time (translated to 'I don't want to take the time') to keep a record of my expenses" to "This is one of the most boring (and painful) tasks I could ever think of doing." In any event, try putting these excuses aside, and carefully examine your current monthly expenses.

YOUR PERSONAL BUDGET QUESTIONS

There are numerous questions you could ask yourself regarding your spending habits. One of the biggest challenges might be to ask the following questions regarding each category of your own personal budget.

1. Am I providing for my individual or family's basic needs?

2. Am I currently spending too much money?

3. Am I able to be more efficient with my spending?

4. Am I too far in debt?

As you consider each of the above questions, it won't be too long before you'll be very proficient in your spending. A few of the benefits to effective spending include:

1. The ability to set money aside for purchasing items to meet future needs and goals.

2. The opportunity to reduce current debts.

3. The freedom of being exempt of all consumer and mortgage debt.

THE PROPOSED MONTHLY BUDGET
A PERCENTAGE GUIDE FOR FAMILY INCOME

How much then, should a family or an individual be spending in each of the basic categories of a budget? Even though the amount of dollars spent within the categories may widely vary throughout the country, the percentages themselves, should in fact, remain fairly constant.

The Percentage Guide For Family Income Table on the next page will give you an idea of the percent spent in the more common budget categories. The guide is based on an average family of four living a modest life style for various levels of income. The

  Solving Your Financial Puzzle

given percentages are intended to provide families a balanced spending plan in which to meet each of their basic needs. Multiply the appropriate percentages by the net spendable income amount for each of the categories of your budget. This calculation will help you determine a realistic amount for each category in the *Proposed Monthly Budget* column of the Budget Planning Worksheet illustrated by Figure 40 on page 82. The proposed budget provides you with a basis from which to measure your future spending. You then have a clear indication of the dollar spending amounts among your various budget categories. The proposed budget is not intended as an absolute or fixed amount; its purpose is to indicate the area or areas of current over, as well as under spending. In this way, you will have an opportunity to identify where adjustments need to be made, if any, and to resolve them before, instead of after, financial crisis occurs.

A PERCENTAGE GUIDE FOR FAMILY INCOME						
Gross Income	$20,000	$35,000	$50,000	$65,000	$80,000	$100,000
Taxes & FICA	17%	19%	22%	25%	28%	30%
Net Spendable Income	$16,600	$28,350	$39,000	$48,750	$57,600	$70,000
Housing	35%	32%	29%	28%	26%	25%
Food	18%	17%	13%	11%	9%	7%
Transportation	13%	13%	10%	9%	7%	6%
Installment Debt	5%	5%	5%	5%	4%	3%
Insurance	5%	5%	5%	4%	4%	4%
Health Care	4%	4%	4%	4%	3%	3%
Clothing	4%	4%	5%	6%	6%	7%
Entertainment	6%	7%	8%	8%	9%	9%
Miscellaneous	5%	5%	7%	8%	9%	10%
Savings & Investments	2%	3%	6%	8%	10%	12%
Margin	3%	5%	8%	9%	13%	14%
Total	100%	100%	100%	100%	100%	100%

Figure 39

THE REVISED MONTHLY BUDGET

Even though you may have established a proposed budget guideline that appears to be realistic on paper, it's very likely that you will need to make adjustments to create a final or revised monthly budget. This is likely to come about through negotiations between spouses or among family members regarding dollar amounts to the various

BUDGET PLANNING WORKSHEET

Monthly Income	$ 2,750			

Monthly Budget Category	Current Budget (Dollars)	Proposed Monthly Budget	Current Budget Minus Proposed Budget	Revised Monthly Budget
Deductions				
2 Federal Taxes	$ 350	$ 310	$ 40	$ 310
3 State/Local Taxes	110	105	5	105
4 FICA	215	210	5	210
5 Retirement/Pension	-----	-----	-----	-----
6 _____	-----	-----	-----	-----
7 **Total Deductions**	$ 675	$ 625	$ 50	$ 625
8 **Net Spendable Income** (per month)	$ 2,075	$ 2,125	$ - 50	$ 2,125
9 Housing	$ 855	$ 738	$ 117	$ 800
10 Food	285	254	31	245
11 Transportation	220	232	- 12	235
12 Installment Debt	295	126	169	275
13 Insurance	80	85	- 5	80
14 Health Care	70	85	- 15	85
15 Clothing	70	105	- 35	85
16 Entertainment	200	190	10	170
17 Children	-----	-----	-----	-----
18 Personal Care	100	126	- 26	100
19 Professional Services	-----	-----	-----	-----
20 Education Expenses	-----	-----	-----	-----
21 Gifts	-----	-----	-----	-----
22 Replacement Accounts	0	58	- 58	50
23 Miscellaneous	-----	-----	-----	-----
24 Savings	15	126	-111	0
25 Investments	-----	-----	-----	-----
26 _____	-----	-----	-----	-----
27 _____	-----	-----	-----	-----
28 **Total Expenses**	$ 2,190	$ 2,125	$ 65	$ 2,125
29 **Net Spendable Income**	$ 2,075	$ 2,125		$ 2,125
30 **Monthly Profit or Loss**	$ -115	$ -0-		$ -0-

Figure 40 - Worksheet page 299

budget categories, as well as to possible changes in the federal, state, local, and FICA *Deduction* portions of your Cash-Flow Worksheet. The following eight points outline the procedure for obtaining a final or revised monthly budget when the *Proposed Monthly Budget* column of your planning worksheet has been completed.

1. Compare each category amount in the *Current Budget (Dollars)* column with the corresponding category amount in the *Proposed Monthly Budget* column.

2. Place the difference of these two amounts in the *Current Budget minus Proposed Budget* column.

    A positive number means an over spending in the category; a negative number indicates a deficit amount was spent.

3. Identify the area(s) of over spending by placing a red check for this category in the *Current Budget minus Proposed Budget* column, as well as next to the item itself in the first column.

4. Decide what category (or categories) you need to reduce to compensate for the over spending in item 3.

5. Determine the amount of decrease for each category you decide that a reduction is to be made.

6. Complete the *Revised Monthly Budget* column according to the changes you made in items 3, 4, and 5 above.

    It may be necessary for you to juggle numbers around often to arrive at the most equitable spending plan.

7. Calculate the total expenses for the *Revised Monthly Budget* column and place this result on line 28.

    The *Total Expenses* amount on line 28 cannot exceed the *Net Spendable Income* amount on line 8 or line 29.

8. Take action and implement your revised monthly budget immediately!

INCOME ALLOCATION

Your budget is now ready for implementation. The Income Allocation Worksheet form shown in Figure 41, page 85 provides a systematic, yet simple way of paying all of your expenses on time. However, before you begin the final task of allocating income and expenses described on pages 84 - 87, review the reasons provided on pages 171 - 173 of the Case Study for the budget adjustments made by Dean and Jane Smith.

Then, by completing the following seven-step procedure, you will not only establish a routine method for paying each of your scheduled monthly expenses (or obligations), you will have money left at the end of the month as well.

Step 1.   Enter the monthly income, along with the dollar allocations for deductions and category expenses on the same numbered line of the *Allocation Amount* column of the Income Allocation Worksheet that you used in the *Revised Monthly Budget* column of the Budget Planning Worksheet.

Step 2.   Total your deductions on lines 2 - 6 and enter this result on line 7, *Total Deductions*. Subtract the amount of the total deductions from your monthly income and place this number on lines 8 and 29, *Net Spendable Income*.

Step 3.   Total your category expenses on lines 9 - 27; place this amount on line 28, *Total Expenses*. Be sure that line 28 does not exceed line 29 (or line 8), *Net Spendable Income*.

Step 4.   Complete lines 2 - 8 for your payment schedule: either bi-weekly, weekly, or monthly. Bi-weekly income and expenses are allocated twice per month as shown in Figure 41 on page 85. Figure 42 on page 86 illustrates the allocation of income and a portion of expenses when receiving a weekly paycheck, while an employee paid on the last work day of the month, in the *Week 4* column, would be identical to the amount in the *Allocation Amount* column as shown in Figure 43.

If you and/or your family receive(s) one paycheck per month, enter your expenses in the appropriate *Week* column (see Figure 43) and proceed to Step 7.

Step 4 is the most important since it will determine the amount and frequency of your net monthly income. If you receive more than one paycheck each month, it is not necessary that you pay the same proportion of each category expense item for that particular pay period. As an example, suppose that you are paid according to the bi-weekly schedule shown in Figure 41. The fact that you are paid twice per month, in two equal payment amounts, does not imply that you pay one half of each category expense for each of the two individual pay periods. As a matter of fact, this may be impossible since home mortgages, automobile loans, and other monthly obligations are not likely to allow you to split monthly payments in accordance to the way you receive your monthly income.

Before you continue to Step 5, review the income and expense allocation decisions on pages 174 - 175 that Dean and Jane Smith made in order to have sufficient funds for each of the category expenses.

INCOME ALLOCATION WORKSHEET
Paid Bi-Weekly - Twice Per Month

1 **Monthly Income**	$2,750		$1,375		$1,375
Category	**Allocation Amount**	**Week 1**	**Week 2**	**Week 3**	**Week 4**
DEDUCTIONS					
2 Federal Taxes	$ 310		$ 155		$ 155
3 State/Local Taxes	105		55		50
4 FICA	210		105		105
5 Retirement/Pension	----		----		----
6 _____	----		----		----
7 **Total Deductions**	$ 625		$ 315		$ 310
8 **Net Spendable Income**	$2,125		$1,060		$1,065
9 Housing	$ 800		$ 140		$ 660
10 Food	245		125		120
11 Transportation	235		85		150
12 Installment Debt	275		165		110
13 Insurance	80		80		0
14 Health Care	85		85		0
15 Clothing	85		85		0
16 Entertainment	170		170		0
17 Children	----		----		----
18 Personal Care	100		100		0
19 Professional Services	----		----		----
20 Education Expenses	----		----		----
21 Gifts	----		----		----
22 Replacement Accounts	50		25		25
23 Miscellaneous	----		----		----
24 Savings	----		----		----
25 Investments	----		----		----
26 _____	----		----		----
27 _____	----		----		----
28 **Total Expenses**	$2,125		$1,060		$1,065
29 **Net Spendable Income**	$2,125		$1,060		$1,065
30 **Monthly Profit or Loss**	0		0		0

Figure 41 - Worksheet page 300

INCOME ALLOCATION WORKSHEET
Paid On A Weekly Basis

Monthly Income	$2,750	$688	$687	$688	$687
Category	Allocation Amount	Week 1	Week 2	Week 3	Week 4
DEDUCTIONS					
Federal Taxes	$ 310	$ 78	$ 77	$ 78	$ 77
State/Local Taxes	105	27	26	26	26
FICA	210	52	53	52	53
Total Deductions	$ 625	$ 157	$ 156	$ 156	$ 156
Net Spendable Income	$2,125	$ 531	$ 531	$ 532	$ 531
Housing	$ 800	$ 100	$ 220	$ 220	$ 260
Food	245	70	70	70	35
Transportation	235	45	40	50	100

Figure 42

INCOME ALLOCATION WORKSHEET
Paid On A Monthly Basis

Monthly Income	$2,750				$2,750
Category	Allocation Amount	Week 1	Week 2	Week 3	Week 4
DEDUCTIONS					
Federal Taxes	$ 310				$ 310
State/Local Taxes	105				105
FICA	210				210
Total Deductions	$ 625				$ 625
Net Spendable Income	$2,125				$2,125
Housing	$ 800				$ 800
Food	245				245
Transportation	235				235

Figure 43

      Solving Your Financial Puzzle

Step 5.   Determine which monthly expenses on lines 9 - 27 must be paid on a specific date, then enter them in the appropriate pay period *Week* column. Mortgage and rent payments are usually required within the first few days of the month. Finance companies and other creditors may be more flexible with receiving their payments as long as they are paid by the same date each month. If you are paid on a weekly basis, it might be necessary to bank certain allocated expense items, such as housing due to mortgage payments (or monthly rent) and transportation, especially if you have an automobile loan, to assure yourself of having sufficient funds available when these monthly payments come due.

Step 6.   Complete each of the remaining expense categories using the budgeted amount in the *Revised Monthly Budget* column of the Budget Planning Worksheet. Be sure to allow some money in each category per pay period when possible.

Most likely you will need to spend some time to juggle dollar amounts among pay periods. It is important that you be patient and not become frustrated in this step with the preparation of your budget. If you are in some degree of debt, or in considerable debt, you must remember that you didn't get to this point with your finances over night so it will take time to correct the situation as well. Now is the time to use self-discipline and restraint with your finances, lower your buying expectations a bit, and make good purchasing decisions on a daily basis to eliminate any debt you currently have. Suggestions for accomplishing debt reduction are discussed in Chapter 6.

Step 7.   Total lines 9 - 27 of the *Week* columns for which you have expenses and enter the amount on line 28, *Total Expenses*. Be sure that the value on line 28 does not exceed your *Net Spendable Income* for that particular pay period. For any pay period that line 28 exceeds line 29 (or line 8), you will need to return to step 5 and step 6 and make the necessary budget adjustments.

☑ ACTION STEPS ☑

❑ Complete an analysis of income versus expenses using your Cash - Flow Statement.

❑ Prepare a chart of your income and expenses to visualize your current financial situation. A picture is worth a thousand words.

❑ Prepare a revised budget compatible to your current income.

❑ Begin debt reduction by destroying your credit cards if your current debt is more than the *Proposed Monthly Budget* column amount.

❑ Follow your Income Allocation Worksheet precisely to insure timely payments for each category expense item.

YOU SHOULD NOW BE ABLE TO:

1. Prepare a current networth statement.

2. Develop a plan for recording expenses and collecting receipts.

3. Devise a general cash-flow plan (or budget) that includes basic categories for sources of income and expenses.

4. Complete an analysis of your income and expenses.

5. Prepare a pie chart graph for any month's income and expenses.

6. Complete an Income Allocation Worksheet for your income pay periods.

CONCLUDING REMARKS

People often associate the word "budget" with punishment; a method to restrict one's spending. A budget, on the other hand, is nothing more than a written plan to help us live within our means. Jim Roan, in his popular audio cassette tape, "Take Charge of Your Life," points out the significance of having a well, thought-out financial program. During his many seminars, he frequently asks participants why they don't have more money. Their reply is often along the lines of, "Mr. Roan, if I had more money, then I'd have a better plan;" to which he instantly responds, "you have this concept backwards, if you had a better plan, then you would have more money." A program consisting of a current networth document and a practical cash-flow statement instills in each of us a sense of awareness, self-discipline, and monetary responsibility. Keeping these two credentials assists us in our quest for financial independence, the principal of which is being prosperous, successful, and thrifty. As Samuel Johnson exemplifies below, thriftiness is a virtue, a sign of wisdom.

"Live within your income. Always have something saved at the end of the year. Let your imports be more than your exports, and you'll never go far wrong."

Samuel Johnson

CHAPTER 4

IMPLEMENTING THE BUDGET

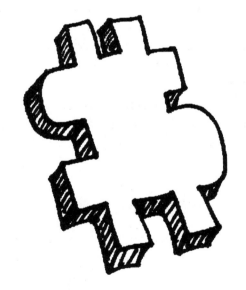

COME ON, DAD

FOCUS ON:

MAINTAINING AN EFFECTIVE BUDGET

1. Adapt a team spirit for implementing your budget system by involving your spouse, or partner, and your children, when appropriate.

2. Develop a budget that can be maintained easily and in a minimum amount of time.

3. Maintain legible and accurate Account Summary forms and a balanced Checkbook Register.

4. Be committed to the category amounts that you and your spouse, or partner, had originally agreed.

5. Use your budget system to responsibly manage your finances.

6. Develop discipline to stop spending in budget categories when Account Summary forms indicate a zero balance.

7. Adjust budget category amounts when financial needs or objectives occur.

8. Develop a habit of saving money regularly in each category of your budget.

9. Insure that your monthly expenses do not exceed your net spendable income for the month.

10. Use your budget as a way of logically reconciling your financial disagreements.

IMPLEMENTING THE BUDGET

"Thrift is not a mere forced rule: it is a virtue; it is a principle. Thrift is not an affair of the pocket, but an affair of character. Thrift is not niggardliness, but wisdom."

S. W. Straus

FINANCIAL RESPONSIBILITY

Chapter 3 provided various ways to organize income and expenses in an effort to prepare a household budget. To be financially responsible, it is essential to develop the habit of living within one's means. The purpose of this chapter is to learn methods that will assist you in maintaining your budget, once it has been established.

CONTROL SPENDING

Keeping within the agreed upon spending plan involves making both decisions and choices, whether it's the food we eat, the clothes we wear, the automobile(s) we drive, or the homes in which we live. Each of us, regardless of age or socio-economic status, have obvious needs, wants, and dreams. This can best be demonstrated by using the purchase of an automobile as an analogy. We can all agree that we definitely need transportation to maintain even the most basic living style. On the other hand, the particular make and model that we ultimately choose is a definite reflection of our wants and dreams.

Now that you have made the decision as to the allocation of your spendable income, it is essential that you regularly maintain records to control spending. The method you use needs to be completed easily, quickly, and accurately; otherwise the chances that you will continue with the system are greatly reduced. The Money Management Flow Chart in Figure 44 on page 94 uses the housing category of Dean and Jane Smith's budget provided on page 173 to outline a process to manage your cash flow. In addition, this procedure will assist you in building cash reserves for each category of your budget.

ACCOUNT SUMMARY INFORMATION

There will be one Account Summary form for each category of your budget; the money you spend will then be recorded on the appropriate form. Each form will be properly labeled in the *Account Category* section (*Housing, Food, Transportation, etc.*) with the monthly budgeted amount placed in the *Monthly Allocated Amount* location. Post the agreed amount to each of the category Account Summary forms from the Income Allocation Worksheet each time a pay period occurs. If you are paid on a monthly basis, you will have exactly one posting per month for each category of your budget. On the other hand, if you are paid twice a month as the young couple included in the Case Study, you may have Account Summary forms with posting for each of the two pay periods. This occurs for such budget categories as *Housing, Food, and Transportation*; while other categories, including *Health Care, Clothing, and Entertainment* have allocated amounts posted for only one of the two pay periods.

Each time a posting entry is made in an Account Summary form, carefully complete the *Date, Transaction Item*, and *Account Balance* columns, along with the *Payment/Withdrawal* or *Deposit/ Credit* column. Be sure that each personal check you write, as well as large cash purchases, are recorded immediately. For pocket money and petty cash expenses, it might be easier, and save time as well, to keep the receipts in an envelope;

> "Extravagance causes financial ills in the nation, but its effects on individual citizens is of primary importance, because no nation can be more prosperous than its people."
>
> T. D. MacGregor

then record them as one entry on a single line of the appropriate Account Summary for that particular pay period. Remember to label each of the receipts with the proper category. When a single receipt contains items for more than one budget category, allocate the specific expenses to the appropriate category, as described on pages 68 - 69, Recording Expenses, before recording them in the proper Account Summary form.

MONEY MANAGEMENT FLOW-CHART

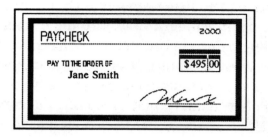

CHECKBOOK REGISTER

RECORD ALL PAYMENTS OR DEPOSITS THAT AFFECT YOUR ACCOUNT

Check Number	Date	Transaction Description	Payment/Withdrawal (-)	Budget Code	Deposit/Credit (+)	Balance $53.75
	1/30	Paycheck Deposits (2)			1,065 00	1,118 75

INCOME ALLOCATION WORKSHEET		WEEK	
Monthly Income	$ 2,750	$ 1,375	$ 1,375
Category	Allocation Amount	Week 2	Week 4
Net Spendable Income	$ 2,125	$ 1,060	$ 1,065
Housing	$ 800	$ 140	$ 660

ACCOUNT SUMMARY

ACCOUNT CATEGORY HOUSING		MONTHLY ALLOCATED AMOUNT $800			
Date	Transaction Item	Check # or Cash	Payment/ Withdrawal	Deposit/ Credit	Account Balance
1/29	Balance On Hand				0 00
1/30	Allocation - Paycheck			660 00	660 00
2/27	Transfer to Allocation Savings: Housing		22 50		0 00

ALLOCATION SAVINGS ACCOUNT

Date	Balance	Housing			
2/27	71 35	22 50			

Figure 44

                    Solving Your Financial Puzzle

You will notice that the Account Summary form for each category is similar to the Checkbook Register form; a format chosen for its familiarity as well as its simplicity in the record keeping process. The purpose of this system is to assist you in the control of your spending by tracking the money spent in each category. This method of budgeting is analogous to the envelope system in which a person's or family's paycheck was divided among the various categories of their budget, then placed in separate envelopes. When the money in a particular envelope was gone, a family quit spending in that particular category of their budget. Instead of placing actual cash in the various envelopes, we have set up an Account Summary for each category item of our budget. Like the reliable and disciplined envelope system, when the balance is zero, the envelope is empty; we must quit spending.

ORGANIZE YOUR FINANCIAL NOTEBOOK

The four sections that make up the major part of the budget section of your notebook are outlined below. Begin by purchasing a three ring binder, a set of color coded dividers with tabs, and copies of the forms listed below. You may wish to separate each of the sections for easier reference by placing colored notebook dividers between them. Review the Case Study on pages 177 - 184 as well as the Money Management Flow-Chart on page 94 to acquaint yourself with each of the four steps below.

Step 1. Checkbook Register (See Figure 97 on pages 177 - 178)

A. Make two copies of form 78 on page 304.

B. Enter the paycheck deposit amounts in the *Deposit/Credit* column of the Checkbook Register. The amount should equal that of the *Net Spendable Income* in the Income Allocation Worksheet for each pay period of the month.

C. Include the date, a description of the transaction, the payment or credited amount, and the new balance in the appropriate columns whenever a deposit is made or a check is written.

D. Indicate any cash taken from the paycheck deposit on a separate line, along with the date, a transaction description, the amount withdrawn, and the resulting balance in the appropriate columns.

Net Spendable Income = Monthly Income - Total Deductions

Step 2. Income Allocation Worksheet (See Figure 98 on page 178)

Refer to Figure 41 on page 85 if assistance is needed to complete this form.

A. Make one copy of form 74 on page 300.

B. Enter the *Monthly Income* (line 1) and the budgeted amount for each *Deduction* (lines 2 - 6) and *Expense* (lines 9 - 27) in the *Week* column for which a paycheck deposit is made.

C. Calculate totals for only those rows on which you entered *Monthly Income, Deductions*, and *Expenses*. The dollar value in the *Allocation Amount* column must equal the sum of the individual *Week* columns for each row of the worksheet.

The value in the *Allocation Amount* column is the same as the value in the corresponding row in the *Revised Monthly Budget* column of the Budget Planning Worksheet (Figure 40 on page 82).

D. Compute the *Total Deductions* (line 7) and the *Total Expenses* (line 28) for the *Allocation Amount* and individual *Week* columns.

E. Calculate the *Net Spendable Income* (lines 8 and 29) in the following manner: *Monthly Income* (line 1) - *Total Deductions* (line 7) = *Net Spendable Income*.

F. Compute the *Monthly Profit or Loss* (line 30) for each column in the following way: *Net Spendable Income* (line 8 or 29) - *Total Expenses* (line 28) = *Monthly Profit or Loss*.

　1. If the result is "positive," you have a profit for the month and should place this amount in *Replacement Accounts* (line 22) or in *Savings* (line 24).

　2. If the result is "negative," you have overspent by this amount for the month and will need to adjust the expense items which caused the overspending.

Step 3. Account Summary (See Figures 99 - 107 on pages 179 - 183)

A. Make one copy for each budget category of form 75 on page 301.

B. Open each Account Summary form in the following manner:

　1. Enter the previous day's date in the *Date* column, balance on hand in the *Transaction Item* column and zero in the *Account Balance* column on the first line of each Account Summary.

　2. Enter the current date in the *Date* Column, allocation - paycheck in the *Transaction Item* column, the amount for each of the budget categories

 　　　　　　　　Solving Your Financial Puzzle

that are to receive monies for the pay period involved in the *Deposit/-Credit* column, and the balance in the *Account Balance* column on the second line.

For individuals (or families) having two or more pay periods per month, there may be categories that will receive funds each pay period while other categories may receive funds from one pay period only.

C. Check that the total amounts for deposits or credits in the Deposit/Credit column is the same as the amount allowed in *Monthly Allocated Amount* column for each individual Account Summary as well as that amount provided each pay period on the Income Allocation Worksheet.

Step 4. Allocation Savings Account (See Figure 109 on page 184)

A. Make one copy of form 76 and one copy of form 77 on pages 302 - 303.

B. Designate a *Savings* column for each expense category of your budget.

C. Transfer any money remaining at the end of every month for each Account Summary to the same *Category Expense* column of the Allocation Savings Account form. This process leaves a zero balance in the *Account Balance* column of each Account Summary before the posting of the next month's allocated paycheck takes place.

D. Enter each date, along with the budget category involved, when a transfer of money is made into or out of any savings account category; then record the resulting balance in the *Balance* column of the form.

The Allocation Savings Account form is designed to help you accumulate a cash reserve for each category of your budget. Therefore, whenever there is money remaining in an Account Summary category account at the end of the month, be sure to allocate the entire amount to the Allocation Savings Account form in the column designated for that particular budgeted category. This will zero out the *Account Balance* column before the deposit on the last day of the month is recorded. Since the extra money is not carried over to the next month on the Account Summary form, it is not as likely to be frivolously spent on unnecessary items. By doing this, you steadily build up a cash reserve over a period of time in each of the categories of your budget, leaving money for unexpected emergencies as well as for possible future buying opportunities. Even more important, you are constantly building discipline and becoming more accountable for the way you are handling your family's money.

"The habit of thrift proves your power to rule your own self. You are captain of your soul. You are able to take care of yourself, and then out of the excess of your strength you produce a surplus."

William A. McKeever

COMMON POSTING SITUATIONS

At this time, some questions might arise for the posting process of certain specific situations. The two cases below illustrate some common situations that frequently occur.

Case 1 How do I record the entry if I write one check for items in two or more categories?

Frequently we write one check for purchases in two or more categories of our budget. Suppose that you purchase four automobile tires for $275.50, a sport's jacket for $62.40, and a VCR and tapes for $345.25. You write the department store clerk a check of $683.15. The following procedure explains the process for completing the entries; Figure 45 on page 99 illustrates the proper use of the forms involved.

A. Checkbook Register

1. Enter the check number and date of purchase in columns 1 - 2.

2. In the column 3, *Transaction Description*, enter the three Account Summaries involving the purchases (Transportation, Clothing, and Housing) and the department store where the purchases were made.

3. Enter $683.15 in the *Payment/Withdrawal* column and appropriate expense codes in the *Budge Code* column.

4. Reduce the balance on the previous line by $683.15 to indicate the new balance amount; place this result in the *Balance* column of your register.

B. Account Summary

1. Enter the date of purchase in column 1 and the correct check number in column 3.

2. Record the store name and item(s) purchased in the *Transaction Item* column.

3. Place the price of the item(s) purchased in the *Payment/Withdrawal* column.

4. Enter the new balance on the appropriate line in the *Account Balance* column.

                    Solving Your Financial Puzzle

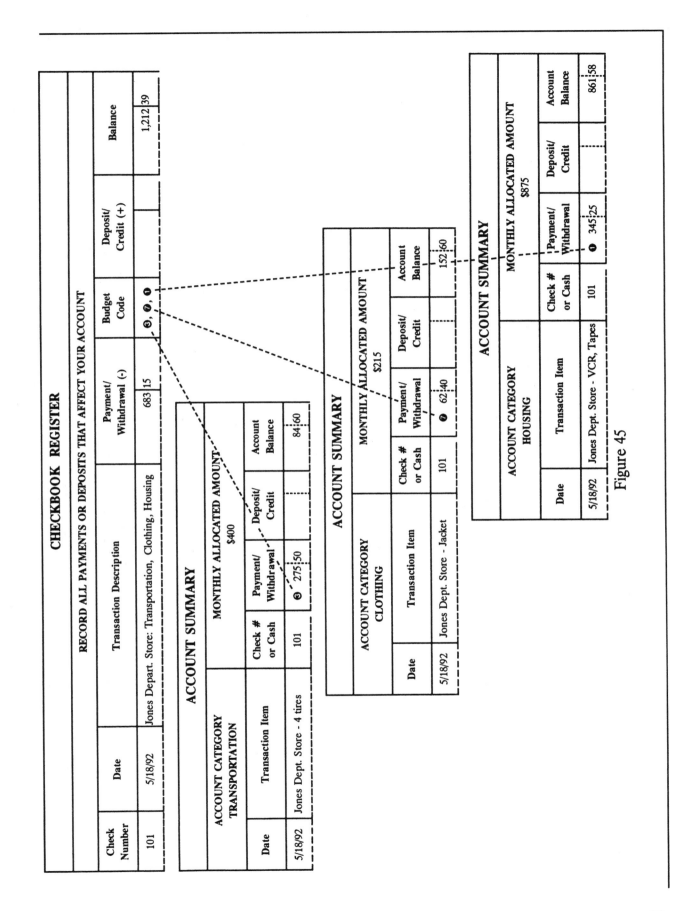

Figure 45

Case 2 How are cash entries posted to the Checkbook Register form?

There are four basic ways that you can enter a cash deposit to this form. Cash can be obtained either as part of a paycheck deposit or with the use of an automatic teller card, a credit card, or by writing a check for cash. The posting procedures for these situations are illustrated in Figures 46 - 48 below and on page 101.

A. Cash obtained with the deposit of a paycheck. (Figure 46)

1. Enter the date of the paycheck deposit in column 2.

2. Enter paycheck deposit in column 3, *Transaction Description*, and the entire paycheck amount in the *Deposit/Credit* column.

3. Enter the new balance in the *Balance* column.

For the amount taken as cash, use the next line in your register, and proceed as follows:

4. Enter the current date in column 2.

5. Record "cash from deposit" in the *Transaction Description* column.

6. Enter the amount taken out as cash in the *Payment/Withdrawal* column with the new balance in the last column.

CHECKBOOK REGISTER						
RECORD ALL PAYMENTS OR DEPOSITS THAT AFFECT YOUR ACCOUNT						
Check Number	Date	Transaction Description	Payment/Withdrawal (-)	Budget Code(s)	Deposit/Credit (+)	Balance $ 684.50
	6/30/92	Paycheck Deposit			1,250 85	1,935 35
	6/30/92	Cash from Deposit	100 00			1,835 35

Figure 46

B. Cash obtained by pocket teller (automatic teller machine) or by credit card. (Figure 47)

1. Enter the date of cash withdrawal in column 2.

2. Write "cash" and the name of card used in the *Transaction Description* column.

3. Enter the amount of cash withdrawn in the *Payment/Withdrawal* column and the new balance in the last column.

                    Solving Your Financial Puzzle

CHECKBOOK REGISTER						
RECORD ALL PAYMENTS OR DEPOSITS THAT AFFECT YOUR ACCOUNT						
Check Number	Date	Transaction Description	Payment/Withdrawal (-)	Budget Code(s)	Deposit/Credit (+)	Balance $ 684.50
	6/30/92	Paycheck Deposit			1,250 85	1,935 35
	6/30/92	Cash from ATM or Credit Card	100 00			1,835 35

Figure 47

C. Cash obtained by writing a check. (Figure 48)

  1. Enter the check number in column 1 and the date of cash withdrawal in column 2.

  2. Write "cash from check" in the *Transaction Description* column.

  3. Enter the cash amount in the *Payment/Withdrawal* column and the resulting balance in the *Balance* column.

CHECKBOOK REGISTER						
RECORD ALL PAYMENTS OR DEPOSITS THAT AFFECT YOUR ACCOUNT						
Check Number	Date	Transaction Description	Payment/Withdrawal (-)	Budget Code(s)	Deposit/Credit (+)	Balance $ 684.50
	6/30/92	Paycheck Deposit			1,250 85	1,935 35
101	6/30/92	Cash from Check	100 00			1,835 35

Figure 48

BUDGET BUSTERS
FINANCIAL STUMBLING BLOCKS

In an effort to control spending effectively, it is absolutely necessary that we retain a portion of each paycheck for those expenses that are contained in our budget, even though they are not paid on a monthly basis. These bills are frequently paid on an annual, semi annual, or quarterly basis, and for this reason are generally known as variable or periodic payments. Common expenses of this type are expected, and can be, as well as should be, planned for well in advance of the payment due date. The more common expenses of this type are shown in Figure 49 at the top of page 102.

VARIABLE OR PERIODIC PAYMENTS

Federal & State Estimated Taxes
Insurance Premiums
- Homeowners or Renters
- Automobile
- Life
- Health
- Disability

Vacations
Property Taxes
Annual Gifts for Special Occasions
College Expenses
- Tuition & Fees
- Room & Board
- Books & Supplies

Figure 49

Besides planning for the variable or periodic payments contained in our budget, we need to set aside a minimum amount of money on a monthly basis for crisis expenses, those unfortunate situations and experiences that always happen to somebody else, but frequently happen to ourselves at the most inopportune time. Such unexpected expenses that are usually not funded in our budget might include those listed in Figure 50 below.

UNEXPECTED OR CRISIS EXPENSES

Repairs
- Home
- Vehicle(s)
- Appliance(s)
Employment
- Time Reduced
- Terminated or Eliminated
Family - Relatives
- Catastrophic Illness
- Nursing Home Care
- Death

Medical - Dental Expenses
- Hospital
- Orthodontist
- Psychiatric Care
- Prescription Medicine
Replacements
- Automobile
- Furnace or Air Conditioner
- Major Appliances
- Theft

Figure 50

FROM STUMBLING BLOCKS TO STEPPING STONES

"There is only one object in economy for any decent person, and that of course is to have the money to spend when you really need it or want it for a useful object."

Albert W. Atwood

Unfortunately, many of the unexpected expenses listed above come at a time when funds are not readily available to make the required payments. A cash reserve fund for emergency expenses can be established through a disciplined habit of saving. Individuals and families alike, will **not** continue to be saddled with the added financial burden of using credit cards as the only alternative to pay for these necessary, and often times costly, expenses and services.

It is absolutely essential that you be thorough with the planning of your budget categories and their monthly allocated amounts in the preparation of the Income Allocation Worksheet. The effectiveness and the usefulness of your Account Summaries, one form for each category of your budget, as well as the success of the Allocation Savings Account, depends entirely on appropriately allocating reasonable and sufficient amounts of money to each area of your budget. One thing you will discover for sure, regardless of your personal or family income, you will never seem to have sufficient money to satisfy each of the categories of your budget. On the other hand, the reason for implementing a budget system is to instill the self discipline necessary to live within your monthly paycheck, while at the same time, to provide adequate funds to cover basic and essential needs.

☑ ACTION STEPS ☑

❑ Prepare an Account Summary for each category of your Revised Budget.

❑ Purchase a three ring binder to organize each of the following forms: Checkbook Register, Income Allocation Worksheet, Account Summaries, and Allocation Savings Account.

❑ Place all monies remaining at the end of each month into the appropriate category Savings Account. The money can be used for future expenses, replacements, and emergencies.

❑ Track all minor and petty cash expenses by keeping receipts and post to the proper budget category at least weekly.

❑ Track carefully each of your variable (periodic) payments and unexpected expenses to plan for the coming year's budget planning process.

❑ Review your budget at least annually or until you have developed a plan for saving each and every month by habit.

YOU SHOULD NOW BE ABLE TO:

1. Prepare your individual or family Money Management Flow-Chart.

2. Organize your financial notebook in a meaningful way.

3. Apply posting procedures for the checkbook register, account summaries, and the allocation savings account in your situation.

4. Identify each of your variable or periodic payment expenses.

5. Identify and begin to set aside an emergency fund for each of the unexpected expenses listed in Figure 50.

6. Develop a sense of awareness for the amount allocated to each category of your budget.

7. Stop spending in any budget category when its balance reaches zero.

CONCLUDING REMARKS

Without any hesitation, perhaps each of us would do well by heeding the following bit of advice. Life is a matter of setting priorities!

"I had my sleeping car in mind for many years. I wanted to build the car and made up my mind that to succeed in my life's dream, it was necessary to have some money and a good deal of it. I began by eliminating a number of things to which I had grown accustomed. Cigars were among them. I had been in the habit of paying five cents apiece for my cigars. I gave them up and many other things too. The total did not amount to much, but the habit was valuable, for I learned I could do without many other things that before that time I thought were absolutely essential to my well-being."

George M. Pullman

CHAPTER 5

MANAGING CREDIT EFFECTIVELY

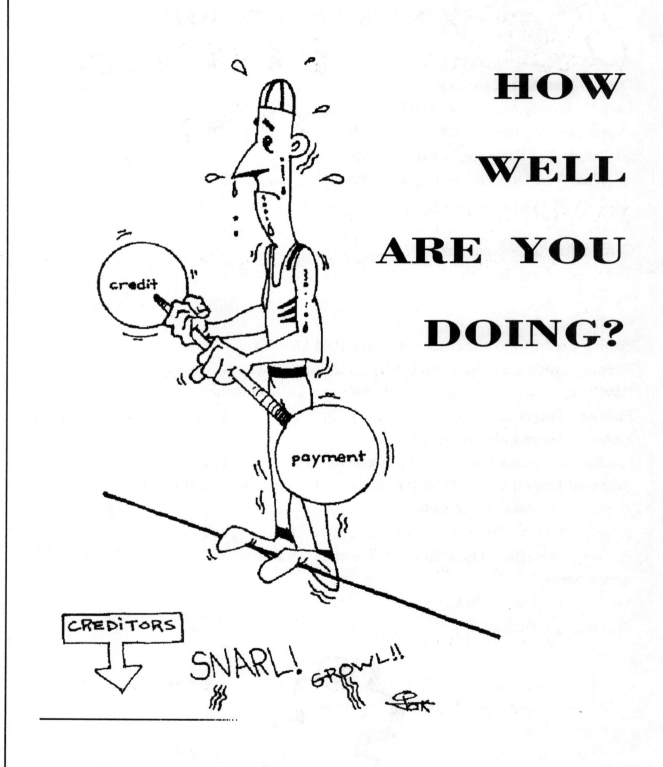

HOW WELL ARE YOU DOING?

     Solving Your Financial Puzzle

FOCUS ON:

MANAGING YOUR CREDIT

1. Use credit cards to meet your financial objectives.

2. Develop a realistic line of credit that conforms to your total financial program.

3. Keep accurate records involving your use of credit.

4. Determine whether your purchase has economic merit before using credit to buy it.

5. Understand the contents of your Cardholder and Disclosure Statement Agreement.

6. Attach the cash register sales receipt to your credit card receipt for each purchase.

7. Check your finance charges and credits regularly against each of your monthly statements.

8. Maintain a sufficient balance in your checking account to pay credit card bills on a monthly basis.

9. Use credit card "cash advances" only in emergencies.

10. Set a goal to pay your credit card bills each month.

MANAGING CREDIT EFFECTIVELY

---

*"There can be no freedom or beauty about a
home life that depends on borrowing and debt."*

Henrik Ibsen

CREDIT - THE AMERICAN WAY

Over the last fifty years, our society has witnessed an incredible growth in its affluence as a nation. We have vast supplies of material resources, along with remarkable advancements in science and technology at our disposal. These enhancements provide our people with unlimited opportunities in which to better themselves over those of past generations. Yet, it is during this same period that debt has gradually become the dominating influence that has dictated the direction of our lives. Isn't it interesting to know that during the time of our grandparents, and perhaps even our parents, that credit cards were unknown, automobile loans were uncommon, and loans for college, vocational, or technical schools were hardly a consideration. It is highly probable that their only debt was a loan on the family home, farm, or business. During those years, it was the teenagers' responsibility to finance their own college education, in addition to being responsive to the needs of the family.

The use of credit as a means to purchase goods and services has become a part of nearly every person's life, from the mid teens to post retirement years. Obtaining credit has often helped us significantly in living more productive lives. Such debts might include home mortgages as well as student and automobile loans. Securing a loan to purchase a home provides one an opportunity to accumulate a major asset. Borrowing for a college or vocational education provides skills for better paying

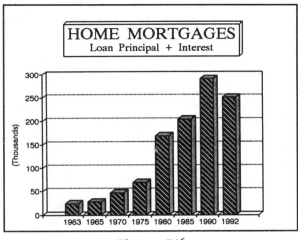

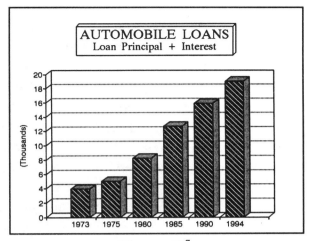

Figure 51[6]   Figure 52[7]

occupations. An automobile is generally regarded as a necessary means of basic transportation. On the other hand, sky-rocketing costs of today make it nearly impossible for the average individual or family to pay cash for such large expenses. (Figures 51 - 52). We need to be aware, that as consumers, getting into debt does not necessarily imply trouble. It is the idea of using credit irresponsibly and letting debt gain control of our financial framework that creates problems. Often times, these problems last for years.

LACK OF MONEY MANAGEMENT SKILLS

One of the hardest lessons to learn in life is how to be financially responsible. Too many people assume they automatically know how to handle their money. However, they fail to realize that handling money effectively is a "trained" skill, like many other skills in life. Acquiring financial knowledge is not a routine part of growing up. The vast majority of today's adults have had little or no training in managing money, setting realistic financial goals and budgets, or dealing with credit. Even though most of us were adequately prepared by the post high school education process to engage in a wide range of employment opportunities, very few institutions of higher learning taught us how to wisely manage our money upon receiving our paychecks.

---

[6]Data to produce the Bar Graph was obtained from Dow Jones & Company, Inc., Your Money Matters: Saving for the Future (Chicopee: The Wall Street Journal Classroom Edition, 1994, Merrill Lynch) 10.

[7]Data to produce the Bar Graph was obtained from Motor Vehicle Manufacturers Association, AAMA Motor Vehicle Facts & Figures (Detroit, 1983, 1994) 63, 57.

Therefore, when we graduated from "I owe U" to begin that first full-time occupation, most of us immediately started acquiring a newer automobile, color television, entertainment center, exercise gear, sports equipment, and the like. It's not uncommon to learn of young couples getting married today who actually believe and expect to amass, in a few short years, the same possessions that took their parents twenty-five years or longer to accumulate. Unfortunately, for the majority of such couples, the only things they accumulated were: a large debt, a great amount of stress, and perhaps a deteriorating relationship. While they had appeared to be raising their standard of living, they were in actuality, drastically lowering it over the long term. According to both Ron Blue[8] and Larry Burkett,[9] noted financial counselors and authors, mismanagement of finances is the leading cause of divorce in America. There seems to be a total lack of teaching the basics of money management to children in their teen age years before they leave home, testing the real world out for themselves. One of the greatest gifts parents can give to their children is a basic understanding of financial planning skills so they will be equipped to make wise financial decisions on their own.

PLASTIC MONEY
BENEFITS OF CREDIT CARDS

"Plastic money" can be a great convenience for today's fast-paced life style. When used with discretion, credit cards become a great asset to an individual or family. Some benefits of owning a credit card are:

1. Improving the standard of living by providing easy access to consumer products.

2. Improving credit ratings by responsibly paying each monthly balance by the statement date.

3. Renting a car unless you have made application and received a "cash" card from the rental company in advance of leasing the vehicle.

---

[8]Ronald W. and Judith W. Blue, Money Matters for Parents and Their Kids (Nashville: Oliver-Nelson Books, 1988) 21.

[9]Larry Burkett, The Complete Financial Guide for Young Couples (Wheaton: Victor Books, 1989) 7, 11.

4. Simplifying record keeping systems by providing an itemized monthly statement.

5. Decreasing bank "check charges" by reducing the number of checks written each month.

6. Itemizing each of the purchases/business transactions with the corresponding amounts to be reimbursed by the company.

7. Reducing the necessity for carrying large quantities of cash.

8. Acting as a safety net in times of a financial emergency.

9. Providing access to instant cash.

10. Providing limited liability if they are lost or stolen.

11. Providing bargaining power when you fail to receive a product or service for which you have paid.

12. Providing "extras" such as monthly cash, free airline mileage, free long distance phone service, etc.

GUIDELINES FOR CHOOSING A CREDIT CARD
WHAT YOU DON'T KNOW CAN HURT YOU

While credit cards add convenience to our life style, they carry a great responsibility as well. When we use them, we are taking out a loan which must be paid back, usually at high rates of interest if the monthly balance is not paid in full. Since all credit cards are not the same, select the one that most meets your objectives and way of life.

It is appropriate to state the difference between **credit** cards and **charge** cards. **Credit** cards allow you to make partial payments from month to month and charge interest on the balance owed (VISA, Mastercard, and Penneys). **Charge** cards, on the other hand, require full payment each month but charge no interest (Diners Club and American Express). Be sure to read the Cardholder Agreement and Disclosure Statement thoroughly before applying to an issuing company. If you have any questions regarding the agreement, ask for clarification from the company representative immediately. The following items vary greatly among card issuers and are significant factors to be considered when shopping for credit cards.

CARD ISSUER DISCLOSURE ITEMS

1. **Expenses and fees**

   Be sure you are aware of all expenses and fees, as well as the duration of each, charged by the issuing company. Typical costs assessed by card issuers include:

   A. Annual membership

   B. Cash advances

   C. Exceeding the credit limit

   D. Late payments

   E. Returned checks for insufficient funds

   F. Duplication of monthly statements, sales drafts, credit vouchers, or other documents requested by the card holder

   G. Lost or stolen card

2. **Grace period**

   The grace period (or free period) is the number of days a card holder has before a credit card company begins charging interest on new purchases. The length of the typical grace period is the number of days from the statement closing date (usually the end of the monthly billing cycle) to the date when interest begins to accrue (generally the payment due date). Currently, the payment must be received by the company, not sent or postmarked by the sender within the grace period to avoid the accumulation of interest charges. Selecting a credit card that offers a grace period allows a major benefit of paying the purchase balance in full each month without incurring finance charges. On the other hand, if you had not paid off your credit card balance in full the previous month, the majority of card issuers will charge you interest on new purchases immediately. You now have, in effect, a typical credit card without a grace or free period on new purchases for the current month. In this case, the company begins charging interest on either the day that the purchase was made or on the day it was posted to the account, depending on the institution's policy as stated in the disclosure agreement. For cards offering a grace period, the credit card company must mail your statement at least fourteen days before your payment is due. This is to insure you adequate time to make the necessary payment by the due date.

                    Solving Your Financial Puzzle

3. Annual percentage rate (APR)

The annual percentage rate, or APR, represents the interest rate charged by the lending institution each year for the use of borrowing their money. Companies disclose this rate to you at three significant times:

A. When you apply for a credit card

B. When you open the account

C. When you receive each of your billing statements

The APR gives the consumer a way to compare different loans, regardless of the amount, length of term, maturity date, or other factors, in the same manner that "unit pricing" gives the consumer a method for comparing prices of the same product contained in various sized packages. This rate will vary from company to company, and can even vary from month to month within the same lending institution. The lender must disclose whether the rate is fixed (constant) or variable (subject to change by the lender). If the rate is variable, the company must tell you how the rate is determined as well as how often it may change.

4. Cash advance

A cash advance is a "cash loan" made through the use of your credit card at a financial institution or automatic teller machine (ATM). The interest rate for cash advances is frequently higher than it is for the purchase of goods and services. In addition, there is usually no grace period, which means you pay interest each day until the cash advance is repaid. The majority of bank cards now impose a transaction fee based on a percentage of the cash borrowed. The fee assessed may be a minimum charge to a stated maximum amount. Be sure to read the Cardholder's Disclosure Agreement for further details regarding finance charges for this situation. The factors mentioned above tend to make credit card cash advances very expensive. It is therefore a good idea to use them only in emergencies.

5. Minimum payment

The minimum payment is the least dollar amount that is required on each month's balance. Depending upon the company, the payment might be as low as two and one half or three percent of the unpaid balance. Keep in mind, the lower the payment, the longer it will take to pay off the balance, and the more interest will be paid. It is always best for the consumer to pay each account balance in full whenever possible. This will allow you to keep money in a bank savings account earning interest for the entire month while using the "borrowing capabilities" of your credit card without cost.

6. Applied payments

Carefully read the order of the items to which the payment is applied. This information is contained in the fine print of the Cardholder and Disclosure Agreement. A typical order may be similar to the following:

A. Finance charges and fees

B. Previous cash advances

C. Previous purchases

D. Current cash advances

E. Current purchases

7. Finance charges

The Finance Charge is the total dollar amount paid to a credit card issuer by a consumer for doing business with a particular lender. This cost includes interest, service or transaction fees, and any carrying charge. The "Truth-in-Lending Act" regulations require card issuers to disclose the computation method used by the company to calculate the balance subject to the interest charged. Standard methods used by the majority of card issuers include:

A. Average daily balance (ADB) excluding new purchases

B. Average daily balance including new purchases

C. Two-cycle average daily balance excluding new purchases*

D. Two-cycle average daily balance including new purchases*
   (*Includes ADB of the previous month.)

Since each issuer can include its own variation for any particular computation method, the task of calculating credit balances is often complicated. It is therefore very likely that an individual having two or more credit cards with the same APR, can make identical purchases and monthly payments with each of the cards, yet have dramatically different finance charges. Even though the calculation of the monthly balance itself might be a mystery, be sure to know the method used by the card issuer. A detailed example comparing calculations of the four methods can be found on pages 201 - 221 of Appendix B.

☑ ACTION STEPS ☑

- ❏ Select a credit card that meets your needs and objectives.
- ❏ Shop around before deciding on a credit card.
- ❏ Read the fine print before selecting a credit card.
- ❏ Keep a minimum number of credit cards.

CARDHOLDER RESPONSIBILITIES

1. Credit limit

The credit limit is the maximum dollar amount of outstanding purchases and cash advances allowed at any time by the card issuer. People who do not have the financial resources or the discipline to be responsible for their original credit limit, should send a written statement to the issuer requesting a lower credit limit. On the other hand, those people who believe that they are entitled to a higher limit, should submit their written request to the lending institution. The lender will generally base their decision on the cardholder's income, existing debt, and card payment history.

2. Lost or stolen cards

Notify the card issuer, through its 800 number <u>immediately</u> when a credit card has been discovered lost or stolen. If the card was used to make unauthorized purchases before the owner reported it lost or stolen, the maximum liability is $50 per card. On the other hand, if only the account number, and not the actual card, was used by an unauthorized person, the card holder is generally not liable for any amount. In this situation, send a follow up letter within 60 days to the credit card issuer containing the following information:

A. Cardholder's name and account number

B. Dollar amount of the suspected or disputed error

C. Date transaction occurred

D. A description of the error

E. An explanation regarding why the item charge is incorrect

The letter must be sent to the address listed on the statement for "billing errors and inquiries." This address may be different from that address where monthly payments are regularly sent. A copy of all correspondence with the card issuer, that is, the issuing company, should be kept by the credit card holder. The Fair Credit Billing Act allows for withholding the disputed amount until the matter has been resolved; all other charges should be paid in the usual manner.

3. Monthly statements

One of the first items in the Cardholder Agreement that accompanies your credit card is "your promise to pay" the total amount of the purchase(s) and/or cash advance(s), as well as any finance charge or other expenses that may be due. Therefore, examine your statement for the following situations before making the monthly payment:

A. Be sure that each of the charges is correct

B. Confirm the date and amount for each expenditure

C. Personally destroy each monthly statement that is not kept

By using your credit card receipts to examine each of the above items, you will not only assure yourself of paying the correct amount, you will be validating the necessity of your expenditures and purchases as well. Furthermore, it's very useful to immediately identify specific items purchased by writing them at the top of the customer copy. For example, you would write "Jim's Nike tennis shoes" at the top of the customer credit card receipt itemized only as sporting goods. See Figure 53 on the following page. Also attach cash register receipts (Figure 54) to your customer copy. This method will save confusion and considerable stress when matching your many credit card receipts with the monthly statement prior to paying the bills.

4. Cancelling a credit card

When you decide to cancel a credit card, write a letter to the issuing company stating this fact. In any event, do **NOT** attempt to cancel a credit card verbally or over the telephone. When a credit card is cancelled, outstanding balances become due immediately. If the issuing company requests that the credit card(s) be returned, cut the card(s) into several pieces and return them in the same envelope with the letter of cancellation. Likewise, upon receiving a new replacement credit card, be sure to cut up the old one and destroy it immediately.

     Solving Your Financial Puzzle

Jim's Nike Tennis Shoes	CASH REGISTER RECEIPT

Jim's Nike Tennis Shoes

Max Sporting Goods
1234 Smith Road
Town, USA Zip
Phone Number

Merchant: 846392-0169
Rec. No.: 822
Date: 8/22/95
Acct. No.: 6732946851477502
Type: VISA/exp. date
Customer: Name
Auth. No.: 035726
VISA ID: 67891012345
Sale: Sporting Goods   84.80
Total   84.80

I AGREE TO PAY ABOVE TOTAL AMOUNT
ACCORDING TO CARD ISSUER AGREEMENT
(MERCHANT AGREEMENT IF CREDIT VOUCHER)

_____

SIGNATURE

RETAIN THIS COPY FOR YOUR RECORDS
White Copy-Merchant Yellow Copy-Customer

Figure 53

CASH REGISTER RECEIPT

846392-0169   822

MAX SPORTING GOODS
1234 Smith Road   Town, USA Zip

8/22/95   4:35PM

Nike Tennis Shoes 12D   80.00
       Subtotal   80.00
       Sales Tax   4.80
       TOTAL   84.80

VISA 6732946851477502
       Charge   84.80

Auth. No. 035726

AMOUNT TENDERED   84.80
       CHANGE   0.00

THANK YOU!

Figure 54

THE CREDIT CARD STATEMENT

Bank card statements contain the same basic information even though the appearance of the statements may differ. The name, address, and toll free telephone number of the card issuer is generally near the top of the statement. If the statement contains the card holder's name and address, the information will also be located near the top. Other information that generally appears near the top of each statement is:

1. Statement (or current billing) date
2. Account number
3. Credit limit
4. Available credit
5. Available cash balance
6. Amount over credit limit
7. Payment due date
8. Minimum payment due
9. Account balance due

The center portion of the statement contains necessary information regarding each purchase or cash advance. Details included are the:

1. Sale or purchase date
2. Posting or transaction date
3. Processing or reference number
4. Merchant name or activity since last statement
5. Merchant or regional billing location
6. Amount of purchase or cash advance
7. Important reminders or advertisement information

The Account Summary is generally located at or near the bottom of the statement. Information contained in this section includes:

1. Previous balance
2. Payments
3. Credits
4. Current charges or purchases
5. Average daily balance
6. Finance charge
7. Monthly periodic rate
8. Annual percentage rate
9. New balance or balance due
10. Minimum payment

The order in which the payments in the Account Summary above are applied to an account is especially important. If the order is not given in detail in the Cardholder Agreement, be sure to have the representative of the card issuing company review this document thoroughly with you. Generally, but not always, payments are applied in the following order:

1. Finance charges and previous fees
2. Previous cash advances
3. Previous purchases
4. Current fees
5. Current cash advances
6. Current purchases

 Solving Your Financial Puzzle

REMEMBER: It is essential when you open a credit card account that you take time to carefully read the Cardholder Agreement and Disclosure fine print that accompanies each of your credit cards. An example of a bank card statement is shown in Figure 55 below.

STATEMENT

City Bank Card System

P. O. Box 6930 CB

Merryfield, Colorado 03302

Telephone (800) - 333 - 1234

Jeffrey R. Smithe

121 Cloverdale Circle

Durant, California 16207

Statement Date	2 10 95
Account Number	156 309 416 897
Credit Limit	2,500.00
Available Credit	1,000.00
Available Cash Balance	1,250.00
Amount Over Credit Limit	0.00
Payment Due Date	3 6 95
Minimum Payment Due	46.00
Account Balance Due	1,521.78

Purchase Date	Posting Date	Processing Number	Merchant Name	Merchant or Regional Billing Location	Amount
02/01/95	02/01/95	1345289T96	Previous Month Payment--Thank You	Ending Balance	500.00 -300.00
01/16/95	01/16/95	241697PT04	Fritz Electronics	Seaville, California	700.00
01/21/95	01/23/95	5764V204K23	Computer Systems	Durant, California	600.00

Important Reminder: Your City Bank Card System account continues to have no annual fees! Our commitment is to provide you with quality service.

Account Summary	Previous Balance	Payments	Credits	Current Charges	Average Daily Balance	Finance Charge	Monthly Periodic Rate(s)	Annual Percentage Rate(s)	Balance Due	Minimum Payment Amount
Purchases	500.00	300.00		1,300.00	1,451.73	21.78	1.5%	18.0%	1,521.78	46.00
Cash Advances							1.6%	19.2%		
Totals	500.00	300.00		1,300.00	1,451.73	21.78			1,521.78	46.00

Figure 55

❑ Familiarize yourself with each of your credit card statements.

❑ Be aware of the general contents of your credit cards' Cardholder Agreement and Disclosure Statements.

CREDIT CARD RECORDS

When you use more than one credit card, it is essential that you keep an inventory of them. The easiest way to accomplish this task is to complete a Credit Card Inventory such as the one illustrated in Figure 56 below and provided on page 307. This information should be kept with your other important records. Be sure to update the material whenever a credit card is added or dropped from your possession.

CREDIT CARD INVENTORY

Date of Record_____

Name(s) of Card Holder	Name of Company	Card Number	Date Card Obtained	Credit Limit	Type/Amount Fee	Company Address	Telephone Number
Jim & Betty Curran	E - Z Buy Finance Co.	C24085	07/15/90	$2,000	Annual - $25.00 Cash Advance - Lesser of 2% or $5 per item	1720 Main St. Pineville, MN	(800)-478-1200 (312)-774-1258
Jim Curran	Best Finance Company	76J427	05/12/88	$1,500	Annual - $10.00 Cash Advance - $2 per time	256 Dale Ave. Morris, CO	(800)-525-4000 (337)-621-1325
Betty Curran	Best Finance Company	62B504	11/07/87	$1,500	Annual - $10.00 Cash Advance - $2 per time	256 Dale Ave. Morris, CO	(800)-525-4000 (337)-621-1325

Figure 56 - Worksheet page 307

POSTING CREDIT CARD EXPENSES
BALANCES PAID MONTHLY

It is imperative that you maintain your budget by knowing the amount you spend for each of the categories. This is true whether you pay your credit card balance in full at the end of each month or allow monthly balances and finance charges to accumulate. In either case, the Cash Method of Accounting is probably the easiest, as well as the most reliable, approach to use in recording your credit card expenses. When using this method, credit purchases are recorded <u>only</u> when a check is written to the credit card company, <u>not</u> when you purchase the item using your card.

The procedure for making credit card entries in the Checkbook Register and Account Summaries are given below. Examples of completed forms appear in Figures 57 and 58.

A. Checkbook Register

1. Indicate the number of your check in column 1.

2. Record the date the check was written in column 2.

3. Enter the name of the credit card, and a description of the item purchased, in the *Transaction Description* column.

4. Record the amount of the purchase(s) in the *Payment/Withdrawal* column, along with the category code in the *Budget Code* column.

5. Finally, enter the new balance in the *Balance* column.

B. Account Summary

1. Record the date that the check was written to the credit card company in column 1.

2. Enter the name of the credit card company, along with the item purchased, in column 2.

3. Record the number of the check in the *Check #* or *Cash* column and the amount for which the check was written in the *Payment/Withdrawal* column.

4. Indicate the new balance in the *Account Balance* column.

A credit card is **not** a license for over spending in any category of your budget. The allocated amount agreed to by the persons involved need to be adhered to, regardless of the method used to make the purchases.

CHECKBOOK REGISTER						
RECORD ALL PAYMENTS OR DEPOSITS THAT AFFECT YOUR ACCOUNT						
Check Number	Date	Transaction Description	Payment/Withdrawal (-)	Budget Code(s)	Deposit/Credit (+)	Balance $ 427.15
714	3/8/92	Best Finance Company Automobile Battery	78⁞50	❸		348⁞65

Figure 57 - Worksheet page 304

ACCOUNT SUMMARY					
ACCOUNT CATEGORY TRANSPORTATION		MONTHLY ALLOCATED AMOUNT $400			
Date	Transaction Item	Check # or Cash	Payment/ Withdrawal	Deposit/ Credit	Account Balance
3/8/92	Balance On Hand				176 33
3/8/92	Best Finance Co. Automobile Battery	714	78 50		97 83

Figure 58 - Worksheet page 301

KEEPING CREDIT CARD BALANCES UNDER CONTROL

Credit cards are an extremely valuable financial tool when expenses resulting from their use are kept under control. In order to maintain a workable plan, it is essential to make sure that sufficient funds exist in budget categories, whether you pay your bills with cash or by credit card. It is necessary to carefully monitor your credit card spending in an effort to bring such expenditures under complete control. This task is accomplished with the use of the Credit Card Obligations form on page 308 and illustrated in Figure 59 below. Complete a separate line of the form each time an item is purchased using credit. You can then be absolutely sure that funds will exist to pay each of your bills in a timely manner. By taking the precautionary step just mentioned, you will be saving yourself from the likely possibility of incurring future anxieties or grief, commonly know as "buyers remorse." When there is no money available to pay for a particular expense, consider the consequences for making the purchase.

CREDIT CARD OBLIGATIONS

Date of Record _____

Name Of Finance Company	Telephone Number	Budget Category & Item	Remaining Payoff Amount	Number Remaining Payments	Current Monthly Payment	Date Payment Made
Valley Bank Credit Card A	(800) 386 - 1213	Transportation Tires	$ 350.74	12	$ 30	2/5
Mesa Finance Credit Card B	(800) 478 - 1100	Housing Refrigerator	$ 659.58	9	$ 75	2/20

Figure 59 - Worksheet page 308

 Solving Your Financial Puzzle

REVOLVING CREDIT
ALLOWING MONTHLY BALANCES TO ACCUMULATE

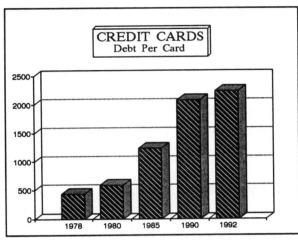

Figure 60[10]

When any type of credit is utilized, whether it's for a purchase or a service, the payment is only deferred (that is, delayed), not forgotten. If used responsibly, credit makes a lot of sense. While it is in the best interests of the card holder to pay the entire amount of the statement each month, in the vast majority of situations, people tend to let monthly balances, as well as finance charges, accumulate. Minimum monthly payments are easily met, and when a line of credit has been reached on one card, it becomes easy to rationalize the necessity for getting another one. The process of carrying over a debt from one month to the next, paying interest on the amount owed, is known as Revolving Credit. The scenario often continues again and again, until purchases finally get out of control. This situation can easily take place during special times of the year, at holidays such as Christmas or during a vacation or extended trip. Consumers have been deluged with radio and television advertising high ticket items - major appliances, home and garden machinery, furniture, carpet, and other such items with the promise that the beginning payment can be delayed three to six months from the date of actual purchase. The average unpaid balance per credit card rose from $263 in 1978 to $1,362 in 1992, a gain of nearly 418%. During the same fourteen year period, the total debt per card (principal + interest) increased from $435 to $2,236 (Figure 60). Is there any wonder then, why individuals and families get into financial difficulty? One objective of this book is to increase your awareness of the "real cost" of maintaining monthly credit card balances and to assist you in eventually reducing all of your credit card statements to zero in the shortest possible time.

[10]Data to produce the Bar Graph was obtained from Dow Jones & Company, Inc., Your Money Matters: Saving for the Future (Chicopee: The Wall Street Journal Classroom Edition, 1994, Merrill Lynch) 10.

FINANCE CHARGES

Paying the minimum balance on credit card bills is generally easy and convenient. Moreover, it gives one an excuse to continue spending on unnecessary items, especially if the card "credit limit" has not yet been reached. It is significant to realize that another monthly expense is created, sometimes unnecessarily, when using revolving credit. The added expense that you pay the finance company each month needs to be placed in your budget. Depending upon your monthly payments, finance charges can indeed represent a substantial amount of money. The amount of each budget category's share of the total monthly payment applied represents both principal and finance charges.

The following example illustrates a convenient form which is used to monitor the amount that is charged to each of your credit cards, as well as the monthly payments and incurring finance charges. The Credit Card Account Form, provided on page 309, will assist you in keeping accurate records. Use <u>one</u> form for each of your credit cards as shown in Figure 62 on page 125.

The Curran family made the following purchases from Jones Department Store using their "E - Z Buy" credit card:

JONES DEPARTMENT STORE			
Date	Item Purchased	Price	Interest Rate
6/1	Children's Clothes	$ 105.00	15 %
6/3	Lawn Mower	390.00	15
6/3	Patio Furniture	220.00	15

Figure 61

Mr. Curran agrees to pay $175 a month until his account is paid in full. The finance company charges an annual rate of 15% or 1.25% per month on the unpaid balance. Mr. Curran chooses to allocate $25 a month to the Clothing account with the remaining $150 of the monthly payment to the Housing account. The budget category is designated in the *Budget Code* column of the form so that the correct portion of each month's payment can be entered on the appropriate Account Summary as illustrated in Figures 64 - 66 on pages 127 - 128.

Notice that the new credit balance is $548.94 rather than $540.00 as might be expected. This is due to the finance charge of $8.94 on July 9th. Since paying finance charges increases spending for each budget category where credit is involved, it is always in the best interest of the consumer to reduce these charges as much as possible, the ultimate goal being to eliminate finance charges completely.

CREDIT CARD ACCOUNT FORM

\multicolumn{8}{c}{Finance Company E - Z Buy}							
Date	Item or Expense Charged	Budget Code	Monthly Payment	Charged Amount	Principal Applied	Finance Charge	Credit Balance
6/1	Children's Clothes	❼		105|00			105|00
6/3	Lawn Mower	❶		390|00			495|00
6/3	Patio Furniture	❶		220|00			715|00
7/9	Payment	❶ , ❼	175|00		166|06	8|94	548|94
8/9	Payment	❶ , ❼	175|00		168|14	6|86	380|80
9/9	Payment	❶ , ❼	175|00		170|24	4|76	210|56
10/9	Payment	❶ , ❼	175|00		172|37	2|63	38|19
11/9	Payment	❶ , ❼	38|67		38|19	|48	0|00
		Totals	738|67	715|00	715|00	23|67	

Figure 62 - Worksheet page 309

FINANCE CHARGE CALCULATIONS

The Credit Card Account Worksheet in Figure 63 on page 126 illustrates a simplified step-by-step process for computing the monthly finance charge of the previous example. The purpose of the calculation is to emphasize the significant amount of finance charge, rather than the tedious computations performed in arriving at the desired results.

The various ways credit card issuers use to calculate monthly balances and finance charges can be very complex. The majority of lenders use variations of the average daily balance to determine their finance charges. Four basic methods are discussed and illustrated in Appendix B on pages 201 - 221. At this point, it is of primary importance that you are aware of the method used to arrive at card expenses for each of your individual credit cards.

CREDIT CARD ACCOUNT WORKSHEET

E - Z Buy Finance Company

Date	Previous Remaining Balance	Finance Charge (%) (1.25%)	Monthly Payment	Finance Charge Amount	Principal Applied Amount	New Remaining Balance
7/9	715|00 x	.0125		= 8|94		
			175|00	- 8|94 =	166|06	
	715|00				- 166|06 =	584|94
8/9	584|94 x	.0125		= 6|86		
			175|00	- 6|86 =	168|14	
	584|94				- 168|14 =	380|80
9/9	380|80 x	.0125		= 4|76		
			175|00	- 4|76 =	170|24	
	380|80				- 170|24 =	210|56
10/9	210|56 x	.0125		= 2|63		
			175|00	- 2|63 =	172|37	
	210|56				- 172|37 =	38|19
11/9	38|19 x	.0125		= |48		
			38|67	= |48 +	38|19	0|00

Figure 63 - Worksheet page 310

Each month's calculations can be broken down into three basic steps.

1. Determine the finance charge by multiplying the credit balance times the monthly periodic rate; 715.00 x 0.0125 (1.25%) = 8.94.

2. Compute the principal amount applied to the loan by subtracting the finance charge from the payment; 175.00 - 8.94 = 166.06.

3. Calculate the new balance by subtracting the principal amount applied to the loan from the previous balance; 715.00 - 166.06 = 548.94.

Compute each monthly payment until the loan is paid in full by continuing with steps 1 - 3 shown above.

The procedure to determine the monthly balance in any particular month can be established by applying the following general formula:

$$\text{Balance Due} = \text{Previous Balance} - \text{Payments} - \text{Credits} + \text{Current Charges} + \text{Finance Charge}$$

                    Solving Your Financial Puzzle

After the finance charge is determined, calculating the balance is a simple matter. It's the myriad of ways credit card issuers choose to calculate the finance charge that makes the entire process complex. Using the general formula listed on page 126, the balance due for July becomes:

Balance Due = $715.00 - $175.00 - $0 + $8.94 = $548.94

POSTING PROCEDURES FOR REVOLVING ACCOUNTS

The procedure for posting credit card payments to the Checkbook Register and to the appropriate account summaries for a revolving account is precisely the same as those steps given on page 121 for an account balance paid in full on a monthly basis. A detail of the Checkbook Register, along with the Housing ❶ and Clothing ❼ Account Summaries for the Curran family, is provided in Figures 64 - 66 that follow.

CHECKBOOK REGISTER						
RECORD ALL PAYMENTS OR DEPOSITS THAT AFFECT YOUR ACCOUNT						
Check Number	Date	Transaction Description	Payment/Withdrawal (-)	Budget Code(s)	Deposit/Credit (+)	Balance $ 427.15
384	7/9	E-Z Buy Clothes, Mower, Patio Furniture	175 00	❶ , ❼		252 15

Figure 64 - Worksheet page 304

ACCOUNT SUMMARY					
ACCOUNT CATEGORY HOUSING		MONTHLY ALLOCATED AMOUNT $850			
Date	Transaction Item	Check # or Cash	Payment/ Withdrawal	Deposit/ Credit	Account Balance
7/8/92	Balance On Hand				645 33
7/9/92	E-Z Buy Mower, Patio Fur	384	150 00		495 33

Figure 65 - Worksheet page 301

ACCOUNT SUMMARY					
ACCOUNT CATEGORY CLOTHING		MONTHLY ALLOCATED AMOUNT $100			
Date	Transaction Item	Check # or Cash	Payment/ Withdrawal	Deposit/ Credit	Account Balance
7/8/92	Balance On Hand				129 36
7/9/92	E-Z Buy Child. Clothes	384	25 00		104 36

Figure 66 - Worksheet page 301

EXCESSIVE USE OF CREDIT CARDS

The impact of excessive credit card use for the purchase of goods and services may not be felt early on, especially if current family income is maintained and financial emergencies are not encountered. However, individuals and families who tend to maximize their credit card limits often lose sight of the larger financial picture that awaits them. In these instances, an interruption of regular income for any reason can make the payment of minimum monthly installments impossible.

VARIABLE VERSUS CONSTANT MONTHLY PAYMENTS

	Method A Decreasing Monthly Payment	Method B Constant Monthly Payment
	Monthly payment decreases from 3% of the initial balance to a minimum payment of $10.	Monthly payment is a constant 3% of the initial principal until the balance is paid in full.
Initial Principal	$1,500.00	$1,500.00
Annual Finance Rate	17.65%	17.65%
Monthly Finance Rate	1.47%	1.47%
Months to Pay Loan	139 months or 11 years, 7 months	47 months or 3 years, 11 months
Total Finance Charge	$1,206.55	$ 576.83
Total Finance Charge is "*" Percent of Principal	* 80.44%	* 38.46%

Figure 67

Consider the situation illustrated in Figure 67 on page 128 showing two methods of paying a credit card balance of $1,500 with an annual rate of 17.65% or 1.47% per month. One plan begins with a $45 monthly payment, then periodically decreases until the $10 minimum payment is reached in the ninety-fourth month. Each payment, to the nearest dollar, is calculated as 3% of the outstanding monthly balance. The schedule of payments and the principal balance remaining is shown in Figures 69 and 70 on pages 131 - 132. It is clear that an item, such as an expensive computer, purchased by this method would likely need to be replaced or updated while the owner continues to make payments on the original model.

A second way would be to pay the same amount each month, regardless of the outstanding balance, until the debt is paid in full. In this case, the monthly payment is calculated as $45.00, which is 3% of the initial principal. Notice the difference in the number of payments made as well as the amount of finance charges incurred. See Figure 71 on page 133. This example shows why it is to the cardholder's advantage to pay as large a monthly installment as possible for each of the credit cards involved.

At this time it might be an excellent idea to ascertain your credit situation by completing the Credit and Loan Summary Worksheet in Figure 68 below to determine whether or not you are in danger of debt overload. If the number in the *Percent of Debt Obligation* row is higher than 15 or 20 percent, you are in the "credit card meltdown stage" and very likely heading towards serious financial problems.

CREDIT AND LOAN SUMMARY WORKSHEET

Name of Creditor or Finance Company	Date of Last Payment	Annual Finance Rate	Monthly Payment Amount	Remaining Card Balance
Total Monthly Payments			$	
Total Of Outstanding Loans				$
Monthly Family Take-Home (Net) Pay			$	
Percent Of Debt Obligation				%

Figure 68 - Worksheet page 311

To illustrate the value of the Credit and Loan Summary Worksheet, consider the following situation. A family of husband, wife, and two teenage children average $1,700 a month take-home pay. Excluding their monthly car loan of $250 and a $725 mortgage payment, they currently pay $285 each month on outstanding credit card balances without a noticeable effect on their present life style. What do you think will be the impact of these debts upon this family's future financial situation and why? A close examination of their current debt can be calculated using the following formula:

$$\textit{Percent of Debt Obligation} = \frac{\textit{Total Monthly Payments}}{\textit{Monthly Net Income}} \times 100$$

Calculating only the credit card obligations, we obtain:

$$\textit{Percent of Debt Obligation} = \frac{\$\ 285}{\$1,700} \times 100 = 17\%$$

However, a more realistic picture of their indebtedness would be to include the amount of the car loan, along with the credit card payments, giving the following results:

$$\textit{Percent of Debt Obligation} = \frac{\$\ 535}{\$1,700} \times 100 = 31\%$$

It is obvious that this family cannot continue on their current "indebtedness program" forever. Immediate attention needs to be given to future possible college education costs for the two teenage children, the remote possibility that one of the wage earners might become disabled, or to a potential medical problem involving a family member. In addition, accumulating retirement income, building an emergency savings fund, or beginning an investment program for future needs is greatly reduced until their debt has been eliminated.

On the other hand, if this family had a fairly substantial savings account, an appropriate question might be, "should they use a portion of their savings to reduce the remaining loan balance and/or their monthly payments?" This would be a possible consideration provided that the family had learned from the uncomfortable experience of being in debt, and pledged to take immediate control of their finances by foregoing the use of each charge account until their entire credit card obligation was resolved. At this time, a commitment would then be made to pay off all future credit card charges on a monthly basis as bills come due.

CREDIT CARD PAYMENT SCHEDULE
MINIMUM PAYMENT VARIES

Initial Payment	Annual Finance Rate	Monthly Finance Rate	Minimum Rate of Principal Balance
$1,500.00	17.65%	1.47%	3%

Number Months	Principal Balance Remaining	Monthly Payment (Rounded to Next Dollar)	Monthly Principal Applied	Monthly Finance Charge	Number Months	Principal Balance Remaining	Monthly Payment (Rounded to Next Dollar)	Monthly Principal Applied	Monthly Finance Charge
1	$1,500.00	$45	$22.94	$22.06	36	$862.29	$26	$13.32	$12.68
2	1,477.06	45	23.27	21.73	37	848.97	26	13.51	12.49
3	1,453.79	44	22.62	21.38	38	835.46	26	13.71	12.29
4	1,431.17	43	21.95	21.05	39	821.75	25	12.91	12.09
5	1,409.22	43	22.27	20.73	40	808.84	25	13.10	11.90
6	1,386.95	42	21.60	20.40	41	795.73	24	12.30	11.70
7	1,365.35	41	20.92	20.08	42	783.44	24	12.48	11.52
8	1,344.43	41	21.23	19.77	43	770.96	24	12.66	11.34
9	1,323.20	40	20.54	19.46	44	758.30	23	11.85	11.15
10	1,302.67	40	20.84	19.16	45	746.45	23	12.02	10.98
11	1,281.83	39	20.15	18.85	46	734.43	23	12.20	10.80
12	1,261.68	38	19.44	18.56	47	722.23	22	11.38	10.62
13	1,242.24	38	19.73	18.27	48	710.86	22	11.54	10.46
14	1,222.51	37	19.02	17.98	49	699.31	21	10.71	10.29
15	1,203.49	37	19.30	17.70	50	688.60	21	10.87	10.13
16	1,184.19	36	18.58	17.42	51	677.73	21	11.03	9.97
17	1,165.61	35	17.86	17.14	52	666.69	21	11.19	9.81
18	1,147.75	35	18.12	16.88	53	655.50	20	10.36	9.64
19	1,129.63	34	17.38	16.62	54	645.14	20	10.51	9.49
20	1,112.25	34	17.64	16.36	55	634.63	20	10.67	9.33
21	1,094.61	33	16.90	16.10	56	623.97	19	9.82	9.18
22	1,077.71	33	17.15	15.85	57	614.14	19	9.97	9.03
23	1,060.56	32	16.40	15.60	58	604.18	19	10.11	8.89
24	1,044.16	32	16.64	15.36	59	594.06	18	9.26	8.74
25	1,027.52	31	15.89	15.11	60	584.80	18	9.40	8.60
26	1,011.63	31	16.12	14.88	61	575.40	18	9.54	8.46
27	995.51	30	15.36	14.64	62	565.86	17	8.68	8.32
28	980.15	30	15.58	14.42	63	557.19	17	8.80	8.20
29	964.57	29	14.81	14.19	64	548.38	17	8.93	8.07
30	949.75	29	15.03	13.97	65	539.45	17	9.07	7.93
31	934.72	29	15.25	13.75	66	530.38	16	8.20	7.80
32	919.47	28	14.48	13.52	67	522.18	16	8.32	7.68
33	905.00	28	14.69	13.31	68	513.86	16	8.44	7.56
34	890.31	27	13.91	13.09	69	505.42	16	8.57	7.43
35	876.40	27	14.11	12.89	70	496.86	15	7.69	7.31

Figure 69

CREDIT CARD PAYMENT SCHEDULE
MINIMUM PAYMENT VARIES
(Continued)

Initial Payment	Annual Finance Rate	Monthly Finance Rate	Minimum Rate of Principal Balance
$1,500.00	17.65%	1.47%	3%

Number Months	Principal Balance Remaining	Monthly Payment (Rounded to Nearest Dollar)	Monthly Principal Applied	Monthly Finance Charge	Number Months	Principal Balance Remaining	Monthly Payment (Rounded to Nearest Dollar)	Monthly Principal Applied	Monthly Finance Charge
71	$489.16	$15	$7.81	$7.19	106	$266.47	$10	$6.08	$3.92
72	481.36	15	7.92	7.08	107	260.39	10	6.17	3.83
73	473.44	15	8.04	6.96	108	254.22	10	6.26	3.74
74	465.40	14	7.15	6.85	109	247.96	10	6.35	3.65
75	458.25	14	7.26	6.74	110	241.61	10	6.45	3.55
76	450.99	14	7.37	6.63	111	235.16	10	6.54	3.46
77	443.62	14	7.48	6.52	112	228.62	10	6.64	3.36
78	436.15	14	7.59	6.41	113	221.99	10	6.73	3.27
79	428.56	13	6.70	6.30	114	215.25	10	6.83	3.17
80	421.86	13	6.80	6.20	115	208.42	10	6.93	3.07
81	415.07	13	6.90	6.10	116	201.48	10	7.04	2.96
82	408.17	13	7.00	6.00	117	194.45	10	7.14	2.86
83	401.18	13	7.10	5.90	118	187.31	10	7.25	2.75
84	394.08	12	6.20	5.80	119	180.06	10	7.35	2.65
85	387.88	12	6.30	5.70	120	172.71	10	7.46	2.54
86	381.58	12	6.39	5.61	121	165.25	10	7.57	2.43
87	375.19	12	6.48	5.52	122	157.68	10	7.68	2.32
88	368.71	12	6.58	5.42	123	150.00	10	7.79	2.21
89	362.13	11	5.67	5.33	124	142.20	10	7.91	2.09
90	356.46	11	5.76	5.24	125	134.30	10	8.02	1.98
91	350.70	11	5.84	5.16	126	126.27	10	8.14	1.86
92	344.86	11	5.93	5.07	127	118.13	10	8.26	1.74
93	338.93	11	6.01	4.99	128	109.87	10	8.38	1.62
94	332.92	10	5.10	4.90	129	101.48	10	8.51	1.49
95	327.82	10	5.18	4.82	130	92.97	10	8.63	1.37
96	322.64	10	5.25	4.75	131	84.34	10	8.76	1.24
97	317.38	10	5.33	4.67	132	75.58	10	8.89	1.11
98	312.05	10	5.41	4.59	133	66.69	10	9.02	0.98
99	306.64	10	5.49	4.51	134	57.68	10	9.15	0.85
100	301.15	10	5.57	4.43	135	48.52	10	9.29	0.71
101	295.58	10	5.65	4.35	136	39.24	10	9.42	0.58
102	289.93	10	5.74	4.26	137	29.81	10	9.56	0.44
103	284.19	10	5.82	4.16	138	20.25	10	9.70	0.30
104	278.37	10	5.91	4.09	139	10.55	10.55	10.55	0.00
105	272.47	10	5.99	4.01	Column	Totals	$2,706.55	$1,500.00	$1,206.55

Figure 70

                Solving Your Financial Puzzle

CREDIT CARD PAYMENT SCHEDULE
CONSTANT MINIMUM PAYMENT

Initial Principal	Annual Finance Rate	Monthly Finance Rate	Constant Minimum Payment
$1,500.00	17.65%	1.47%	$45.00

Number Months	Principal Balance Remaining	Monthly Principal Applied	Monthly Finance Charge	Number Months	Principal Balance Remaining	Monthly Principal Applied	Monthly Finance Charge
1	$1,500.00	$22.94	$22.06	26	$812.95	$33.04	$11.96
2	1,477.06	23.27	21.73	27	779.91	33.53	11.47
3	1,453.79	23.62	21.38	28	746.38	34.02	10.98
4	1,430.17	23.96	21.04	29	712.36	34.52	10.48
5	1,406.21	24.32	20.68	30	677.84	35.03	9.97
6	1,381.89	24.67	20.33	31	642.81	35.55	9.45
7	1,357.21	25.04	19.96	32	607.26	36.07	8.93
8	1,332.18	25.41	19.59	33	571.19	36.60	8.40
9	1,306.77	25.78	19.22	34	534.60	37.14	7.86
10	1,280.99	26.16	18.84	35	497.46	37.68	7.32
11	1,254.83	26.54	18.46	36	459.78	38.24	6.76
12	1,228.29	26.93	18.07	37	421.54	38.80	6.20
13	1,201.35	27.33	17.67	38	382.74	39.37	5.63
14	1,174.02	27.73	17.27	39	343.37	39.95	5.05
15	1,146.29	28.14	16.86	40	303.42	40.54	4.46
16	1,118.15	28.55	16.45	41	262.88	41.13	3.87
17	1,089.60	28.97	16.03	42	221.75	41.74	3.26
18	1,060.63	29.40	15.60	43	180.01	42.35	2.65
19	1,031.23	29.83	15.17	44	137.66	42.98	2.02
20	1,001.39	30.27	14.73	45	94.68	43.61	1.39
21	971.12	30.72	14.28	46	51.07	44.25	0.75
22	940.41	31.17	13.83	47	6.83	6.83	0.00
23	909.24	31.63	13.37	48	0.00		
24	877.61	32.09	12.91				
25	845.52	32.56	12.44	Column	Totals	$1,500.00	$576.83

Figure 71

TENDENCY TO ACCUMULATE DEBT

"It's easier to keep up with the Joneses if you can get their bank to extend you the same credit line."

Author Unknown

How many times have you used credit cards for purchases that would not have been made if you had to pay cash? Accumulating debt by the acquisition of things that were bought in a period of weakness or on the spur of the moment have caused significant stress for people when it comes time for paying their bills. Figure 72 below reveals some of the difficulties people must face when they overspend without first consulting either their checkbook or cash reserve fund to first verify that money is available for such acquisitions. You can easily monitor your tendency to borrow by annually updating the Personal Networth Document discussed on page 65. Since this document provides a snap-shot of your current financial situation at any one particular time, it can also be used to determine your tendency to borrow.

CREDIT CARD FACTS

☑ Americans average two and one-half bank cards and eight credit cards in all.

☑ Five years ago, about half of all cardholders paid their balances in full each month. Now only one-third do so.

☑ 392,000 people contacted consumer credit counseling offices for help in 1990.

☑ Over 713,000 Americans declared personal bankruptcy in 1990.

☑ Over a million consumers lost their cars or trucks to the "repo man" in 1990.

Figure 72[11]

Frequently, financial counselors use the current value of a client's assets and liabilities to give the individual or family immediate feed back regarding their tendency to borrow. Using the formula at the top of page 135,

---

[11]Source: Credit card companies, Federal Reserve Board, Bankcard Holders of America. The Cedar Rapids Gazette, Wednesday, November 20, 1991: 8C.

                    Solving Your Financial Puzzle

$$\boxed{\text{Tendency to Borrow} \ = \ \frac{\text{Current} \ \$ \ \text{Liabilities}}{\text{Current} \ \$ \ \text{Assets}} \ \text{x} \ 100}$$

the counselor will be able to determine the percent of assets that were obtained through acquiring debt. As an example, if one's tendency to borrow is 45%, forty-five cents of each dollar spent is accomplished with either loaned or borrowed money. The significance of this calculation should now be apparent. The higher the percent, the greater the tendency is for a person to borrow. One hundred percent indicates that all of an individual's or family's purchases have been acquired through borrowing. Furthermore, if they were to sell everything they possess, but don't necessarily own, they would likely remain in debt. In addition, the chances for leaving themselves or their family in a bankrupt situation are virtually guaranteed.

On the other hand, the Tendency to Borrow formula can be utilized to regularly monitor progress in achieving financial independence. In order to attain this goal, the tendency to borrow must be zero. You will then have no liabilities as payment is made by cash or check for goods and services, and any expenses using credit cards, will be paid off on a monthly basis. What a significant difference from financing each possession with borrowed money!

The importance of the Tendency to Borrow principle can best be illustrated by considering two simple applications utilizing the Personal Networth Statement in the Case Study of Dean and Jane Smith on page 167. The first application includes all current assets and liabilities; that is, existing loans, credit card balances, and the outstanding home mortgage. The numbers used in the calculation are given on the *Total Assets* and *Total Liabilities* lines.

Application 1

Using the general formula provided above and including the current value of the home with the remaining mortgage, the tendency to borrow would be:

$$\text{Tendency to Borrow} \ = \ \frac{\$ \ 97,750}{\$ \ 148,050} \ \text{x} \ 100 \ = \ 66\%$$

Notice that when the current asset value and outstanding mortgage of a home are taken into consideration, the mortgage balance is frequently a substantial portion of the debt, thereby creating an unusually high liability amount. In this way, the mortgage liability might give an unrealistic picture of the overall tendency of a family or individual to accumulate debt. This would be especially true if the persons involved were "debt free" except for the mortgage on their home.

The second application includes all those current assets and liabilities in application 1 on page 135 <u>less</u> the present market value of the home ($95,000) and the remaining mortgage ($75,000).

Application 2

Excluding the current market value of the home and remaining mortgage, the tendency to borrow in the second application would be:

$$\text{Tendency to Borrow} = \frac{\$22,750}{\$53,050} \times 100 = 43\%$$

It is an excellent idea to calculate your tendency to borrow percent by excluding both the market value and outstanding mortgage of your home as in the second application. When these two values are excluded, you will be able to monitor your spending for those items that have the greatest potential to trap families and individuals. Expensive hobbies, luxurious vacations, and costly automobiles are frequent ways people accumulate unnecessary debt. By focusing on purchased possessions, you will be able to determine precisely what percent of each dollar spent is done with loaned or borrowed money. Unless the family or individual involved has a number of credit card debts and/or outstanding loans, the tendency to borrow percent in this situation will be significantly less than in the first application.

You now have a specific procedure to use to monitor the tendency to borrow. By annually updating the Networth Document and focusing on areas of excess spending, such as automobile loans, credit card debt, and finance charges, you will be able to quickly determine which of the areas involved needs immediate and urgent attention. Again, it is generally an excellent idea to perform the calculations with and without considering the value of your home and the outstanding mortgage.

HOW MUCH DEBT CAN YOU AFFORD?

Is an ounce of prevention worth a pound of cure? This often used cliche can be applied to the amount of debt that we can afford to undertake. Knowing the amount of monthly payments in advance, and the immediate impact of additional installment debt on our budget, would encourage us to think a second time when financing a major purchase. This definitely could affect the purchase in mind, especially if it didn't improve our standard of living.

The Debt Retirement Table on page 353, a portion of which appears in Figure 73 below, is of immediate assistance in knowing the monthly payment necessary to retire any given debt in a specific number of years. Suppose that your family has been considering the purchase of a used camper costing $5,000. You are able to obtain a loan at 16% and you want the camper paid for in five years. By using the Debt Retirement Table, you know that monthly payments of $121.59 are required to retire the debt. This gives you an additional "financial planning tool," to determine whether or not a desired purchase is readily affordable, as well as makes economic sense to you and your family. In this way, you don't need to make a substantial purchase before discovering that you have made a big mistake.

DEBT RETIREMENT TABLE					
Outstanding Debt	Annual Finance Rate	Approximate Monthly Payment To Retire Outstanding Debt In:			
		3 Years	4 Years	5 Years	6 Years
$ 500	14%	17.09	13.66	11.63	10.30
	16%	17.58	14.17	12.16	10.85
$ 1,000	14%	34.18	27.33	23.27	20.61
	16%	35.16	28.34	24.32	21.69
$ 5,000	14%	170.89	136.63	116.34	103.03
	16%	175.79	141.70	121.59	108.46

Figure 73 - Table page 353

▼ PLANNING STRATEGIES ▼
OPTIONAL APPLICATIONS

The examples given below and on page 139 offer additional applications using the Debt Retirement Table on page 353.

1. To calculate monthly payments for a debt amount not in the table, but with the interest rates and time periods contained in the table.

   A. Find the monthly payment necessary to retire a $1,500 debt at an annual rate of 16% in four years.

      1. Using the table, find the monthly payment necessary to retire a debt of $500 at 16% in four years. The required payment found in the *4 Year* column is $14.17.

      2. Multiply $14.17 x 3 = $42.51 to obtain the correct monthly payment. (You multiply $14.17 by three since there are three $500's in $1,500.)

   B. Find the approximate monthly payment necessary to retire a loan of $6,000 at an annual rate of 14% in three years.

      1. From the table, find the monthly payment to retire a $5,000 loan at 14% in three years. The necessary payment found in the *3 Year* column is $170.89.

      2. Use the table to locate the necessary monthly payment to retire a $1,000 debt at 14% in three years. The value is $34.18.

      3. Add the results found in the table from (A) and (B) above to obtain the complete monthly payment. $170.89 + $34.18 = $205.07. (The results in this example are added since $5,000 + $1,000 = $6,000 which is the value of the original loan.)

2. To find a close approximation for the annual rates of 11%, 13%, 15%, and 17% when the amount of debt and time period can be obtained from the table.

   A. Compute the monthly payment necessary to retire a credit card debt of $5,000 at an annual rate of 15% in four years.

      1. Use the table to determine the approximate monthly payment to pay off a debt of $5,000, both at rates of 14% and 16% in four years. From the table, the monthly payment would be $136.63 at 14% and $141.70 at 16%.

2. Calculate the average of the two monthly payments from (A) above by adding the two numbers together, then dividing that result by two as shown below.

   a. $136.63 + $141.70 = $278.33

   b. $278.33 ÷ 2 = $139.17 (Approximate monthly payment required for the retirement of a $5,000 at an annual rate of 15% in four years.)

3. The Debt Retirement Table will **not** work for a situation of the following type. To calculate monthly payments for a debt and interest rates obtained from the table, but for periods of time **not** contained in the table.

A. Find the monthly payment to retire a debt of $5,000 at 16% in ten years. (In this case, you are able to obtain the correct answer from the table directly.)

   1. Determine the monthly payment for $5,000 at 16% for five years from the table. The required payment is $121.59 per month.

   2. Divide the amount of $121.59 in step A above by two since the time period required is 2 x 5 = 10 years. The result of $121.59 ÷ 2 = $60.80 is **not** the correct answer. Notice from the table on page 353 that the correct answer is $83.76.

☑ ACTION STEPS ☑

- ❑ Create a credit card inventory listing each of your credit cards.

- ❑ Complete a record of your credit card obligations.

- ❑ Pay the entire amount of each card's monthly billing statement in an effort to eliminate revolving credit.

- ❑ Determine the method used to calculate the finance charge for each of your credit cards.

- ❑ Compute your *percent of debt obligation* as illustrated by the Credit and Loan Summary Worksheet.

- ❑ Calculate your tendency to borrow using the two applications on pages 135 - 136.

YOU SHOULD NOW BE ABLE TO:

1. Intelligently select credit cards that best meet your financial needs and goals.

2. Read and interpret your monthly credit card statements.

3. Put together and maintain a credit card filing system.

4. Develop a realistic plan to pay each of your current debts.

5. Determine the moment you begin taking on too much debt.

6. Follow the procedure on pages 115 - 116 to inform your card issuer that your credit card has been lost or stolen.

CONCLUDING REMARKS

Each of us has or will use credit sometime in our life, whether it is to purchase clothing, household items, an automobile, or a home. We also hope that these purchases will enhance or improve our life style. It is therefore essential that we have the knowledge to select loans and credit cards that best meet our needs and objectives. Furthermore, we must realize that having the right to credit comes a responsibility to manage it as well. Its misuse has placed far too many of us in a situation that has jeopardized our personal well-being or that of our family. It is up to each of us to be prudent whenever credit is involved.

Each of us might profit from the following bit of advice:

> "I have discovered the philosopher's stone, that turns everything into gold: It is, 'pay as you go.'"[12]
>
> John Randolph, 1802

---

[12]Reproduced with the permission of Simon & Schuster from The MacMillan Book of Business & Economic Quotations by Michael Jackson. MacMillan Publishing Company (New York, 1984) 59.

CHAPTER 6

OVERCOMING FINANCIAL BONDAGE

Solving Your Financial Puzzle

FOCUS ON:

RECOGNIZING & RESOLVING INDEBTEDNESS

1. Admit to yourself that you are in financial trouble when forced to purchase basic necessities with credit.

2. Accept responsibility for your indebtedness, then be determined to resolve it.

3. Be more conservative by reducing purchases to essential items.

4. Place all credit cards except one, two at most, in your safe deposit box until each of your creditors have been paid in full.

5. Develop a realistic and systematic debt payment plan and implement it immediately.

6. Notify each creditor immediately to make alternative payment arrangements when unable to maintain a regular payment schedule.

7. Utilize caution when borrowing from family members or friends.

8. Reduce entertainment expenses, such as eating out, movies, and sports, by improvising with creative ideas.

9. Consult with your spouse when you are in doubt if a purchase is essential.

10. Declare bankruptcy **only** as a last resort.

OVERCOMING FINANCIAL BONDAGE

"Debt is a trap which a man sets and baits himself -- and catches himself."

Josh Billings

TAKING THE PATH OF LEAST RESISTANCE

Many years ago, I attended a seminar in which the following question was asked to the participants: "Why doesn't a river flow in a straight line from its source to its destination?" The answer can be found in the title to this section. The river, from its beginning, in its rush downstream to its destination, will take the path of least resistance. In a similar manner, in our own efforts to rush "downstream" to accumulate possessions and wealth, we also take the path of least resistance and wind up greatly in debt, with liabilities exceeding assets, or in a bankrupt state of affairs.

Rest assured, regardless of your income, it never seems enough to satisfy your needs. Individuals and families alike, at any particular income level, can rapidly accumulate debt to a dangerous degree. Possible symptoms, or outside warning signs, of incurring too much personal debt are:

WARNING SIGNS OF DEBT OVERLOAD

1. Your monthly expenditures exceed the amount of income.

2. You procrastinate with the opening of monthly bills and expenses.

3. You have more than 20% of your take-home pay committed to credit payments, not including rent or home mortgage.

  Solving Your Financial Puzzle

4. You make only partial payments or pay the minimum balance due on credit card accounts.

5. Your major purchases are being paid over the longest period of time.

6. You tap into a savings account to pay current or routine expenses.

7. You're using credit to pay for routine living expenses (groceries, utilities, and personal items) that were previously paid with cash.

8. You seriously believe that your credit card limit minus the current balance is an "emergency savings fund."

9. You get post due notices and/or telephone calls from creditors.

10. You get behind in utility, rent, or mortgage payments.

11. You are threatened with repossession of your car, denied credit, or intimidated with other legal action.

12. You postdate checks so they won't bounce.

13. You and/or your spouse work overtime or take a second job to help make ends meet, or a second household salary is used exclusively to pay debts.

14. You take out a new loan to make payments on existing loans or use cash advances from one credit card to make payments on another card.

15. You ask for loans from parents, relatives, and/or friends.

16. You regularly buy things on impulse to make yourself feel better.

17. Your liabilities are greater in value than your assets, thereby giving a negative Networth.

18. You feel as if you have totally lost control of your life.

19. You obtain a cash advance from a credit card to have enough money on which to live until the next paycheck arrives.

20. You delay routine and/or necessary visits to the physician or dentist because you can't afford their services.

21. You experience frequent unexplained emotional and/or physical illness, mounting or increasing pressure, tension headaches, abdominal pain, neck and/or back tension, sleepless nights.

22. You and your spouse either fail to communicate or are dishonest with each other regarding finances and/or use of credit.

23. You begin or increase the number of arguments with spouse, family members, and/or business associates.

IDENTIFYING THE PROBLEM

These warning signs or symptoms are outside indicators that usually accompany a far deeper problem. People often begin by taking the easy way out, which is trying to "fix" the symptom. However, this quick fix or band-aid approach generally results with a temporary solution, and another symptom usually pops up somewhere else. This method is seldom permanent, it's like trying to cure cancer by taking aspirin or solving your dandelion problem by cutting off the flower. Therefore, statements such as "If I only made an additional $200 a month" or "If my annual salary were only $75,000 a year, then I wouldn't have all these financial headaches," is putting it bluntly, a lot of bunk!

It may take considerable time, patience, and energy to discover the actual root or source of the problem(s). It's almost certain that the debt overload didn't occur in a day, week, or even a month. The current situation may have resulted from an excessive use of credit card expenditures over a continued period of time. Likewise, it may take days, months, or even a few years, depending on the amount of debt and commitment of the individual(s) involved, to resolve the problem. Individuals or families will need to make the necessary effort and agree to do what ever it takes, to determine the cause of the debt. The great news is there is generally a solution; the problem is usually solvable. The first step to recovery is admitting that a problem does exist. The second step is to identify the specific predicament, along with why, how and when it started.

Before listing possible causes for your debt overload at this time, complete the following worksheet to identify the financial reason(s) for your particular economic situation.

STEPS TO IDENTIFY FINANCIAL PROBLEMS

1. Define the problem as you <u>now</u> perceive it. Be specific and list only one problem at a time.

_____

_____

_____

Figure 74 - Worksheet page 312

 Solving Your Financial Puzzle

2. List ways you believe the problem can be solved. Write down all possible solutions that come to mind. Do not make a value judgment at this time.

_____

_____

_____

3. Evaluate each of the solutions you listed in step 2.

_____

_____

_____

Are the solutions workable, practical, and agreeable to everyone involved? Can you combine alternatives?

_____

_____

_____

4. Now, select <u>one</u> desired solution. Outline the steps.

_____

_____

_____

5. List any obstacles that might prevent you from solving the problem. What sacrifices are you willing to make in order to reach a solution that will be agreed to by each person involved? What outside support do you need to reach a final consensus?

_____

_____

_____

Figure 75 - Worksheet page 312

To illustrate the usefulness of this worksheet, consider the following family situation:
An average family of four members includes the husband (35) and wife (37), and two

children, ages six and nine. The husband has full time employment and is paid every two weeks; the wife works thirty hours a week and is paid at the end of each week. The family's monthly income and take home pay is more than adequate to meet their needs; however, they tend to spend their money frivolously with little or no accountability. They often need to use credit cards to buy essentials, such as groceries, before the next paycheck is received. As a result of their current spending habits, their credit card debts increase on a weekly basis. They are currently on each other's nerves and at their wits end.

STEPS TO RESOLVE FINANCIAL PROBLEMS

In an attempt to find the source of this family's financial problem, together with a realistic and practical solution, they proceed as follows.

1. Define the problem as you now perceive it.

    A. We continue to run out of money before receiving the next paycheck.

    B. We regularly spend money without knowing exactly where it is being spent.

    C. We tend to buy nonessential things.

    D. We seldom, if ever, communicate with our spouse when making purchases.

2. List ways you believe the problem can be solved.

    A. Track our expenditures more carefully.

    B. Wait at least two days before purchasing nonessential items; make time to evaluate the importance of the item being considered.

    C. When in doubt if an item is essential, first discuss its purchase with spouse to obtain a second opinion.

    D. Agree to consult spouse for each purchase in excess of $15.00.

3. Evaluate each of the solutions you listed in step 2.

    A. Track each of the expenditures by either requesting a receipt or by writing the item or service down in a 3" x 5" spiral notebook. (Each spouse has agreed to carry a 3" x 5" notebook with them.)

    B. Agree to a two day waiting period before buying nonessential items; however, if still in doubt after the two days, consult with spouse <u>prior</u> to making the purchase.

                    Solving Your Financial Puzzle

4. Select one desired solution. Outline the steps.

  A. Carefully track each and every expenditure.

    1. Request a receipt from each purchase made and from each service rendered, and place each one in a business size envelope.

    2. Record every expense in a 3" x 5" spiral notebook for each receipt not obtained.

  B. Monitor checking account balance at the end of each day; enter each daily balance on a separate line in a 8 1/2" x 11" spiral notebook.

  C. Agree not to buy nonessential items for two months.

  D. Lock up all credit cards, except one bank card, in bank safe deposit box. Bank card will be used only in an emergency with consent of spouse.

  E. Inform spouse when spending in excess of $15.00 on nonessential items.

5. List obstacles to overcome, sacrifices to be made, and outside support used when solving the problem.

  A. Obstacles

    1. Lack of self discipline when dealing with finances.

    2. Current record keeping system is in total disarray.

    3. Lack of knowledge requiring the preparation of a realistic budget.

  B. Sacrifices

    1. Limit vacations to one-day trips for the next 9 - 12 months.

    2. Limit family eating out to once per week.

    3. Rent videos instead of going to the movies every two weeks.

  C. Outside Support

    1. Make an appointment with a credit counseling service within the next three days.

    2. Both husband and wife agree to attend a basic 8 week financial budgeting class offered by the local community college adult education department.

REASONS FOR FINANCIAL BONDAGE

The actual events leading to debt overload, known as financial bondage, can range from a single difficulty to a combination of many complex problems. A careful analysis of the previous example revealed several factors which led to this family's continual over spending. Some of the more common reasons for people to be held hostage to their creditors include:

1. An independent attitude regarding money. This is my money, that is his/her money. Therefore each can do whatever he/she wishes regarding their own money. On the other hand, each family member - husband, wife, children - needs some weekly or monthly money to spend entirely the way they desire.

2. Failure to set financial goals. Without written goals, there can be no plan, only wishes.

3. Inadequate or non existent records. Records are essential for controlling any financial plan; they indicate both your income, as well as your outgo.

4. Failure to establish a basic spending plan or budget. Without a specific plan or budget, it is next to impossible to establish spending priorities.

5. Lack of communication. Communication is essential to maintain any kind of relationship, especially where finances are involved.

6. Lack of responsibility. It is essential that the family maintain adequate financial accounts. Whichever spouse is the better financial record keeper should take the leadership role in this responsibility; however, both spouses should share an active role in this regard.

7. Ignoring the problem. This is also known as the ostrich technique; if I leave it alone, if I can forget about it for awhile, then the problem will go away and I won't have to worry about it anymore.

8. Lack of information. The more complex our society becomes, the more we need to know about the management of our finances, whether it is organizing our record keeping system or preparing a realistic individual or family budget.

"The way to stop financial joy-riding is to arrest the chauffeur, not the automobile."

Woodrow Wilson

 Solving Your Financial Puzzle

☑ **ACTION STEPS** ☑

❏ Determine whether or not you're in financial bondage.

❏ Take immediate steps to identify <u>and</u> resolve any financial problems.

❏ Don't take on any more debt than you are able to pay.

REDUCING DEBT REQUIRES SACRIFICE

People don't often consider the implication of the debt they're creating for themselves until they come to the startling realization that they are way over their heads with monthly payment obligations and no money to pay them. The fact that the Smiths, pages 168 - 170, overspent their January budget by $115 is quite common in our "buy what you want -- have it now" society today. On the other hand, suppose that, instead of seeking immediate financial counseling, they continued their over spending habits for only five years.

The table in Figure 76 on page 152 illustrates a five year period of over spending a monthly budget by <u>only</u> $100 a month, followed by a five year period of deficit reduction, as well as one of consistent sacrifice. Interest was compounded monthly, on the unpaid balance, at an annual rate of 12% or at 1% per month. Notice that the *Total Debt Cost* in this illustration is the sum of the *Annual Interest Paid* column and the *Debt + Interest Repayment* column or a total of $11,490. Moreover, the amount of the *Total Debt Cost* does not even include the $1,200 per year ($6,000 for the five year term) sacrifice the family was required to make while reducing the debt from $6,000 to zero. If that amount were added, the actual cost of the debt incurred would then be $17,490. From this example, the financial long-range disadvantage resulting from short-range pleasures of over spending can be seen.

A PLAN FOR DEBT REDUCTION

Unfortunately, getting out of debt can be far more difficult than getting into it. The good news is that with perseverance, sacrifice, discipline, and time, it is possible to eliminate debt. Figure 77 on page 152 illustrates various expenses and purchases made by a family, using revolving credit with incurring finance charges, to accumulate a debt of $17,265. This example clearly shows that by paying cash for each item and service or the balance due each month, a total of $2,803 ($17,265 - $14,462) or 19% of the entire debt amount would have been saved.

DEBT ACCUMULATION CHART						
Year	Annual Debt	Accumulative Debt	Annual Interest Paid	Accumulative Interest Paid	Debt + Interest Repayment	Total Debt Cost
1	$ 1,200	$ 1,200	$ 78	$ 78	$ 0	$ 78
2	1,200	2,400	222	300	0	222
3	1,200	3,600	366	666	0	366
4	1,200	4,800	510	1,176	0	510
5	1,200	6,000	654	1,830	0	654
6		4,800	654	2,484	1,854	2,508
7		3,600	510	2,994	1,710	2,220
8		2,400	366	3,360	1,566	1,932
9		1,200	222	3,582	1,422	1,644
10		0	78	3,660	1,278	1,356
Total	$ 6,000		$ 3,660	$ 3,660	$ 7,830	$ 11,490

Figure 76

FINANCIAL DEBTS			
Item or Service	Debt Amount	Debt + Interest	Interest Rate
Patio Furniture	$ 366	$ 375	15 %
Hospital Expenses	618	640	12
Credit Card	677	750	18
New Computer	1,825	2,000	15
Motor Cycle	6,164	7,500	10
Student Loan	4,812	6,000	7
Totals	$ 14,462	$ 17,265	

Figure 77 - Worksheet page 313

The family decided that they could budget $555 a month until the entire debt was retired. A financial counselor helped them set up a Debt Retirement schedule that would satisfy each of the creditors involved, as well as eliminate each of the debts in the shortest possible time. The payment schedule that this couple agreed to follow is shown in Figure 78 on page 154. Notice that the six obligations begin with Patio Furniture, the debt requiring the fewest number of payments, and concluding with the Student Loan obligation, the debt requiring the greatest number of payments.

When the Patio Furniture obligation is paid, or retired, the $75 monthly payment is then applied to the second debt; in this case, Hospital Expenses. This process is also known as the Roll-Over Method, since, when one creditor is paid off, that particular monthly payment is rolled-over, or applied to the following debt. This procedure continues until the entire monthly payment of

> "Economy is not meanness. True economy consists in always making the income exceed the outgo."
>
> P. T. Barnum

$555 can be applied to the final obligation; in this case, the Student Loan. By the time the final payment has been made, it is hoped that enough discipline has been learned to allocate the entire amount of $555 as a regular monthly contribution towards a cash reserve or emergency savings account, an additional contribution towards a retirement program, a long-range investment program, or an additional amount towards a home mortgage payment. In addition to the possibilities just mentioned, it may be the case that the $555 monthly amount not available for 32 months will not be significantly missed, thus making saving relatively easy for this family in the future.

RESTRUCTURING YOUR DEBT PLAN WHEN MINIMUM PAYMENTS CAN'T BE MET

Occasionally, there arise circumstances beyond our control that make it impossible for us to make even the minimum payment each month. Can you imagine what you would do if you had installment payments totaling $555 a month, then two weeks later you were informed by your boss that you would be laid off after the current month? Situations such as loss of employment, the death of a spouse, divorce, or medical expenses can easily cause sudden panic in a family and throw their finances into complete chaos. Indeed, in such emergencies, minimum payments might be impossible to make. The first step would be to reevaluate your current budget expenses, scaling back living necessities to bare bone amounts. After you determined a realistic amount for installment debt, contact each creditor to explain your plan to them. Do **not** wait for them to contact you! It is always best to contact the creditor in person; otherwise, send them a letter such as the one shown on page 156.

DEBT REDUCTION WORKSHEET
ROLL-OVER METHOD

Date Month/Year	Patio Furniture ($375)	Hospital Expenses ($640)	Credit Card ($750)	New Computer ($2,000)	Motor Cycle ($7,500)	Student Loan ($6,000)	Total Monthly Payment
Jan. 1990	75	80	50	125	150	75	555
Feb. 1990	75	80	50	125	150	75	555
Mar. 1990	75	80	50	125	150	75	555
Apr. 1990	75	80	50	125	150	75	555
May 1990	75	80	50	125	150	75	555
Jun. 1990		155	50	125	150	75	555
Jul. 1990		85	50	125	150	75	555
Aug. 1990			120	125	150	75	555
Sep. 1990			205	125	150	75	555
Oct. 1990			125	205	150	75	555
Nov. 1990				330	150	75	555
Dec. 1990				330	150	75	555
				135	345	75	555
Jan. 1991					480	75	555
Feb. 1991					480	75	555
Mar. 1991					480	75	555
Apr. 1991					480	75	555
May 1991					480	75	555
Jun. 1991					480	75	555
Jul. 1991					480	75	555
Aug. 1991					480	75	555
Sep. 1991					480	75	555
Oct. 1991					480	75	555
Nov. 1991					480	75	555
Dec. 1991					480	75	555
					225	330	555
Jan. 1992						555	555
Feb. 1992						555	555
Mar. 1992						555	555
Apr. 1992						555	555
May 1992						555	555
Jun. 1992						555	555
Jul. 1992						555	555
Aug. 1992						60	60
Sep. 1992							
Oct. 1992							
Nov. 1992							
Dec. 1992							

Figure 78 - Worksheet page 314

Solving Your Financial Puzzle

Be sure to inform each creditor regarding:

1. the cause or reason for your inability to pay the minimum payment.
2. your current family monthly take home pay.
3. your money available for debt repayment after basic necessities are met.
4. your other financial obligations.
5. a brief statement listing your assets and liabilities.
6. what you can realistically afford to pay each month.
7. the month, day, and year of the first payment.
8. the number of monthly payments to be made.

DEBT PAYMENT OPTIONS

Now that you have adjusted your budget to the reduced monthly take home pay, you are able to determine the specific portion applied to debt payment. In this example, the couple will only be able to pay $250, instead of the $555 per month as they had been paying earlier. The three options that follow illustrate common ways to adjust minimum payments, provided the creditor is willing to accept the proposed payment. The three options are illustrated below and on pages 157 to 159.

Option I. The adjusted payment is equal to the percent of the total debt represented by each of the individual debts.

OPTION I - PERCENT OF TOTAL DEBT

Debt	Individual Debt	Percent of Total Debt	Original Monthly Payment	Adjusted Payment
Patio Furniture	$ 375	2.2 %	$ 75	$ 5.50
Hospital Expenses	640	3.7	80	9.25
Credit Cards	750	4.3	50	10.75
New Computer	2,000	11.6	125	29.00
Motor Cycle	7,500	43.4	150	108.50
Student Loan	6,000	34.8	75	87.00
Total Debt	$ 17,265	100.0 %	$ 555	$ 250.00

Figure 79 - Worksheet page 315

FINANCIAL DIFFICULTIES SAMPLE LETTER

Cardholder's Address
City, State, Zip Code
Current Date

Name of Creditor
Street Address or P.O. Box
City, State, Zip Code

Attention: Delinquent Accounts

Re: Cardholder's Name
     Account Number
     Balance Due on Account

Dear Sir/Madam:

This letter is to inform you that I am experiencing financial problems. I am behind with making my monthly payment due to {*cause or reason*}. I am therefore asking for your assistance in arriving at a repayment plan that is acceptable to you and affordable to me (us).

I have taken the following steps in a serious attempt to resolve my current financial position: (1) received assistance from {*name of counselor or organization*} in an effort to evaluate my financial situation; (2) prepared a written budget to allocate realistic amounts for each of my living expenses; (3) developed a plan to pay each of my creditors; and (4) agreed to stop using credit cards until each of my creditors is paid in full. I am asking each of my creditors to accept a reduced payment until funds are available to increase the amount.

I owe {*number of*} creditors in excess of $ {*total debt to all creditors*}. The value of my assets is {*list, e.g. my home worth $_____ with a mortgage of $_____; an automobile with a book value of $_____; home furnishings of $____; and personal possessions of $____; etc.*} My monthly take home pay is $ {*list exactly*}. My proposed budget allows $ {_____} for basic living expenses with the remaining $ {_____} for debt repayment. I am asking that you accept payments of $ {_____} each month for {_____} months which will allow me to repay my debt to your company. I will make the first payment on {*month, day, year*}.

I greatly appreciate your assistance on my behalf.
Sincerely,

Your Signature

Your Name

Figure 80

                           Solving Your Financial Puzzle

When option I is selected, the creditors will be paid in full at approximately the same time. In this illustration, the time period is either sixty nine or seventy months. Use the two general formulas below to determine the percent of total debt and the adjusted payment for each of your creditors. The amount for patio furniture would be calculated as follows:

$$\textbf{Percent of Total Debt} = \frac{\text{Individual Debt}}{\text{Total Debt}}$$

$$\text{Percent of Total Debt} = \frac{\$\ 375}{\$\ 17,265} = 0.022 = 2.2\%$$

$$\textbf{Adjusted Payment} = \text{Total Adjusted Payment} \times \text{Percent of Total Debt}$$

$$\text{Adjusted Payment} = \$250.00 \times 0.022 = \$5.50$$

Option II. The adjusted payment is equal to a pro-rated portion of the original payment based on the total money available for paying of debts.

OPTION II - PRO-RATED PERCENT

Debt	Individual Debt	Original Monthly Payment	Pro-rated Share	Adjusted Payment	Number of Adjusted Payments
Patio Furniture	$ 375	$ 75	0.45	$ 34	12
Hospital Expenses	640	80	0.45	36	18
Credit Cards	750	50	0.45	23	34
New Computer	2,000	125	0.45	56	36
Motor Cycle	7,500	150	0.45	68	112
Student Loan	6,000	75	0.45	34	178
Total Debt	$ 17,265	$ 555		$ 251	

Figure 81 - Worksheet page 316

When option II is selected only $250 of the $555 is available for debt payment. Therefore, each creditor will receive a 45% pro-rated share of the original payment as shown by the following calculations for the patio furniture:

$$\textbf{Pro-rated Percent} = \frac{\text{Adjusted Debt Payment}}{\text{Original Debt Payment}}$$

$$\text{Pro-rated Percent} = \frac{\$\,250}{\$\,555} = 0.45 = 45\%$$

$$\textbf{Adjusted Payment} = \text{Pro-rated Share} \times \text{Original Payment}$$

$$\text{Adjusted Payment} = 0.45 \times \$75 = \$33.75 = \$34$$

OPTION III. The adjusted payment is equal to the total debt repayment available divided by the number of creditors.

The total debt repayment portion of $250 is divided equally among the six creditors. Therefore, each creditor will receive the same monthly payment of $41.67 or $42.

OPTION III - ADJUSTED PER NUMBER OF CREDITORS

Debt	Individual Debt	Original Monthly Payment	Adjusted Monthly Payment	Number of Adjusted Payments
Patio Furniture	$ 375	$ 75	$ 42	9
Hospital Expenses	640	80	42	16
Credit Cards	750	50	42	18
New Computer	2,000	125	42	48
Motor Cycle	7,500	150	42	180
Student Loan	6,000	75	42	144
Total Debt	$ 17,265	$ 555	$ 252	

Figure 82 - Worksheet page 317

                        Solving Your Financial Puzzle

This method of payment is most beneficial to creditors financing the smallest debt (patio furniture) and of least benefit to creditors financing the largest debts (student loan). Furthermore, the adjusted monthly payments will need to be recalculated when an individual creditor is paid in full, thereby reducing the number of creditors by one, or when the financial situation of the individual making the payments changes significantly to alter the amount of his/her payments. By using the roll-over method illustrated on pages 153 - 154, the number of months for reducing the debt can be greatly reduced. The calculations to determine the adjusted payments for option III are provided in the illustration below.

$$\textbf{Adjusted Payment} = \frac{\text{Total Debt Payment Available}}{\text{Total Number of Creditors}}$$

$$\text{Adjusted Payment} = \frac{\$250.00}{6} = \$41.67 = \$42$$

☑ ACTION STEPS ☑

- ☐ Use your credit cards with discretion.
- ☐ Pay each monthly credit card bill in full.
- ☐ Make minimum card payments only as a last resort.
- ☐ Seek professional counseling before financial problems get out of hand.

YOU SHOULD NOW BE ABLE TO:

1. Recognize warning signs of debt overload.
2. Identify and take action to resolve financial problems.
3. Prepare a realistic budget when experiencing financial difficulties.
4. Communicate effectively with each creditor when you're not able to make the minimum payment.
5. Determine when financial counseling is advisable and take immediate action.

CONCLUDING REMARKS

People generally get themselves into financial difficulty without realizing it. Annual increases in family income give rise to the buying of more "things." This is especially true when minimum loans and credit card payments are easily met. Warning signs are either ignored or soon forgotten. Family life and increased spending continue on a merry roll until there is a major change in family income. This may be created by the occurrence of major medical expenses, the birth of a child, or one of the spouses facing temporary or permanent unemployment.

Disagreements or lack of communication between spouses regarding finances are one of the major reasons for the breakup of families today. The family unit of past decades does not exist in our "I need it today" or "I've got to have it my way" society. It is therefore imperative that financial problems be detected in their infancy and warning signs dealt with immediately if our family unit is to survive. Fortunately, we have the benefit of a variety of financial counseling services available to us. These agencies range from providing financial assistance through churches and state and local consumer credit counseling organizations which are either free or very modest in cost to fee based financial counselors who provide their clients with a set budget and strategies for its implementation. In any case, there is now assistance for those families and individuals who find themselves "held hostage" to their finances. The time to act, however, is **now**, not later.

> "Credit buying is much like being drunk. The buzz happens immediately, and it gives you a lift . . . The hangover comes the day after."[13]
>
> Joyce Brothers, 1971

---

[13]Reproduced with the permission of Simon & Schuster from The MacMillan Book of Business & Economic Quotations by Michael Jackson. Ibid 51.

          Solving Your Financial Puzzle

CHAPTER 7

A REAL LIFE SITUATION

IT'S A FAMILY MATTER

FOCUS ON:

APPLYING REAL LIFE PRINCIPLES

1. Clarify your financial goals.

2. Determine your financial needs and objectives.

3. Prepare your documents and asset location list.

4. Keep accurate records of your income and expenses.

5. Prepare your networth statement.

6. Develop a filing system for your current expenses, eg. utilities, telephone, credit cards, automobile loans, and mortgage payments, etc.

7. Prepare a realistic budget or cash-flow system.

8. Evaluate the necessity for each of your credit cards, eg. interest rate, annual fee, credit limit, grace period, etc.

9. Devise a realistic method to pay each of your monthly bills as they come due.

10. Develop a plan to be debt free, including home mortgage payments, by the time you retire.

A REAL LIFE SITUATION

"Economy makes happy homes and sound nations; instill it deep."

George Washington

A FAMILY DILEMMA

The names of the young couple are Dean and Jane Smith. Dean is 28 years old and works in sales for a growing computer firm. He has a base salary of $750 a month with commissions after his base sales reach $5,000. Last year he earned $8,700 in commissions. Dean has both health insurance and a retirement program through his company; however, he does not receive life insurance or dental insurance benefits. His retirement program, which has done very well, has a current value of $12,500.

Jane is 29 years of age and works as a nurse in a doctor's office. Her current salary is $1,275 a month with an expected increase in the next six or seven months. She receives health insurance coverage, but like Dean, she receives no life insurance or dental insurance benefits at the present time. The doctor's office has no retirement program for their employees.

The couple has been married four and a half years, has no children and purchased a very nice home in the Midwest approximately three years ago for $95,000. They bought a new 1987 automobile for $15,000 and still owe $8,250 on it but own a 1980 van free and clear. In addition to their home mortgage of $75,000, the Smiths owe $8,000 on their two school loans and another $6,500 on several credit cards. At the current time their joint checking account has a balance of $50 with another $4,000 in savings. They inherited $6,500 of which $5,000 was invested in a two year Certificate of Deposit which comes due in four months and will have a total value of $5,725. The remaining $1,500 was invested in a growth mutual fund through a financial planning firm. Dean has an individual disability income policy if he should become disabled at any time. He also has $1,500 of cash value in an individual life insurance policy. Jane has no life insurance or disability protection at this time.

By January, 1990 this young couple was experiencing much stress. While the Smiths had a beautiful home, a new automobile, and several possessions, they became aware of the fact that more money was going "out" than coming "in." They found themselves in a desperate financial situation and marital problems were beginning to surface. They decided to seek immediate financial counseling through a local organization. The budget and records included throughout this chapter illustrate what they did to solve their crisis, and the progress they have made in recent months.

A REVIEW OF THE SITUATION
REASONS FOR CONCERN

Reviewing the previous family scenario may bring out aspects of your own financial situation that cause you similar concerns. Items on your list might include:

1. Does the decision to buy an expensive first home fit the Smith's budget allowance for the *Housing* category? If, for any reason, either Dean or Jane were not able to work, how would they continue their *Housing* expenses, as well as their other expenses, on one income?

2. Was their decision to purchase a new, luxury automobile wise relative to their other debts?

3. What were the reasons for this couple to spend more money than their income was providing? Were they actually aware that this situation was occurring?

4. Were purchases made consistent with their system of values, goals, and priorities?

5. How could this couple have reduced their stress level placed on their marriage as a result of the mismanagement of their finances?

6. Is a credit card debt of $6,500 and a student loan debt of $8,000 reasonable?

7. Is it possible to mismanage money regardless of a person's age, education, or profession? Explain.

8. Do you feel the over spending of a month's income as illustrated in the Cash-Flow Statement (pages 168 - 169) is quite common in our society today. Why?

9. Would financial counseling by this young couple be considered a wise and mature decision, or one of weakness? Why?

10. Is the time and effort required to develop and implement an effective budget worthwhile for an individual or family to do so? Why or why not?

The previous ten concerns, and possibly more, may surface as you analyze A Family Dilemma on pages 164 - 165. You may wish to use it as a model to apply to your own particular situation. Perhaps you or a family member can relate to some of the financial circumstances this couple had to deal with during the last three to four years.

APPLICATION OF DOCUMENTS AND WORKSHEETS

The Case Study of the young married couple, Dean and Jane Smith, is included to demonstrate how materials in previous chapters might be applied to a real life situation. Documents and worksheets illustrated in this chapter include the following:

1. Networth (Financial) Statement to determine current assets and liabilities.

2. Cash-Flow (Budget) Statement with pie charts of income and expenses of the original spending plan that was creating regular monthly deficits.

3. Budget Planning Worksheet explaining the procedure used to arrive at a balanced revised budget.

4. Income Allocation Worksheet with financial decisions that had to be made to appropriate each month's income to individual budget categories.

5. The final revised monthly spending plan of income and expenses with pie charts illustrating the amount of each budget category.

6. A Flow Chart For Financial Accountability to illustrate an entire month's posting procedures for the Checkbook Register and primary Account Summary Worksheets.

7. A summary of Cash Expenditures that were not recorded in the Checkbook Register but needed to be posted to appropriate Account Summaries.

8. An Allocated Savings Account Worksheet to receive remaining monies from budget categories that were not spent during the month.

9. A chart of the Smith's financial debts and a Debt Reduction Worksheet illustrating the "roll-over" method used for the repayment of their installment debt.

10. The benefits which this young couple gained from the four and one half years of struggling with overspending, how it got out of control, and the discipline used to halt their run away spending habits.

PERSONAL NETWORTH STATEMENT
January, 1990

Liquid Assets
Checking Account	$	50
Savings Account		4,000
Total Liquid Assets	**$**	**4,050**

Investment Assets
Certificate of Deposit	$	5,000
Mutual Funds		1,500
Life Insurance Cash Value		1,500
Total Investment Assets	**$**	**8,000**

Property Assets
Home	$	95,000
Automobile		9,500
Personal, Household Items		15,000
Second Car (Van)		4,000
Total Property Assets	**$**	**123,500**

Other Assets
Retirement Plan	$	12,500
Total 'Other' Assets	**$**	**12,500**

TOTAL ASSETS	**$**	**148,050**

Liabilities
Home Mortgage	$	75,000
Automobile Loan		8,250
Credit Card Debt		6,500
Student Loans		8,000
TOTAL LIABILITIES	**$**	**97,750**

PERSONAL NETWORTH	**$**	**50,300**

(Total Assets - Total Liabilities)

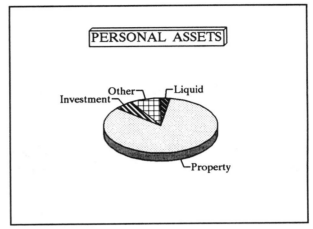

Figure 83

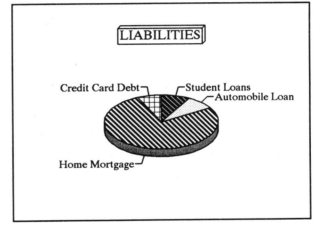

Figure 84

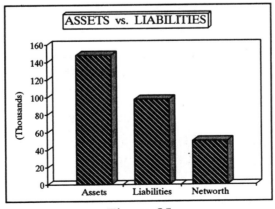

Figure 85

CASH - FLOW STATEMENT
January, 1990

Sources Of Income

Salaries	$ 2,025
Commission	725
TOTAL GROSS INCOME	**$ 2,750**

Less Deductions

Federal Taxes	$ 350
State, Local Taxes	110
FICA	215
TOTAL DEDUCTIONS	**$ 675**
NET SPENDABLE INCOME	**$ 2,075**

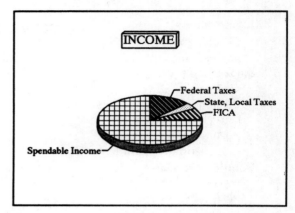

Figure 86

CURRENT BUDGET
(Dollars)

Housing

Mortgage	$ 560
Insurance	15
Property Taxes	70
Gas, Electric Utilities	55
Water, Sanitation	10
Home Improvements	40
Telephone	35
Maintenance, Repairs	30
Home Furnishings	40
Total Housing	**$ 855**
Food	**$ 285**

Transportation

Automobile Payment	$ 150
Automobile Insurance	25
Gas	40
Lube & Oil	20
License & Taxes	10
Total Transportation	**$ 245**

Installment Debt

Student Loan Payments	$ 75
Credit Cards	220
Total Installment Debt	**$ 295**

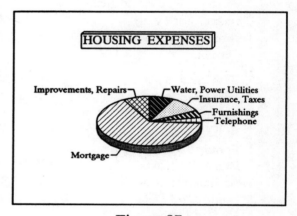

Figure 87

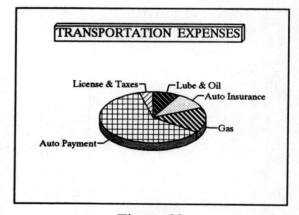

Figure 88

                    Solving Your Financial Puzzle

CASH - FLOW STATEMENT
Page 2

CURRENT BUDGET
(Dollars)

Insurance

Medical, Health	$	15
Disability Income		35
Life Insurance		30
Total Insurance	**$**	**80**

Health Care

Doctors	$	30
Dentists		25
Prescriptions		15
Total Health Care	**$**	**70**

Clothing

Purchases	$	60
Cleaning		10
Total Clothing	**$**	**70**

Entertainment

Eating Out	$	60
Sports Events, Movies		20
Travel, Vacation		95
Family Outings		25
Total Entertainment	**$**	**200**

Personal Care

Allowances	$	40
Subscriptions		10
Gifts, Cards		15
Hairdresser, Barber		30
Cosmetics		5
Total Personal Care	**$**	**100**

Savings	**$**	**15**
TOTAL EXPENSES, SAVINGS		**$ 2,190**

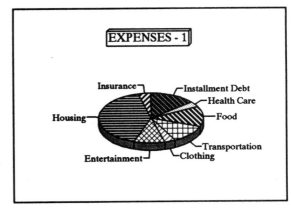

Figure 89

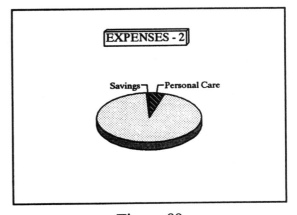

Figure 90

"The trouble with the average family budget is that at the end of the money there's too much month left."

Anonymous

The Pie Chart graph illustrated in Figure 90 represents money spent in <u>excess</u> of the amount provided by the family's paychecks, or Net Spendable Income.

BUDGET PLANNING WORKSHEET
Dean & Jane Smith

Monthly Income	$2,750				
Monthly Payment Category	**Current Budget (Dollars)**	**Current Budget (Percent)**	**Proposed Monthly Budget**	**Column 2 Minus Column 4**	**Revised Monthly Budget**
Deductions					
Federal Taxes	$ 350	13%	$ 310	$ 40	$ 310
State/Local Taxes	110	4%	105	5	105
FICA	215	8%	210	5	210
Total Deductions	$ 675	25%	$ 625	$ 50	$ 625
Net Spendable Income (per month)	$2,075	100%	$2,125	$ -50	$2,125
Housing	$ 855	41%	$ 738	$ 117	$ 800
Food	285	14%	254	31	245
Transportation	220	11%	232	- 12	235
Installment Debt	295	14%	126	169	275
Insurance	80	4%	85	- 5	80
Health Care	70	3%	85	- 15	85
Clothing	70	3%	105	- 35	85
Entertainment	200	10%	190	10	170
Personal Care	100	5%	126	- 26	100
Replacement Accounts			58	- 58	50
Savings	15	1%	126	-111	0
Total Expenses	$2,190	106%	$2,125	$ 65	$2,125
Net Spendable Income	$2,075	100%	$2,125		$2,125
Monthly Profit Or Loss	$ -115	-6%	$ -0-		$ -0-

Figure 91

   Solving Your Financial Puzzle

BUDGET ADJUSTMENTS
THE REVISED MONTHLY BUDGET

The Revised Monthly Budget was determined by the budget adjustments described below.

Taxes/FICA:
(Federal/State)
There was a significant amount of over withholding by the employer. A W-4 was used in this situation to reduce withholding amounts.

Housing:
A $55 reduction was made in this category. The result of $800 now represents 38% of this couple's *Net Spendable Income*. Conservation of individual items within the *Housing* category needs attention.

Food:
Since this family has no children, a $40 reduction was made in this area of their budget to allow additional money to be applied to the *Transportation* and *Replacement Accounts* categories. Wise shopping with attention to sales will greatly help to reduce expenditures.

Transportation:
An increase of $15 a month was necessary to provide for basic expenses until the completion of the $150 per month car payments on their automobile loan of $8,250. The loan was further reduced by $1,500 when the life insurance cash value was applied in April.

Installment Debt:
The couple agreed to a reduction of $20 a month in this area. All credit cards were destroyed except one, which was placed in their bank safe deposit box until all debts were paid. Some of their creditors agreed to smaller monthly payments. The Smith's made a commitment to have just <u>one</u> credit card after all debts were settled. They further agreed to use this card only in emergencies and to pay their credit card bills in full each month. The Financial Debts chart and the Debt Reduction Worksheet on pages 185 - 186 illustrates the manner in which their debts were paid.

Insurance:
No monthly change was made in the Insurance category of their budget. However, due to their young age, the financial counselor suggested that the couple purchase a term policy with consider-

ably more protection on Dean, as well as a policy with the same amount of protection on Jane. The cancellation of the original policy was to be completed <u>only</u> after the new policy had been received and their insurance program was securely in place. At that time Dean requested the $1,500 of cash value contained in his original policy. Upon receiving this money, he then cancelled his "participating cash value" life insurance program on himself.

Health Care: The *Health Care* portion of their budget was increased from $70 to $85 a month since some of their credit card debt was used to pay doctor and dentist bills. They will now be able to pay extra amounts on their *Installment Debt* with the money they do not use each month in this category.

Clothing: An increase of $15 a month was allocated to this area. Again, some of their credit card debt was used to buy clothes.

Entertainment: A $30 monthly reduction was made in this category. The couple made a commitment to reduce their dining out to twice a month, and to apply this savings to the reduction of their current debt.

Personal Care: No change was made in the *Personal Care* category. However, the couple agreed to adhere closely to their individual allowances of $20 a month.

Replacement Accounts: Money that was not spent on necessary budget items was placed in this account. When significant funds are accumulated, additional *Installment Debt* payments will be made. After all debt payments are completed, additions to these accounts will continue until a sufficient reserve, as determined by the Smith's, has been established.

Savings: The couple agreed to apply the total amount of $5,725 that recently came due in their Certificate of Deposit account to their student and automobile loans, as well as to their credit card C debt of $4,875. In addition, no money will be added to the *Savings* category of their budget until all current debts are paid. The couple then agreed to evaluate their budget and save at least $150 a month, part of which will be placed into conservative investment accounts.

Net Spendable Income: The *Revised Monthly Budget* column spending (Figure 91, page 170) can **not** exceed the *Net Spendable Income* of $2,125 per month allowed by the *Allocation Amount* column of the Income Allocation Worksheet shown in Figure 92 below.

INCOME ALLOCATION WORKSHEET
Dean & Jane Smith

Monthly Income	$2,750		$1,375		$1,375
Category	Allocation Amount	Week 1	Week 2	Week 3	Week 4
Deductions					
Federal Taxes	$ 310		$ 155		$ 155
State/Local Taxes	105		55		50
FICA	210		105		105
Total Deductions	$ 625		$ 315		$ 310
Net Spendable Income (per month)	$2,125		$1,060		$1,065
Housing	$ 800		$ 140		$ 660
Food	245		125		120
Transportation	235		85		150
Installment Debt	275		165		110
Insurance	80		80		0
Health Care	85		85		0
Clothing	85		85		0
Entertainment	170		170		0
Personal Care	100		100		0
Replacement Accounts	50		25		25
Savings	0		0		0
Total Expenses	$2,125		$1,060		$1,065

Figure 92

INCOME ALLOCATION DECISIONS

Dean and Jane Smith receive their income twice a month in equal amounts. Even though the *Net Spendable Income* is the same for each pay period, it is not a necessity that the allocated category amounts be divided evenly between the paycheck received in *Week 2* and the paycheck received in *Week 4*. The essential thing is that whenever bills come due, money is available in the appropriate category to pay them. For payments that are due on the first of the month, it will be necessary to build a surplus in each of those accounts to insure that adequate funds are available at the time of payment.

The greatest portion of the Smith family's *Housing* expenses is their monthly mortgage payment of $645. The $660 received in *Week 4* is to pay the mortgage due on the first of each month. Utility, telephone, and other on going *Housing* expenses will then come from the allocated amount of $140 received in *Week 2*.

The *Food* and *Replacement Accounts* were two budget categories divided into near equal amounts in an effort to keep the *Net Spendable Income* in balance for each of the two pay periods.

The *Transportation* account was divided in such a way as to make certain that $150 would be available for the car payment due on the first of each month. The $85 allocated in *Week 2* would then be required to cover remaining automobile expenses for the entire month.

The allocated amount for paying *Installment Debts* was done in a manner to pay a credit card company $150 by the 20th of the month. The other creditors were flexible with receiving reduced payments when they were convinced that the Smith's were seriously committed to a budget for responsibly paying their debts. As a matter of fact, they were able to increase their monthly payments to creditors by reducing expenses in other category areas.

Since insurance premiums were due by the 20th of each month, the entire allocated amount for *Insurance* was taken out of the *Week 2* paycheck.

Health Care, Clothing, and *Personal Care* are variable accounts that require infrequent funding. Therefore, the allocated funds for these three categories were taken from the *Week 2* paycheck. Both Dean and Jane were to take their guilt free monthly allowance of $20 each to spend as they desired. The money that was not spent during the month in any of the three categories was to be placed in a savings account until a time when the funds were needed.

    Solving Your Financial Puzzle

The remaining *Entertainment* category of $170 was allocated from *Week 2* in order to balance the *Net Spendable Income* for each of the pay periods. This also challenged the couple to plan their monthly recreational activities around a specified dollar amount instead of spending money on spur of the moment events.

The revised and more realistic Spending Plan for the Smith family's Income and Expenses is shown by the tables, together with the corresponding pie charts in Figures 93 - 96 that follow.

REVISED MONTHLY INCOME

Monthly Income	$ 2,750	
Monthly Deductions	**Revised Monthly Amount**	**Revised Monthly Percent**
Federal Taxes	$ 310	11.3 %
State/Local Taxes	105	3.8
FICA	210	7.6
Total Deductions	$ 625	22.7 %
Net Spendable Income	$ 2,125	77.3 %

Figure 93

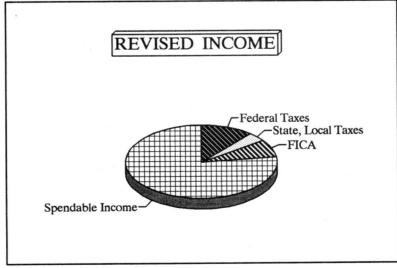

Figure 94

© 1996 by John M. Orth, Iowa City, IA.

REVISED MONTHLY EXPENSES

Monthly Category		Revised Monthly Amount	Revised Monthly Percent
Net Spendable Income		$ 2,125	100.0 %
	Budget Code		
Housing	❶	$ 800	37.6 %
Food	❷	245	11.5
Transportation	❸	235	11.1
Installment Debt	❹	275	12.9
Insurance	❺	80	3.8
Health Care	❻	85	4.0
Clothing	❼	85	4.0
Entertainment	❽	170	8.0
Personal Care	❾	100	4.7
Replacement Account	❿	50	2.4
Savings	⬤	0	0.0
Total Expenses		$ 2,125	100.0 %
Amount Over/Under Spent		$ 0	0 %

Figure 95

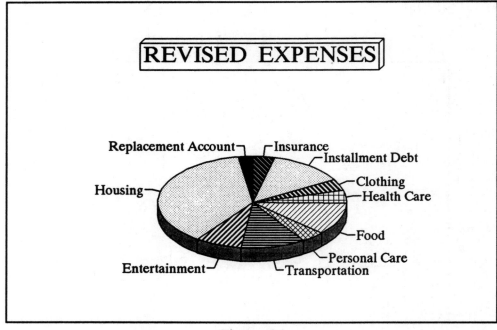

Figure 96

    Solving Your Financial Puzzle

FLOW-CHART FOR FINANCIAL ACCOUNTABILITY

The movement of this couple's income from receiving their paychecks to the posting of the allocated amounts in the individual Account Summary pages is now complete. It is essential that you are able to follow the cash-flow process throughout the illustrations provided on pages 177 to 186 so that you will be able to apply these principles to your own individual or family situation. By placing the category number in the *Budget Code* column of the Checkbook Register as shown in Figure 97, you will increase your awareness significantly for spending your monthly income.

CHECKBOOK REGISTER

RECORD ALL PAYMENTS OR DEPOSITS THAT AFFECT YOUR ACCOUNT

Check Number	Date	Transaction Description	Payment/Withdrawal (-)	Budget Code	Deposit/Credit (+)	Balance
	1/29					53 75
	1/30	Paycheck Deposit			1,065 00	1,118 75
	1/30	Cash From Deposit	50 00			1,068 75
	1/30	Allocation To Accounts				1,068 75
401	2/01	Mortgage - PITI	645 00	❶		423 75
402	2/01	Car Payment	150 00	❸		273 75
403	2/02	Groceries	45 60	❷		228 15
404	2/05	Credit Card A	30 00	❹		198 15
405	2/05	Credit Card B	20 00	❹		178 15
406	2/07	Home Maintenance	15 00	❶		163 15
407	2/09	Groceries	34 35	❷		128 80
408	2/10	Paid On Dental Account	25 00	❻		103 80
409	2/10	Newspaper - 3 Months	22 50	❾		81 30
410	2/13	Replacement Account	25 00	❿		56 30
	2/14	Paycheck Deposit			1,060 00	1,116 30
	2/14	Cash From Deposit	60 00			1,056 30
	2/14	Allocation To Accounts				1,056 30
411	2/15	Home Furnishings	12 50	❶		1,043 80
412	2/15	Groceries	22 30	❷		1,021 50
413	2/15	Gas	10 00	❸		1,011 50
414	2/15	Student Loan	75 00	❹		936 50
415	2/17	Car Repair	20 00	❸		916 50
416	2/18	Credit Card C	150 00	❹		766 50
417	2/18	Gift - Friend	7 50	❾		759 00
418	2/19	Hairdresser, Barber	30 00	❾		729 00
419	2/20	Home Gas, Electricity	65 00	❶		664 00
420	2/20	Water, Sanitation	10 00	❶		654 00
421	2/20	Groceries	48 25	❷		605 75
422	2/20	Health, Life, Disability Ins.	80 00	❺		525 75
423	2/20	Paid On Doctor Account	60 00	❻		465 75
424	2/21	Weekend Trip	115 60	❽		350 15
425	2/22	Telephone	30 00	❶		320 15
426	2/25	Jane, Dean - Clothes	74 30	❼		245 85

Check Number	Date	Transaction Description	Payment/Withdrawal (-)	Budget Code	Deposit/Credit (+)	Balance
427	2/25	Car Insurance	25 00	❸		220 85
428	2/26	Groceries	58 75	❷		162 10
429	2/26	Replacement Savings Account	25 00	❿		137 10
430	2/27	Gas	12 00	❸		125 10
	2/27	Transfer to Allocation Savings -	71 35			53 75
		Housing	- 22 50	❶		53 75
		Food	- 4 60	❷		53 75
		Transportation	- 18 00	❸		53 75
		Clothing	- 10 70	❼		53 75
		Entertainment	- 15 55	❽		53 75
	2/28	Paycheck Deposit			1,065 00	1,118 75
	2/28	Cash From Deposit	50 00			1,068 75
	2/28	Allocation To Accounts				1,068 75

Figure 97

INCOME ALLOCATION WORKSHEET			WEEK	
Monthly Income		$ 2,750	$ 1,375	$ 1,375
Category		**Allocation Amount**	**Week 2**	**Week 4**
Deductions				
Federal Taxes		$ 310	$ 155	$ 155
State/Local Taxes		105	55	50
FICA		210	105	105
Total Deductions		$ 625	$ 315	$ 310
Net Spendable Income		$ 2,125	$ 1,060	$ 1,065
	Budget Code			
Housing	❶	$ 800	$ 140	$ 660
Food	❷	245	125	120
Transportation	❸	235	85	150
Installment Debt	❹	275	165	110
Insurance	❺	80	80	0
Health Care	❻	85	85	0
Clothing	❼	85	85	0
Entertainment	❽	170	170	0
Personal Care	❾	100	100	0
Replacement Accounts	❿	50	25	25
Savings	●	0	0	0
Total Expenses		$ 2,125	$ 1,060	$ 1,065

Figure 98

 Solving Your Financial Puzzle

ACCOUNT SUMMARY

ACCOUNT CATEGORY HOUSING		MONTHLY ALLOCATED AMOUNT $800.00			
Date	Transaction Item	Check # or Cash	Payment/ Withdrawal	Deposit/ Credit	Account Balance
1/29	Balance On Hand				0 00
1/30	Allocation - Paycheck			660 00	660 00
2/01	Mortgage - PITI	401	645 00		15 00
2/07	Maintenance	406	15 00		0 00
2/14	Allocation - Paycheck			140 00	140 00
2/15	Furnishings	411	12 50		127 50
2/20	Gas, Electricity	419	65 00		62 50
2/20	Water, Sanitation	420	10 00		52 50
2/22	Telephone	425	30 00		22 50
2/27	Transfer to Allocation		22 50		0 00
2/27	Savings: Housing				
2/28	Allocation: Paycheck			660 00	660 00

Figure 99

ACCOUNT SUMMARY

ACCOUNT CATEGORY FOOD		MONTHLY ALLOCATED AMOUNT $245.00			
Date	Transaction Item	Check # or Cash	Payment/ Withdrawal	Deposit/ Credit	Account Balance
1/29	Balance On Hand				0 00
1/30	Allocation - Paycheck			120 00	120 00
2/02	Groceries	403	45 60		74 40
2/09	Groceries	407	34 35		40 05
2/12	Groceries	Cash	31 15		8 90
2/14	Allocation - Paycheck			125 00	133 90
2/15	Groceries	412	22 30		111 60
2/20	Groceries	421	48 25		63 35
2/26	Groceries	428	58 75		4 60
2/27	Transfer to Allocation		4 60		0 00
2/27	Savings: Food				
2/28	Allocation - Paycheck			120 00	120 00

Figure 100

ACCOUNT SUMMARY

ACCOUNT CATEGORY TRANSPORTATION			MONTHLY ALLOCATED AMOUNT $235.00		
Date	Transaction Item	Check # or Cash	Payment/ Withdrawal	Deposit/ Credit	Account Balance
1/29	Balance On Hand				0:00
1/30	Allocation - Paycheck			150:00	150:00
2/01	Car Payment	402	150:00		0:00
2/14	Allocation - Paycheck			85:00	85:00
2/15	Gas	413	10:00		75:00
2/17	Repair	415	20:00		55:00
2/25	Car Insurance	427	25:00		30:00
2/27	Gas	430	12:00		18:00
2/27	Transfer to Allocation Savings: Transportation		18:00		0:00
2/28	Allocation - Paycheck			150:00	150:00

Figure 101

ACCOUNT SUMMARY

ACCOUNT CATEGORY INSTALLMENT DEBT			MONTHLY ALLOCATED AMOUNT $275.00		
Date	Transaction Item	Check # or Cash	Payment/ Withdrawal	Deposit/ Credit	Account Balance
1/29	Balance On Hand				0:00
1/30	Allocation - Paycheck			110:00	110:00
2/05	Credit Card A	404	30:00		80:00
2/05	Credit Card B	405	20:00		60:00
2/14	Allocation - Paycheck			165:00	225:00
2/15	Student Loan	414	75:00		150:00
2/18	Credit Card C	416	150:00		0:00
2/27	Transfer to Allocation Savings: Install. Debt		0:00		0:00
2/28	Allocation - Paycheck			110:00	110:00

Figure 102

    Solving Your Financial Puzzle

ACCOUNT SUMMARY

ACCOUNT CATEGORY INSURANCE		MONTHLY ALLOCATED AMOUNT $80.00			
Date	Transaction Item	Check # or Cash	Payment/ Withdrawal	Deposit/ Credit	Account Balance
1/29	Balance On Hand				0 00
1/30	Allocation - Paycheck			0 00	0 00
2/14	Allocation - Paycheck			80 00	80 00
2/20	Health, Life, Disability Insurance Premiums	422	80 00		0 00
2/27	Transfer to Allocation Savings: Insurance		0 00		0 00
2/28	Allocation - Paycheck			0 00	0 00

Figure 103

ACCOUNT SUMMARY

ACCOUNT CATEGORY HEALTH CARE		MONTHLY ALLOCATED AMOUNT $85.00			
Date	Transaction Item	Check # or Cash	Payment/ Withdrawal	Deposit/ Credit	Account Balance
1/29	Balance On Hand				0 00
1/30	Allocation - Paycheck			0 00	0 00
2/10	Dental Account	408	25 00		- 25 00
2/14	Allocation - Paycheck			85 00	60 00
2/20	Doctor's Account	423	60 00		0 00
2/27	Transfer to Allocation Savings: Health Care		0 00		0 00
2/28	Allocation - Paycheck			0 00	0 00

Figure 104

ACCOUNT SUMMARY

ACCOUNT CATEGORY CLOTHING		MONTHLY ALLOCATED AMOUNT $85.00			
Date	Transaction Item	Check # or Cash	Payment/ Withdrawal	Deposit/ Credit	Account Balance
1/29	Balance On Hand				0 00
1/30	Allocation - Paycheck			0 00	0 00
2/14	Allocation - Paycheck			85 00	85 00
2/25	Jane, Dean Clothes	426	74 30		10 70
2/27	Transfer to Allocation Savings: Clothing		10 70		0 00
2/28	Allocation - Paycheck			0 00	0 00

Figure 105

ACCOUNT SUMMARY

ACCOUNT CATEGORY ENTERTAINMENT		MONTHLY ALLOCATED AMOUNT $170.00			
Date	Transaction Item	Check # or Cash	Payment/ Withdrawal	Deposit/ Credit	Account Balance
1/29	Balance On Hand				0 00
1/30	Allocation - Paycheck			0 00	0 00
2/10	Dining Out - Cafeteria	Cash	8 85		- 8 85
2/10	Evening Movie	Cash	10 00		- 18 85
2/14	Allocation - Paycheck			170 00	151 15
2/21	Weekend Trip	424	115 60		35 55
2/22	Trip Misc. Expenses	Cash	20 00		15 55
2/27	Transfer to Allocation Savings: Entertainment		15 55		0 00
2/28	Allocation - Paycheck			0 00	0 00

Figure 106

  Solving Your Financial Puzzle

ACCOUNT SUMMARY

ACCOUNT CATEGORY PERSONAL CARE		MONTHLY ALLOCATED AMOUNT $100.00			
Date	Transaction Item	Check # or Cash	Payment/ Withdrawal	Deposit/ Credit	Account Balance
1/29	Balance On Hand				0 00
1/30	Allocation - Paycheck			0 00	0 00
2/10	Newspaper - 3 months	409	22 50		- 22 50
2/14	Allocation - Paycheck			100 00	77 50
2/15	Allowances		40 00		37 50
2/18	Gift - Friend	417	7 50		30 00
2/19	Hairdresser, Barber	418	30 00		0 00
2/27	Transfer to Allocation Savings: Personal Care		0 00		0 00
2/28	Allocation - Paycheck			0 00	0 00

Figure 107

The table below summarizes the expenditures of the cash withdrawals taken January 30 for $50 and February 14 for $60. Even though these expenses were not recorded in the Checkbook Register, they do need to be posted to the various Account Summary pages since they were paid with cash as budgeted expenses.

SUMMARY OF CASH EXPENDITURES

Date	Account Category	Transaction Item	Cash Amount
2/10	Entertainment	Dining Out - Cafeteria	8 85
2/10	Entertainment	Evening Movie	10 00
2/12	Food	Groceries	31 15
2/15	Personal Care	Allowances	40 00
2/22	Entertainment	Trip Misc. Expenses	20 00
		Total Cash Expenses	110 00

Figure 108

ACCOUNT SUMMARY

ACCOUNT CATEGORY HOUSING — **MONTHLY ALLOCATED AMOUNT $800.00**

Date	Transaction Item	Check # or Cash	Payment/ Withdrawal	Deposit/ Credit	Account Balance
2/20	Gas, Electricity	419	65.00		62.50
2/20	Water, Sanitation	420	10.00		52.50
2/22	Telephone	425	30.00		22.50
2/27	Trans. to Allocation Savings: Housing		22.50		0.00
2/28	Allocation-Paycheck			660.00	660.00

ACCOUNT SUMMARY

ACCOUNT CATEGORY TRANSPORTATION — **MONTHLY ALLOCATED AMOUNT $235.00**

Date	Transaction Item	Check # or Cash	Payment/ Withdrawal	Deposit/ Credit	Account Balance
2/17	Repair	415	20.00		55.00
2/25	Car Insurance	427	25.00		30.00
2/27	Gas	430	12.00		18.00
2/27	Trans. to Allocation Savings: Transp'n		18.00		0.00
2/28	Allocation-Paycheck			150.00	150.00

ACCOUNT SUMMARY

ACCOUNT CATEGORY FOOD — **MONTHLY ALLOCATED AMOUNT $245.00**

Date	Transaction Item	Check # or Cash	Payment/ Withdrawal	Deposit/ Credit	Account Balance
2/15	Groceries	412	22.30		111.60
2/20	Groceries	421	48.25		63.35
2/26	Groceries	428	58.75		4.60
2/27	Trans. to Allocation Savings: Food		4.60		0.00
2/28	Allocation-Paycheck			120.00	120.00

ACCOUNT SUMMARY

ACCOUNT CATEGORY REPLACEMENT ACC'T — **MONTHLY ALLOCATED AMOUNT $50.00**

Date	Transaction Item	Check # or Cash	Payment/ Withdrawal	Deposit/ Credit	Account Balance
2/13	Replacement Acc'ts	410	25.00		0.00
2/14	Allocation-Paycheck			25.00	25.00
2/26	Replacement Acc'ts	429	25.00		0.00
2/27	Trans. to Allocation Savings: Replace't		0.00		0.00
2/28	Allocation-Paycheck			25.00	25.00

ALLOCATED SAVINGS ACCOUNT

Date	Balance	Housing	Food	Transportation	Installment Debt	Clothing	Entertainment
2/25	0.00				0.00		
2/27	71.35	22.50	4.60	18.00		10.70	15.55

Figure 109

Solving Your Financial Puzzle

Item	Debt Amount	Amount of Certificate of Deposit Applied	Remaining Debt	Remaining Debt + Interest	Interest Rate
FINANCIAL DEBTS					
Credit Card C	$ 4,875	$2,725	$ 2,150	$ 2,383	15 %
Credit Card A	975		975	1,160	15
Credit Card B	650		650	786	15
Automobile Loan	8,250	2,000	6,250	7,200	12
Student Loan	8,000	1,000	7,000	8,139	6
Totals	$22,750	$5,725	$17,025	$19,668	

Figure 110

DEBT REDUCTION WORKSHEET
ROLL-OVER METHOD

Date Month/Year	Credit Card C ($2,383)	Credit Card A ($1,160)	Credit Card B ($786)	Automobile Loan ($7,200)	Student Loan ($8,139)	Total Monthly Payment
Jan. 1990	150	30	20	150	75	425
Feb. 1990	150	30	20	150	75	425
Mar. 1990	150	30	20	150	75	425
Apr. 1990	150	30	20	1,650	75	1,925
May 1990	150	30	20	150	75	425
Jun. 1990	150	30	20	150	75	425
Jul. 1990	150	30	20	150	75	425
Aug. 1990	150	30	20	150	75	425
Sep. 1990	150	30	20	150	75	425
Oct. 1990	150	30	20	150	75	425
Nov. 1990	150	30	20	150	75	425
Dec. 1990	150	30	20	150	75	425
Jan. 1991	150	30	20	150	75	425
Feb. 1991	150	30	20	150	75	425
Mar. 1991	150	30	20	150	75	425
Apr. 1991	133	47	20	150	75	425
May 1991		180	20	150	75	425
Jun. 1991		180	20	150	75	425

Date Month/Year	Credit Card C ($2,383)	Credit Card A ($1,160)	Credit Card B ($786)	Automobile Loan ($7,200)	Student Loan ($8,139)	Total Monthly Payment
DEBT REDUCTION WORKSHEET **ROLL-OVER METHOD** (Continued)						
Jul. 1991		180	20	150	75	425
Aug. 1991		123	77	150	75	425
Sep. 1991			200	150	75	425
Oct. 1991			129	221	75	425
Nov. 1991				350	75	425
Dec. 1991				350	75	425
Jan. 1992				350	75	425
Feb. 1992				350	75	425
Mar. 1992				350	75	425
Apr. 1992				350	75	425
May 1992				229	196	425
Jun. 1992					425	425
Jul. 1992					425	425
Aug. 1992					425	425
Sep. 1992					425	425
Oct. 1992					425	425
Nov. 1992					425	425
Dec. 1992					425	425
Jan. 1993					425	425
Feb. 1993					425	425
Mar. 1993					425	425
Apr. 1993					425	425
May 1993					425	425
Jun. 1993					425	425
Jul. 1993					318	318
TOTALS	$ 2,383	$ 1,160	$ 786	$ 7,200	$ 8,139	$ 19,668

Figure 111

 Solving Your Financial Puzzle

CONCLUSION

To make the Income Allocation system work, it is necessary to discipline yourself to stop spending when the allocated amount for each category is spent. Therefore, accurate records need to be kept. Moreover, borrowing money from one category account to pay for purchases or bills in another will only lead to a break down of the entire system. If this didn't happen, an allocation system wouldn't have been necessary in the first place.

By following the structured allocated amounts for the given categories of their budget and using the "roll-over" method of debt payment illustrated on pages 185 - 186, Dean and Jean Smith were able to pay off their three credit card obligations and automobile loan in 29 months. Their student loan was repaid in 43 months, leaving them with only their monthly mortgage payment of $645. Notice the significant amount of savings received, both in terms of interest paid and in months required, by applying the "roll-over" method to the payment of debts as compared to spending money as soon as each of the debts were paid in full (Figure 112 below).

More important, the discipline they gained over this period of time led to their ability to acquire the habit of accumulating definite amounts of money necessary to pay each of the monthly installment debts. As soon as the last payment had been made, the Smiths opened a cash reserve savings account and committed themselves to add $350 on a monthly basis. This fund was ear marked for emergency expenses (medical, dental, hospital, etc.) and for the replacement of major household necessities (furnace, air conditioner, automobile, etc.). The remaining $75 they used to pay installment debts was applied as principal towards their mortgage balance.

DEBT PAYMENT COMPARISON CHART

		Credit Card C	Credit Card A	Credit Card B	Auto Loan	Student Loan	Totals
Roll-Over Method Used	Number Months	16	20	22	29	43	
	Interest	$233	$185	$136	$950	$1,139	$2,643
Without the Roll-Over Method	Number Months	16	42	42	39	127	
	Interest	$250	$284	$189	$1,075	$2,525	$4,323

Figure 112

REAPING THE BENEFITS

The greatest satisfaction for this young couple may well have been the knowledge and wisdom they gained while committing themselves to a workable solution of their current financial situation. Listed below are some of the benefits the Smiths received.

1. They always seemed to have enough money to meet their basic needs and necessities. They seldom, if ever, had to deprive themselves of essential items.

2. The communication in nearly all areas of their lives, as well as finances, began to rapidly improve.

3. They were able to formulate and set financial goals, as well as other life goals, and to begin their subsequent implementation.

4. Probably the most important benefit was that Dean and Jean attained a peace of mind by wisely managing their assets, as well as protecting these resources with the proper types of insurance programs.

YOU SHOULD NOW BE ABLE TO:

1. Complete a Networth (Financial) Statement for yourself or your family.
2. Write financial goals that agree with your personal values.
3. Make purchase decisions that are consistent with your needs, goals, and priorities.
4. Prepare a realistic budget based on your income and expenses.

FINAL THOUGHTS

"Perhaps each one of us can picture ourselves receiving one or more of these attainable benefits. However, they come only with an immediate beginning of a disciplined system by which we analyze our current spending, and then, appropriately allocating our Spendable Income to fit each of our individual or family situations. Only then, will the possibility exist to have the necessary financial resources to reach our desired goals as well as our dreams!"

John M. Orth

APPENDIX A

FINANCIAL GOALS NEEDS ANALYSIS

Chapter one established the importance of setting financial goals. These can be classified as: short-term (less than twelve months), medium-term (one to five years), or long-term (five years and longer). Occasionally, financial goals involve calculated projections that necessitate the saving or wise investing of money. Others may consist of paying a modest amount on a regular basis to protect us and our families against a catastrophic loss or financial crisis.

During our lifetime, each of us will face situations requiring long-range planning. In some circumstances, waiting until the last moment can result in disastrous consequences. This might include the need for appropriate life insurance protection, providing sufficient college or private school education funds for children, maintaining a respectable and livable income during retirement years without depending entirely on social security. Even though it may not appear obvious at the moment, there are several benefits from pursing the following needs analysis applications that apply in your situation. They will:

1. Provide flexibility by increasing the number of options, as well as the scope of each option, when planning for education funds and retirement income.

2. Reduce monthly investment amounts as well as risk by allowing you to invest over a longer period of time. This concept is known as "dollar cost averaging."

3. Reduce anxiety and stress by providing you with significantly more time to plan for major education funding and retirement decisions.

4. Insure financial stability for surviving family members by providing adequate insurance protection in the event of an untimely death.

5. Assist you and your family in planing your immediate and long-term goals by allowing you time to hire appropriate professionals to carry out your desires satisfactory.

6. Enable family members to communicate with each other in addressing financial problems and concerns.

The modified case study that follows illustrates how a young professional family dealt with three significant conditions that the majority of families face. Alan (35) and Dorey (34) Jones meet with their personal financial planner and insurance advisor. Their objectives are to determine an appropriate amount of life insurance in the event of their premature deaths, to inquire about college funding for their children, and to plan

Making Ends Meet Plus More © 1996 by John M. Orth, Iowa City, IA. 189

PERSONAL NETWORTH STATEMENT

Liquid Assets

Checking Accounts	$ 2,015
Saving Accounts	3,500
Certificates of Deposit	2,500
College Funds - Brad	10,000
College Funds - Susie	8,500
Total Liquid Assets	**$ 26,515**

Property Assets

Home	$ 135,000
Automobiles (2)	15,000
Personal Items	8,000
Total Property Assets	**$ 158,000**

Other Assets

Retirement Plan - Dorey	$ 6,500
IRA - Dorey	8,820
Pension - Alan	12,000
401(k) - Alan	11,400
Total 'Other' Assets	**$ 38,720**

TOTAL ASSETS	**$ 223,235**

Liabilities

Home Mortgage	$ 108,500
Credit Cards	2,500
Automobile Loans	7,250
Student Loans	3,500
TOTAL LIABILITIES	**$ 121,750**

PERSONAL NETWORTH	**$ 101,485**
(Total Assets - Total Liabilities)	

Figure 113

for their own retirement. The Jones have two children: Brad, 14, and a ninth grader, and Susie, 11, and a sixth grader. Alan, an aerospace engineer with VanAllen Research Laboratories, has an annual salary of $47,500. His company benefits include a health insurance policy that covers him and the two children. The annual deductible is $1,000 for the three of them, after which the policy pays 90% of the expenses with 100% coverage after $2,500 out-of-pocket expenses have been incurred. The company provides a term life insurance policy equal to his annual salary, as well as a disability insurance program that pays 60% of his current salary for life after a 90 day waiting period. Alan's current retirement program includes a lump sum payout equal to 80% of his last year's salary; the amount of which can be rolled over to an IRA account. In addition, he has an optional 401(k) plan which the company matches 50 cents for each dollar Alan contributes. He contributes $100 a month to a 401(k) that has a market value of $11,400. In the event of Alan's death, Dorey would receive the value of his 401(k) plan, a lump sum distribution of his company retirement program, and the value of his company life insurance.

Dorey is employed as a surgical nurse at Carver Memorial Hospital. Her annual salary is $30,500. She has an individual health insurance policy that provides her full coverage after an annual $500 deductible amount. Dorey is provided with a $10,000 life insurance policy but has no disability protection coverage through the hospital. Her retirement program provides a life annuity, paid in monthly installments equal to 60% of her final year's salary. In the event of her death before retirement, Alan will receive 60% of her current salary in a lump sum payout and life insurance of $10,000. Dorey has decided not to contribute to a supplemental retirement program until their loans and credit card debts are paid in full.

    Solving Your Financial Puzzle

The Jones' contribute $300 each month towards future college expenses for Brad and Susie to attend one of the two in-state universities. Their goal is to have saved enough for a four-year college education for the children by the completion of each child's senior year. Both Brad and Susie will be expected to contribute towards their own college expenses if further funding should become necessary. The Networth Statement on page 190 gives an overview of the family's assets and liabilities.

COMPLETING THE ANALYSIS WORKSHEETS

Each of the following three analysis plans is only one way of estimating appropriate funds necessary for adequate insurance, education, and retirement. Companies often provide their employees with information so that each individual may determine whether additional insurance and retirement savings will be advantageous. Be sure that you have a current copy of your company's policy and benefits handbook. Know the type and approximate amount of insurance protection (health, disability, and life) your firm provides, as well as the amount of retirement (or pension) fund, and how it is calculated. This information can be obtained from your employee benefits or human resources (relations) department.

In addition to your employment information mentioned above, the following requirements are critical to the needs analysis worksheets:

1. Keep meticulous records.

2. Develop a reasonable assessment of your spending habits.

3. Determine your ability to set money aside each pay period for necessities and emergencies.

4. Contact the Social Security Administration every three years for an updated Earnings and Benefit Estimate Statement.

5. Keep annual records of the inflation rate or consumer price index (CPI).

6. Update the earnings, rate of growth, and market value for each of your investments on an annual basis.

7. Determine whether you will have a home mortgage, credit card debts, or outstanding loans during your retirement.

Update each analysis every three to five years to determine your progress in attaining your current objectives. The usefulness and accuracy of the estimates will depend largely on the precision of the data used.

INSURANCE NEEDS ANALYSIS

Insurance Needs For Alan Jones	Age 35	Date 02 - 15 - 95

Information & Documentation

1. Capital Needs

  A. Death Expenses

1. Funeral, burial costs	$ 6,500	Funeral home
2. Medical expenses not covered by insurance	1,500	Outstanding bills due hospital, doctors, etc.
3. Estate, inheritance taxes	3,500	Attorney
4. Attorney, court fees	8,000	
Total Death Expenses	$ 19,500 (1)	Numbers above each parenthesis are used in calculations throughout the insurance analysis.

  B. Liabilities

		Personal networth statement
1. Home mortgage balance	$ 108,500	Monthly statements
2. Installment debt	2,500	Monthly statements
3. Personal loans	10,750	Lender or monthly statements
Total Liabilities	$ 121,750 (2)	

  C. Future Obligations

1. Children's education fund	$ 51,100	Additional college funds to be accumulated
2. Emergency fund	1,000	Cushion for emergency expenses
3. Short-term income (6 mo.)	16,625	Estimated to be 70% of 6 months salary
4. Other _____	0	
Total Future Obligations	$ 68,725 (3)	

Total Capital Needs	$ 209,975 (4)	Sum of lines 1, 2, & 3 from above

2. Available Capital

  A. Liquid Assets

		Personal networth statement
1. Checking account(s)	$ 2,015	Liquid assets include cash and assets easily converted to cash, even though a penalty might be incurred.
2. Savings, money market accounts	3,500	
3. Certificates of deposit	2,500	
4. Other _____	0	
Total Liquid Assets	$ 8,015 (5)	

Figure 114 - Worksheet pages 318 - 320

 Solving Your Financial Puzzle

INSURANCE NEEDS ANALYSIS
Page 2

Information & Documentation

B. Investible Assets		
1. Stocks	$	0
2. Bonds		0
3. Mutual funds		0
4. Other _____		0
Total Investible Assets	$	0
		(6)

Investible assets are found on the personal networth statement. These assets are generally designated for medium- and long-term growth.

C. Employee Benefit Proceeds		
("Lump sum" payments only)		
1. Company insurance	$	47,500
2. Retirement program death benefit		38,000
Total Employee Benefit Proceeds	$	85,500
		(7)

See employee benefits or human resources department for information in this section.
Equal to Alan's current salary
Equal to 80% of Alan's current salary ($47,500 x 0.80 = $38,000)

D. Other Assets		
("Lump sum" payments only)		
1. IRA, TSA, 401(K), etc.	$	11,400
2. Current personal insurance		0
3. Other _____		0
Total Other Assets	$	11,400
		(8)

Consider "lump sum" payments only for this section.
Supplemental retirement programs
Current value of Alan's 401(k)
Personal insurance programs

Total Available Capital	$	104,915
(Add lines 5, 6, 7, 8)		(9)

Sum of lines 5, 6, 7, 8

3. Care Of Survivors

A. Annual Income Needs		
(A general rule is 75% of net income)		
1. Spouse	$	40,950
2. Children		6,000
3. Parent(s)		0
Total Annual Survivor Income Needs	$	46,950
		(10)

Annual income needs generally ranges between 70 - 80% of take-home pay.
Estimated a 30% tax bracket
$78,000 x (1 - 0.30) {0.70} x 0.75 = $40,950
Additional $500/month needed

Figure 115

INSURANCE NEEDS ANALYSIS
Page 3

Information & Documentation

B. Annual Income of Survivors		
1. Spouse's income	$ 30,500	Current salary of spouse (Dorey)
2. Social security survivors' benefits	14,400	Estimated income from social security Contact Social Security Administration
3. Current investment income	0	
4. Survivors' benefits from retirement programs (If paid in installments)	0	List only survivor benefits paid in installments on this line. Contact benefits office or human resources department.
5. Other income _____	0	
Total Annual Survivor(s) Income	$ 44,900 (11)	

4. Calculations To Determine Life Insurance Needs

A. Net Capital Required (Line 4 - line 9)	$ 105,060 (12)	Total capital needs - total capital available $209,975 - 104,915 = $105,060
B. Net Annual Income Needs (Line 10 - line 11)	$ 2,050 (13)	Additional "annual" income required $46,950 - $44,900 = $2,050
C. Rate Of Investment Return You Expect After Taxes	8% (14)	Realistic, after tax, rate of return expected from wise investing.
D. Additional Capital Required (Divide line 13 by the investment return on line 14)	$ 25,625 (15)	Additional capital required to produce annual income needed on line 13. ($2,050 ÷ 0.08 = $25,625)
E. Estimated Insurance Needs (Add line 12 + line 15)	$ 130,685 (16)	Net capital needs (line 12) + capital necessary to produce annual income deficiency (line 15).

Figure 116

Solving Your Financial Puzzle

EDUCATION NEEDS ANALYSIS

Education Needs For Susie Jones	Age 11	Date 02 - 15 - 95

Information & Documentation

1. Number of years before child enters college	7
2. Current annual cost of selected college	$ 5,500
3. Annual inflation rate for selected college	7%
4. Inflation factor from the Cost of Living Adjustment (COLA) table	1.606
5. Approximate cost for child's first year of college (Multiply line 2 x line 4)	$ 8,833
6. Multiplication factor for annual college cost increases	1.07

Students entering college are generally 18 years old.

Contact the selected college for current costs: tuition, board & room, books, fees, etc., as well as the average increase in costs the past four to six years.

Use the Cost of Living Adjustment (COLA) table on page 351. See explanation on pages 13 - 14.

The cost for the first year of college is calculated by multiplying the "current" annual cost by the COLA factor on line 4.

See explanation immediately below.

Figure 117 - Worksheet page 321

Since the projected rate of inflation is considered to be 7% a year, the increase in college expenses will be 107% (100% + 7% increase) per year for each of the next two - four years or until the child graduates. Therefore, to estimate the annual cost for each year of college, multiply the cost of the current year by the "multiplication factor" in line 6.

Information & Documentation

7. Approximate cost for child's second year of college (Multiply line 5 x line 6)	$ 9,451
8. Approximate cost for child's third year of college (Multiply line 7 x line 6)	$ 10,113
9. Approximate cost for child's fourth year of college (Multiply line 8 x line 6)	$ 10,821

$8,833 x 1.07 = $9,451

$9,451 x 1.07 = $10,113

$10,113 x 1.07 = $10,821

Figure 118

EDUCATION NEEDS ANALYSIS

Page 2

Information & Documentation

10. Approximate cost for each additional year of college (Continue as in line 9)	$ 0	
11. Approximate cost for child's college education (Add lines 5, 7, 8, 9, 10)	$ 39,218	
12. Current value of education savings and investments	$ 8,500	
13. Remaining education funds required (Line 11 - line 12)	$ 30,718	
14. Number of years to complete college savings and investments	11	

Susie will rely on herself for college funding after four years.

From Networth Statement on page 190.

See following explanation.

Figure 119

If you intend to have all of the college funds accumulated when your child enters college, use the number on line 1 as the number for line 14. On the other hand, if you plan to continue investing until your child graduates, add the number of years that you anticipate he/she will be in college to the value on line 1. For example, if you expect your son or daughter to graduate in four years, you would place the number 11 (7 + 4) on line 14.

Information & Documentation

15. Investment rate of return you expect after taxes	9%	
16. Savings factor from the Annual Savings Accumulation table to produce the required capital	0.057	
17. Annual savings required to achieve college funding (Multiple line 13 x line 16)	$ 1,751	
18. Monthly savings required to achieve college funding (Divide line 17 by 12)	$ 146	

Use Annual Savings Accumulation table on page 352. See explanation on pages 14 - 15.
$30,718 x 0.057 = $1,750.93 ($1,751)

$1,751 ÷ 12 = $145.91 ($146)

Figure 120

                    Solving Your Financial Puzzle

RETIREMENT INCOME NEEDS ANALYSIS

Retirement Income Needs For Alan & Dorey Jones	Ages 35 & 34	Date 02 - 15 - 95

Information & Documentation

1. General Retirement Information		
A. Current family salary(ies)	$ 78,000	For the purpose of this illustration, both Alan and Dorey will retire the same year.
B. Desired annual income at retirement (Usually 70 - 80% of current take-home pay)	38,025	Alan and Dorey's combined salary Estimating 35% for federal & state taxes, and 75% of net income desired for retirement, calculations would be as follows: $78,000 x (100% - 35%) x 75% = $78,000 x 0.65 x 0.75 = $38,025 Increase percentage if payments will be made on home mortgage, credit cards, or other loans during your retirement years.
C. Number of years until retirement	20	Alan will retire at 55, Dorey at 54
D. Age to which annual retirement income must continue before beginning to consume assets	75	This age must be carefully considered since consuming assets immediately may leave you without either retirement funds or sufficient assets for later years. Increasing this age will allow you flexibility to reduce monthly income during retirement years if necessary.
E. Number of years to age on line 1D	40	
F. Projected annual increase in the cost of living (inflation) until retirement	3%	Usually the consumer price index or CPI.
G. Inflation factor from the Cost of Living Adjustment (COLA) table	3.262	Use the COLA table on page 351 to calculate this number. See explanation on pages 13 - 14.
H. Future annual needs in today's dollars (Multiply line 1B by line 1G)	$ 124,038	Multiply $38,025 x 3.262 = $124,038. This value approximates your desired annual income, adjusted for inflation, in 40 years.

Figure 121 - Worksheet pages 322 - 324

RETIREMENT INCOME NEEDS ANALYSIS

Page 2

2. Projected Annual Retirement Benefits		
A. Estimated annual social security benefits (Contact the Social Security Administration for an Earnings and Benefit Estimate Statement)	$ 18,300	Enter the combined estimated amounts. For this illustration, Alan will receive $12,200 and Dorey $6,100.
B. Estimated annual company pension or retirement plan in today's dollars (Contact your employee benefits office for this information)	$ 48,788	Annual income from Dorey's retirement annuity. This value is based on 25 years of service with annual salary increases of 4%. Dorey's annual income would then be 60% of her final year's salary; that is, $30,500 x 2.666 (COLA table) x 0.60 (60%) = $48,788.
C. Total projected annual retirement benefits (Add line 2A + line 2B)	$ 67,088	Combined social security benefits + annual income from Dorey's retirement annuity $18,300 + $48,788 = $67,088.
D. Annual income required from savings, investments, and other sources at retirement (Subtract line 1H - line 2C)	$ 56,950	$124,038 - $67,088 = $56,950
3. Investment Capital Necessary For Desired Income At Retirement		
A. Projected "average" rate of annual return on retirement investments	9%	Investments include: IRA's, TSA's (403 b's), 401(k)'s, SEP's, ESOP's, personal insurance annuities, etc.
B. Capital sum in today's dollars required to produce the annual income desired on line 2D (Divide line 2D by line 3A)	$ 632,778	Divide $56,950 by 0.09 (9%) = $632,778
C. Estimated value in today's dollars employee pension (or retirement) fund to be received as a <u>lump sum</u> distribution at retirement (Contact your employee benefits office for this information)	$ 100,814	It is very unlikely that an employee will receive retirement funds for benefits mentioned on both line 2B and line 3C. Alan's benefit is calculated as follows: $47,500 x 2.653 x 0.80 (80%) = $100,814. The COLA factor of 2.653 assumes a 5% increase in salary each year for the next 20 years.

Figure 122

RETIREMENT INCOME NEEDS ANALYSIS

Page 3

Information & Documentation

D. Current value of investments and savings designated for retirement	$ 0	No investments or savings were designated for retirement.
E. Current value of IRA's	$ 8,820	This is the current value of Dorey's IRA.
F. Current value of employee supplemental retirement plans	$ 11,400	This is the current value of Alan's 401(k). Notice that Dorey's retirement plan of $6,500 and Alan's pension of $12,000 can <u>not</u> be included in this section since they were previously included as a part of employee benefits on lines 2B and 3C.
G. Total current value of investment programs for retirement funding (Add lines 3D, 3E, and 3F)	$ 20,220	$8,820 + $11,400 = $20,220
H. Investment growth factor from the Cost of Living Adjustment (COLA) table (Use line for 1C and column for 3A)	$ 5.604	The inflation factor for 20 years at 9% annually needs to be determined.
I. Future value of investment capital (line 3G) in today's dollars (Multiply line 3G x line 3H)	$ 113,313	$20,220 x 5.604 = $113,313
J. Additional capital to be accumulated during the next ___ (line 1C) years until retirement (Line 3B - line 3C - line 3I)	$ 418,651	This is the capital that Alan and Dorey need to accumulate in the next 20 years to provide for their "desired" annual income during retirement.
4. Savings Program to Accumulate Necessary Capital		
A. Savings factor from the Annual Savings Accumulation table to produce the required capital (Use line for 1C and column for 3A)	0.020	The annual savings accumulation factor to produce the required monthly savings needs to be determined. The couple have 20 years and believe that they can average an annual 9% return on their investments. Use the Annual Savings Accumulation table on page 352. See explanation on pages 14 - 15 if necessary.

Figure 123

RETIREMENT INCOME NEEDS ANALYSIS
Page 4

Information & Documentation

B. Capital to be invested annually for ___ (line 1C) years until retirement (Multiply line 3J x line 4A)	$	8,373
C. Monthly investment required (Divide line 4B by 12)	$	698
D. Weekly investment required (Divide line 4B by 52)	$	161

This is the <u>projected</u> annual investment necessary to produce the desired retirement income in 20 years (line 1C) <u>provided</u> that the input data in this analysis are accurate. No assets will be consumed until the age given on line 1D.

$8,373 ÷ 12 = $698 per month

$8,373 ÷ 52 = $161 per week

Figure 124

Retirement Analysis Conclusion

Even though Alan is investing $100 a month (his company is matching $50 a month), in a supplemental 401(k) retirement program, monthly investments need to be increased an additional $548 to reach their desired annual income during retirement. Preparing an analysis 20 years prior to their intended retirement gives Alan and Dorey valuable time to consider a variety of options that would not have existed had they waited until a few years before their retirement to begin planning.

Many retirees will find new careers, take education classes, or pursue a hobby that has held their interest. Alan may want to consider consulting as there most likely will be a great demand for his expertise. On the other hand, Alan and Dorey may want to explore various part time opportunities to provide additional income during retirement. These are just a few of the many options for them to contemplate, and possibly prepare themselves, in the 20 years that follow. One thing is certain, the fact that they took time to plan in advance will reduce their stress level tremendously when the decision to retire is eventually made.

APPENDIX B

AVERAGE DAILY BALANCE CALCULATIONS

Pages 201 - 221 are inserted for persons who wish to perform the meticulous calculations used in arriving at various results for computing average daily balances. It is not necessary to comprehend the following twenty pages in order to appreciate or understand the appropriate use of credit cards.

CREDIT CARD EXPENSES

Even though federal regulations require credit card issuers to disclose the interest and fees to their customers in a clear and uniform manner, the way that a "balance" may be calculated is completely unregulated. The variations used by lenders are so subtle that it is nearly impossible to determine the procedure they used. Furthermore, to complicate the situation, it is not uncommon for issuers to use a combination of the standard methods, thereby creating an entirely new one. To compare the four methods in the calculation of the "average daily balance" as precisely as possible, the following factors were considered:

1. Guidelines
2. Information
3. Data

4. Format
   A. Monthly Statements
   B. Monthly Worksheets

5. Summary
6. Conclusion

GUIDELINES

The parameters, as well as the order in which they are applied, determine the average daily balance (ADB), and therefore, the finance charge for a credit card issuer. The guidelines for calculating the ADB that follow are very similar to those used by a national bankcard issuer. The guidelines and their order are:

1. To calculate the *ADB previous month:*
   The date the charge posted to the cycle (statement) date = the number of days, multiplied by (x) the amount of the charge, divided by (/) the number of days in the previous cycle.

2. To calculate the *ADB month end total:*
   The day <u>after</u> the cycle date to the day <u>before</u> the payment = the number of days, multiplied by the amount of the ending statement balance, divided by the number of days in the current cycle.

3. To calculate the *ADB payment:*
   The day of the payment to the day of the cycle = the number of days, multiplied by [the month end total (or monthly ending balance) <u>minus</u> the payment] divided by the number of days in the current cycle.

4. To calculate the *ADB current purchases:*
   The date the charge is posted to the cycle date = the number of days, multiplied by the amount of the charge, divided by the number of days in the current cycle.

INFORMATION

The information used to determine the average daily balance for each of the four standard methods is:

1. The account was opened December 5, 1994; no purchases were made during the month of December.

2. The Grace Period is 25 days.

3. The Statement Date is the 10th of each month.

4. The Annual Percentage Rate (APR) is 18%; the monthly rate is 1.5%.

5. The Minimum Payment is 3% of the Monthly Ending Balance.

DATA

The data used for each of the methods is provided in the tables below and on page 203. When calculating the average daily balance, use the posting, rather than the purchase date, if the two dates are not the same.

JANUARY STATEMENT
Statement Date: 1/10/95
Payment Due Date: 2/3/95
31 Days in Cycle

Purchase Date	Posting Date	Payment Date	Posted Amount
1/5/95	1/5/95		500.00

Figure 125

FEBRUARY STATEMENT
Statement Date: 2/10/95
Payment Due Date: 3/6/95
31 Days in Cycle

Purchase Date	Posting Date	Payment Date	Posted Amount
1/16/95	1/16/95		700.00
1/21/95	1/23/95		600.00
	2/1/95	2/1/95	-300.00

Figure 126

MARCH STATEMENT
Statement Date: 3/10/95
Payment Due Date: 4/3/95
28 Days in Cycle

Purchase Date	Posting Date	Payment Date	Posted Amount
2/15/95	2/15/95		400.00
	3/3/95	3/3/95	-500.00

Figure 127

FORMAT
MONTHLY STATEMENT

The monthly statements illustrated on the following pages are named by the month that the statement is printed, that is, by the statement or cycle date. For example, the statement dated 1/10/95 would be considered the January statement since it was printed on January 10th. This is especially important when calculating finance charges for revolving accounts because the previous cycle purchases are often used when computing the average daily balance. This procedure will be explained in detail for the monthly worksheets in the next section. At this time, you may wish to review the material on pages 117 - 119 which gives the information and its general location on a typical bank-card statement.

FORMAT
MONTHLY STATEMENT WORKSHEET

Each of the four standard methods illustrated contain three monthly statements followed by a Monthly Statement's Worksheet. The information and calculations contained on the worksheet are used to generate each of the three monthly statements received by Jeffrey R. Smithe. The Monthly Statements Worksheets are divided into two sections, one for the <u>previous</u> month's cycle, the other for the <u>current</u> month's cycle. Notice that a subtotal of the average daily balances is calculated for each cycle, as some card issuers give a separate average daily balance for the previous cycle as well as for the current one. The final total is placed in the *total ADB* row. Information that does not apply for a particular month or cycle is indicated by shading.

To assist you in verifying the number of days for each cycle, the dates are given immediately above the specific computation each time an average daily balance is calculated. For example, consider the *ADB month end total* row of the *February* column under the previous cycle on page 208. The number of days from 1/11/95 to 1/31/95 is 21 days as both the first and last days must be counted. To compute the number of days between any two specific dates, simply subtract the two numbers, then add one {31 - 11 = 20; 20 + 1 = 21} to obtain the correct result. The answer can be easily verified by counting the dates on the calendar; in this case, beginning with 11 and ending with 31. The *month end total* is calculated by using guideline 2 on page 202. Use the ending statement balance of $500 obtained from the *balance due* column of the January Statement found on page 205 since January is the <u>previous</u> month for the February Statement.

For the average daily balance period that extends into a second month, the calculations are <u>exactly</u> the same. Notice that the *ADB month end total* of the *March* column under the *previous cycle* on page 208 contains an ADB period from 2/11/95 to 3/2/95. Break the ADB into two parts, from 2/11/95 - 2/28/95 and 3/1/95 - 3/2/95. By subtracting the dates for each of the monthly periods, then adding one, you will obtain the desired number of days for each part as shown below:

February 11 - 28 {28 - 11 = 17, 17 + 1 = 18} and

March 1 - 2   {2 - 1 = 1, 1 + 1 = 2}

February 11 - March 2 {18 + 2 = 20 Days}

Since the *balance due* column for the February statement is $1,520.37 and the number of days in the March cycle is 28, the correct computation for the March *ADB month end total* becomes:

20 Days x $1,520.37/28 (Days) = $1,085.98

AVERAGE DAILY BALANCE
INCLUDING NEW PURCHASES

JANUARY STATEMENT

City Bank Card System

P. O. Box 6930 CB

Merryfield, Colorado 03302

Telephone (800) - 333 - 1234

Jeffrey R. Smithe

121 Cloverdale Circle

Durant, California 16207

Statement Date	1 10 95
Account Number	156 309 416 897
Credit Limit	2,500.00
Available Credit	2,000.00
Available Cash Balance	1,000.00
Amount Over Credit Limit	0.00
Payment Due Date	2 3 95
Minimum Payment Due	15.00
Account Balance Due	500.00

Purchase Date	Posting Date	Processing Number	Merchant Name	Merchant or Regional Billing Location	Amount
01/05/95	01/05/95	75834J27PR43	Previous Month Jay's Department Store	Ending Balance Red Rock, California	000.00 500.00

Reminder: Your City Bank Card System account continues to have no annual fees! Our commitment is to provide you with quality service.

Account Summary	Previous Balance	Payments	Credits	Current Charges	Average Daily Balance	Finance Charge	Monthly Periodic Rate(s)	Annual Percentage Rate(s)	Balance Due	Minimum Payment Amount
Purchases				500.00			1.5%	18.0%	500.00	15.00
Cash Advances							1.6%	19.2%		
Totals				500.00					500.00	15.00

Figure 128

AVERAGE DAILY BALANCE
INCLUDING NEW PURCHASES

FEBRUARY STATEMENT

City Bank Card System

P. O. Box 6930 CB

Merryfield, Colorado 03302

Telephone (800) - 333 - 1234

Jeffrey R. Smithe

121 Cloverdale Circle

Durant, California 16207

Statement Date	2 10 95
Account Number 156 309 416 897	
Credit Limit	2,500.00
Available Credit	979.63
Available Cash Balance	490.00
Amount Over Credit Limit	0.00
Payment Due Date	3 6 95
Minimum Payment Due	46.00
Account Balance Due	1,520.37

Purchase Date	Posting Date	Processing Number	Merchant Name	Merchant or Regional Billing Location	Amount
01/16/95	01/16/95	241697PT04	Previous Month	Ending Balance	500.00
01/21/95	01/23/95	5764V204K23	Fritz Electronics	Seaville, California	700.00
02/01/95	02/01/95	1345289T96	Computer Systems	Durant, California	600.00
			Payment--Thank You		-300.00

Due to your excellent credit rating, your cash advance limit has been increased to 55% of your credit limit beginning March 1, 1955.

To obtain basic information regarding your account 24 hours a day or 7 days a week, just dial 800 - 333 - 1238.

Account Summary	Previous Balance	Payments	Credits	Current Charges	Average Daily Balance	Finance Charge	Monthly Periodic Rate(s)	Annual Percentage Rate(s)	Balance Due	Minimum Payment Amount
Purchases	500.00	300.00		1,300.00	1,358.07	20.37	1.5%	18.0%	1,520.37	46.00
Cash Advances							1.6%	19.2%		
Totals	500.00	300.00		1,300.00	1,358.07	20.37			1,520.37	46.00

Figure 129

                    Solving Your Financial Puzzle

AVERAGE DAILY BALANCE
INCLUDING NEW PURCHASES

MARCH STATEMENT

City Bank Card System

P. O. Box 6930 CB

Merryfield, Colorado 03302

Telephone (800) - 333 - 1234

Jeffrey R. Smithe

121 Cloverdale Circle

Durant, California 16207

Statement Date	3 10 95
Account Number	156 309 416 897
Credit Limit	2,500.00
Available Credit	1,053.82
Available Cash Balance	580.00
Amount Over Credit Limit	0.00
Payment Due Date	4 3 95
Minimum Payment Due	44.00
Account Balance Due	1,446.18

Purchase Date	Posting Date	Processing Number	Merchant Name	Merchant or Regional Billing Location	Amount
02/15/95 02/15/95 03/03/95	03/03/95	74RJ16P32Q5 1345289T96	Previous Month George's Transmission Payment--Thank You	Ending Balance Webster, California	1,520.37 400.00 -500.00

For more efficient processing of your account, please include the stub provided with your statement, and write your account number on your check.

Account information is provided to you 24 hours a day; dial toll free 800 - 333 - 1235.

Account Summary	Previous Balance	Payments	Credits	Current Charges	Average Daily Balance	Finance Charge	Monthly Periodic Rate(s)	Annual Percentage Rate(s)	Balance Due	Minimum Payment Amount
Purchases	1,520.37	500.00		400.00	1,720.37	25.81	1.5%	18.0%	1,446.18	44.00
Cash Advances							1.6%	19.2%		
Totals	1,520.37	500.00		400.00	1,720.37	25.81			1,446.18	44.00

Figure 130

AVERAGE DAILY BALANCE INCLUDING NEW PURCHASES

MONTHLY STATEMENTS' WORKSHEET

PREVIOUS CYCLE

Statement For	January 31 Days 12/11/94 - 1/10/95	February 31 Days 1/11/95 - 2/10/95	March 28 Days 2/11/95 - 3/10/95
ADB Previous Month			
ADB Month End Total Guideline 2		1/11/95 - 1/31/95 21 Days x 500/31 = 338.71	2/11/95 - 3/2/95 20 Days x 1,520.37/28 = 1,085.98
ADB Payment Guideline 3		2/1/95 - 2/10/95 10 Days x (500 - 300)/31 = 64.52	3/3/95 - 3/10/95 8 Days x (1,520.37-500.00)/28 = 291.53
Subtotal ADB		338.71 + 64.52 = 403.23	1,085.98 + 291.53 = 1,377.51

CURRENT CYCLE

Statement For	January 31 Days 12/11/94 - 1/10/95	February 31 Days 1/11/95 - 2/10/95	March 28 Days 2/11/95 - 3/10/95
ADB Current Purchases Guideline 4	1/5/95	1/16/95 - 2/10/95 26 Days x 700/31 = 587.10 1/23/95 - 2/10/95 19 Days x 600/31 = 367.74	2/15/95 - 3/10/95 24 Days x 400/28 = 342.86
Subtotal ADB	First Month, Does Not Apply	587.10 + 367.74 = 954.84	342.86
TOTAL ADB	0.00	403.23 + 954.84 = 1,358.07	1,377.51 + 342.86 = 1,720.37
Finance Charge	0.00	1,358.07 x 0.015 = 20.37	1,720.37 x 0.015 = 25.81
Balance Due	500.00	500 - 300 + 1,300 + 20.37 = 1,520.37	1,520.37 - 500.00 + 400.00 + 25.81 = 1,446.18

Figure 131

 Solving Your Financial Puzzle

AVERAGE DAILY BALANCE
EXCLUDING NEW PURCHASES

JANUARY STATEMENT

City Bank Card System

P. O. Box 6930 CB

Merryfield, Colorado 03302

Telephone (800) - 333 - 1234

Jeffrey R. Smithe

121 Cloverdale Circle

Durant, California 16207

Statement Date	1 10 95
Account Number	156 309 416 897
Credit Limit	2,500.00
Available Credit	2,000.00
Available Cash Balance	1,000.00
Amount Over Credit Limit	0.00
Payment Due Date	2 3 95
Minimum Payment Due	15.00
Account Balance Due	500.00

Purchase Date	Posting Date	Processing Number	Merchant Name	Merchant or Regional Billing Location	Amount
01/05/95	01/05/95	75834J27PR43	Previous Month Jay's Department Store	Ending Balance Red Rock, California	000.00 500.00

Reminder: Your City Bank Card System account continues to have no annual fees!

Our commitment is to provide you with quality service.

Account Summary	Previous Balance	Payments	Credits	Current Charges	Average Daily Balance	Finance Charge	Monthly Periodic Rate(s)	Annual Percentage Rate(s)	Balance Due	Minimum Payment Amount
Purchases				500.00			1.5%	18.0%	500.00	15.00
Cash Advances							1.6%	19.2%		
Totals				500.00					500.00	15.00

Figure 132

AVERAGE DAILY BALANCE
EXCLUDING NEW PURCHASES

FEBRUARY STATEMENT

City Bank Card System

P. O. Box 6930 CB

Merryfield, Colorado 03302

Telephone (800) - 333 - 1234

Jeffrey R. Smithe

121 Cloverdale Circle

Durant, California 16207

Statement Date	2 10 95
Account Number	156 309 416 897
Credit Limit	2,500.00
Available Credit	993.95
Available Cash Balance	497.00
Amount Over Credit Limit	0.00
Payment Due Date	3 6 95
Minimum Payment Due	46.00
Account Balance Due	1,506.05

Purchase Date	Posting Date	Processing Number	Merchant Name	Merchant or Regional Billing Location	Amount
01/16/95	01/16/95	241697PT04	Previous Month	Ending Balance	500.00
01/21/95	01/23/95	5764V204K23	Fritz Electronics	Seaville, California	700.00
02/01/95	02/01/95	1345289T96	Computer Systems	Durant, California	600.00
			Payment--Thank You		-300.00

Due to your excellent credit rating, your cash advance limit has been increased to 55% of your credit limit beginning March 1, 1995.

To obtain basic information regarding your account 24 hours a day or 7 days a week, just dial 800 - 333 - 1238.

Account Summary	Previous Balance	Payments	Credits	Current Charges	Average Daily Balance	Finance Charge	Monthly Periodic Rate(s)	Annual Percentage Rate(s)	Balance Due	Minimum Payment Amount
Purchases	500.00	300.00		1,300.00	403.28	6.05	1.5%	18.0%	1,506.05	46.00
Cash Advances							1.6%	19.2%		
Totals	500.00	300.00		1,300.00	403.28	6.05			1,506.05	46.00

Figure 133

Solving Your Financial Puzzle

AVERAGE DAILY BALANCE
EXCLUDING NEW PURCHASES

MARCH STATEMENT

City Bank Card System

P. O. Box 6930 CB

Merryfield, Colorado 03302

Telephone (800) - 333 - 1234

Jeffrey R. Smithe

121 Cloverdale Circle

Durant, California 16207

Statement Date	3 10 95
Account Number	156 309 416 897
Credit Limit	2,500.00
Available Credit	1,073.50
Available Cash Balance	591.00
Amount Over Credit Limit	0.00
Payment Due Date	4 3 95
Minimum Payment Due	43.00
Account Balance Due	1,426.50

Purchase Date	Posting Date	Processing Number	Merchant Name	Merchant or Regional Billing Location	Amount
02/15/95 03/03/95	02/15/95 03/03/95	74RJ16P32Q5 1345289T96	Previous Month George's Transmission Payment--Thank You	Ending Balance Webster, California	1,506.05 400.00 -500.00

For more efficient processing of your account, please include the stub provided with your statement, and write your account number on your check.

Account information is provided to you 24 hours a day; dial toll free 800 - 333 - 1235.

Account Summary	Previous Balance	Payments	Credits	Current Charges	Average Daily Balance	Finance Charge	Monthly Periodic Rate(s)	Annual Percentage Rate(s)	Balance Due	Minimum Payment Amount
Purchases	1,506.05	500.00		400.00	1,363.19	20.45	1.5%	18.0%	1,426.50	43.00
Cash Advances							1.6%	19.2%		
Totals	1,506.05	500.00		400.00	1,363.19	20.45			1,426.50	43.00

Figure 134

AVERAGE DAILY BALANCE EXCLUDING NEW PURCHASES

MONTHLY STATEMENTS' WORKSHEET

PREVIOUS CYCLE

Statement For	January 31 Days 12/11/94 - 1/10/95	February 31 Days 1/11/95 - 2/10/95	March 28 Days 2/11/95 3/10/95
ADB Previous Month			
ADB Month End Total Guideline 2		338.71	2/11/95 - 3/2/95 20 Days x 1,506.05/28 = 1,075.75
ADB Payment Guideline 3		64.52	3/3/95 - 3/10/95 8 Days x (1,506.05-500.00)/28 = 287.44
Subtotal ADB		338.71 + 64.52 = 403.23	1,075.75 + 287.44 = 1,363.19

CURRENT CYCLE

Statement For	January 31 Days 12/11/94 - 1/10/95	February 31 Days 1/11/95 - 2/10/95	March 28 Days 2/11/95 - 3/10/95
ADB Current Purchases			
Subtotal ADB			
TOTAL ADB	0.00	403.28	1,363.19
Finance Charge	0.00	403.28 x 0.015 = 6.05	1,363.19 x 0.015 = 20.45
Balance Due	500.00	500.00 - 300.00 + 1,300.00 + 6.05 = 1,506.05	1,506.05 - 500.00 + 400.00 + 20.45 = 1,426.50

Figure 135

          Solving Your Financial Puzzle

TWO - CYCLE AVERAGE DAILY BALANCE
INCLUDING NEW PURCHASES

JANUARY STATEMENT

City Bank Card System

P. O. Box 6930 CB

Merryfield, Colorado 03302

Telephone (800) - 333 - 1234

Jeffrey R. Smithe

121 Cloverdale Circle

Durant, California 16207

Statement Date	1 10 95
Account Number	156 309 416 897
Credit Limit	2,500.00
Available Credit	2,000.00
Available Cash Balance	1,000.00
Amount Over Credit Limit	0.00
Payment Due Date	2 3 95
Minimum Payment Due	15.00
Account Balance Due	500.00

Purchase Date	Posting Date	Processing Number	Merchant Name	Merchant or Regional Billing Location	Amount
01/05/95	01/05/95	75834J27PR43	Previous Month Jay's Department Store	Ending Balance Red Rock, California	000.00 500.00

Reminder: Your City Bank Card System account continues to have no annual fees!

Our commitment is to provide you with quality service.

Account Summary	Previous Balance	Payments	Credits	Current Charges	Average Daily Balance	Finance Charge	Monthly Periodic Rate(s)	Annual Percentage Rate(s)	Balance Due	Minimum Payment Amount
Purchases				500.00			1.5%	18.0%	500.00	15.00
Cash Advances							1.6%	19.2%		
Totals				500.00					500.00	15.00

Figure 136

TWO - CYCLE AVERAGE DAILY BALANCE
INCLUDING NEW PURCHASES

FEBRUARY STATEMENT

City Bank Card System

P. O. Box 6930 CB

Merryfield, Colorado 03302

Telephone (800) - 333 - 1234

Jeffrey R. Smithe

121 Cloverdale Circle

Durant, California 16207

Statement Date	2 10 95
Account Number	156 309 416 897
Credit Limit	2,500.00
Available Credit	978.18
Available Cash Balance	490.00
Amount Over Credit Limit	0.00
Payment Due Date	3 6 95
Minimum Payment Due	46.00
Account Balance Due	1,521.82

Purchase Date	Posting Date	Processing Number	Merchant Name	Merchant or Regional Billing Location	Amount
01/16/95	01/16/95	241697PT04	Previous Month	Ending Balance	500.00
01/21/95	01/23/95	5764V204K23	Fritz Electronics	Seaville, California	700.00
02/01/95	02/01/95	1345289T96	Computer Systems	Durant, California	600.00
			Payment--Thank You		-300.00

Due to your excellent credit rating, your cash advance limit has been increased to 55% of your credit limit beginning March 1, 1995.

To obtain basic information regarding your account 24 hours a day or 7 days a week, just dial 800 - 333 - 1238.

Account Summary	Previous Balance	Payments	Credits	Current Charges	Average Daily Balance	Finance Charge	Monthly Periodic Rate(s)	Annual Percentage Rate(s)	Balance Due	Minimum Payment Amount
Purchases	500.00	300.00		1,300.00	1,454.84	21.82	1.5%	18.0%	1,521.82	46.00
Cash Advances							1.6%	19.2%		
Totals	500.00	300.00		1,300.00	1,455.84	21.82			1,521.82	46.00

Figure 137

Solving Your Financial Puzzle

TWO - CYCLE AVERAGE DAILY BALANCE
INCLUDING NEW PURCHASES

MARCH STATEMENT

City Bank Card System

P. O. Box 6930 CB

Merryfield, Colorado 03302

Telephone (800) - 333 - 1234

Jeffrey R. Smithe

121 Cloverdale Circle

Durant, California 16207

Statement Date	3 10 95
Account Number	156 309 416 897
Credit Limit	2,500.00
Available Credit	1,038.03
Available Cash Balance	571.00
Amount Over Credit Limit	0.00
Payment Due Date	4 3 95
Minimum Payment Due	44.00
Account Balance Due	1,461.97

Purchase Date	Posting Date	Processing Number	Merchant Name	Merchant or Regional Billing Location	Amount
02/15/95 03/03/95	02/15/95 03/03/95	74RJ16P32Q5 1345289T96	Previous Month George's Transmissions Payment--Thank You	Ending Balance Webster, California	1,521.82 400.00 -500.00

For more efficient processing of your account, please include the stub provided with your statement, and write your account number on your check.

Account information is provided to you 24 hours a day; dial 800 - 333 - 1235.

Account Summary	Previous Balance	Payments	Credits	Current Charges	Average Daily Balance	Finance Charge	Monthly Periodic Rate(s)	Annual Percentage Rate(s)	Balance Due	Minimum Payment Amount
Purchases	1,521.82	500.00		400.00	2,676.66	40.15	1.5%	18.0%	1,461.97	44.00
Cash Advances							1.6%	19.2%		
Totals	1,521.82	500.00		400.00	2,676.66	40.15			1,461.97	44.00

Figure 138

TWO - CYCLE AVERAGE DAILY BALANCE INCLUDING NEW PURCHASES

MONTHLY STATEMENTS' WORKSHEET

PREVIOUS CYCLE

Statement For	January 31 Days 12/11/94 - 1/10/95	February 31 Days 1/11/95 - 2/10/95	March 28 Days 2/11/95 - 3/10/95
ADB Previous Month Guideline 1		1/5/95 - 1/10/95 6 Days x 500/31 = 96.77	587.10 + 367.74 = 954.84
ADB Month End Total Guideline 2		1/11/95 - 1/31/95 21 Days x 500/31 = 338.71	2/11/95 - 3/2/95 20 Days x 1,521.82/28 = 1,087.01
ADB Payment Guideline 3		2/1/95 - 2/10/95 10 Days x (500.00-300)/31 = 64.52	3/3/95 - 3/10/95 8 Days x (1,521.82-500.00)/28 = 291.95
Subtotal ADB		96.77 + 338.71 + 64.52 = 500.00	954.84 + 1,087.01 + 291.95 = 2,333.80

CURRENT CYCLE

Statement For	January 31 Days 12/11/94 - 1/10/95	February 31 Days 1/11/95 - 2/10/95	March 28 Days 2/11/95 - 3/10/95
ADB Current Purchases Guideline 4	1/5/95	1/16/95 - 2/10/95 26 Days x 700/31 = 587.10 1/23/95 - 2/10/95 19 Days x 600/31 = 367.74	2/15/95 - 3/10/95 24 Days x 400/28 = 342.86
Subtotal ADB	First Month, Does Not Apply	587.10 + 367.74 = 954.84	342.86
TOTAL ADB	0.00	500.00 + 954.84 = 1,454.84	2,333.80 + 342.86 = 2,676.66
Finance Charge	0.00	1,454.84 x 0.015 = 21.82	2,676.66 x 0.015 = 40.15
Balance	500.00	500.00 - 300.00 + 1,300.00 + 21.82 = 1,521.82	1,521.82 - 500.00 + 400.00 + 40.15 = 1,461.97

Figure 139

Solving Your Financial Puzzle

TWO - CYCLE AVERAGE DAILY BALANCE
EXCLUDING NEW PURCHASES

JANUARY STATEMENT

City Bank Card System

P. O. Box 6930 CB

Merryfield, Colorado 03302

Telephone (800) - 333 - 1234

Jeffrey R. Smithe

121 Cloverdale Circle

Durant, California 16207

Statement Date	1 10 95
Account Number	156 309 416 897
Credit Limit	2,500.00
Available Credit	2,000.00
Available Cash Balance	1,000.00
Amount Over Credit Limit	0.00
Payment Due Date	2 3 95
Minimum Payment Due	15.00
Account Balance Due	500.00

Purchase Date	Posting Date	Processing Number	Merchant Name	Merchant or Regional Billing Location	Amount
01/05/95	01/05/95	75834J27PR43	Previous Month Jay's Department Store	Ending Balance Red Rock, California	000.00 500.00

Reminder: Your City Bank Card System account continues to have no annual fees!

Our commitment is to provide you with quality service.

Account Summary	Previous Balance	Payments	Credits	Current Charges	Average Daily Balance	Finance Charge	Monthly Periodic Rate(s)	Annual Percentage Rate(s)	Balance Due	Minimum Payment Amount
Purchases				500.00			1.5%	18.0%	500.00	15.00
Cash Advances							1.6%	19.2%		
Totals				500.00					500.00	15.00

Figure 140

TWO - CYCLE AVERAGE DAILY BALANCE
EXCLUDING NEW PURCHASES

FEBRUARY STATEMENT

City Bank Card System

P. O. Box 6930 CB

Merryfield, Colorado 03302

Telephone (800) - 333 - 1234

Jeffrey R. Smithe

121 Cloverdale Circle

Durant, California 16207

Statement Date	2 10 95
Account Number	156 309 416 897
Credit Limit	2,500.00
Available Credit	992.50
Available Cash Balance	497.00
Amount Over Credit Limit	0.00
Payment Due Date	3 6 95
Minimum Payment Due	46.00
Account Balance Due	1,507.50

Purchase Date	Posting Date	Processing Number	Merchant Name	Merchant or Regional Billing Location	Amount
01/16/95	01/16/95	241697PT04	Previous Month	Ending Balance	500.00
01/21/95	01/23/95	5764V204K23	Fritz Electronics	Seaville, California	700.00
02/01/95	02/01/95	1345289T96	Computer Systems	Durant, California	600.00
			Payment--Thank You		-300.00

Due to your excellent credit rating, your cash advance limit has been increased to 55% of your credit limit beginning March 1, 1995.

To obtain basic information regarding your account 24 hours a day or 7 days a week, just dial 800 - 333 - 1238.

Account Summary	Previous Balance	Payments	Credits	Current Charges	Average Daily Balance	Finance Charge	Monthly Periodic Rate(s)	Annual Percentage Rate(s)	Balance Due	Minimum Payment Amount
Purchases	500.00	300.00		1,300.00	500.00	7.50	1.5%	18.0%	1,507.50	46.00
Cash Advances							1.6%	19.2%		
Totals	500.00	300.00		1,300.00	500.00	7.50			1,507.50	46.00

Figure 141

Solving Your Financial Puzzle

TWO - CYCLE AVERAGE DAILY BALANCE
EXCLUDING NEW PURCHASES

MARCH STATEMENT

City Bank Card System

P. O. Box 6930 CB

Merryfield, Colorado 03302

Telephone (800) - 333 - 1234

Jeffrey R. Smithe

121 Cloverdale Circle

Durant, California 16207

Statement Date	3 10 95
Account Number 156 309 416 897	
Credit Limit	2,500.00
Available Credit	1,057.71
Available Cash Balance	582.00
Amount Over Credit Limit	0.00
Payment Due Date	4 3 95
Minimum Payment Due	44.00
Account Balance Due	1,442.29

Purchase Date	Posting Date	Processing Number	Merchant Name	Merchant or Regional Billing Location	Amount
02/15/95 02/15/95 03/03/95	03/03/95	74RJ16P32Q5 1345289T96	Previous Month George's Transmission Payment--Thank You	Ending Balance Webster, California	1,507.50 400.00 -500.00

For more efficient processing of your account, please include the stub provided with your statement, and write your account number on your check.

Account information is provided to you 24 hours a day; dial toll free 800 - 333 - 1235.

Account Summary	Previous Balance	Payments	Credits	Current Charges	Average Daily Balance	Finance Charge	Monthly Periodic Rate(s)	Annual Percentage Rate(s)	Balance Due	Minimum Payment Amount
Purchases	1,507.50	500.00		400.00	2,319.49	34.79	1.5%	18.0%	1,442.29	44.00
Cash Advances							1.6%	19.2%		
Totals	1,507.50	500.00		400.00	2,319.49	34.79			1,442.29	44.00

Figure 142

TWO - CYCLE AVERAGE DAILY BALANCE EXCLUDING NEW PURCHASES

MONTHLY STATEMENTS' WORKSHEET

PREVIOUS CYCLE

Statement For	January 31 Days 12/11/94 - 1/10/95	February 31 Days 1/11/95 - 2/10/95	March 28 Days 2/11/95 - 3/10/95
ADB Previous Month		96.77	587.10 + 367.74 = 954.84
ADB Month End Total Guideline 2		338.71	20 Days x 1,507.50/28 = 1,076.79
ADB Payment Guideline 3		64.52	8 Days x (1,507.50-500.00)/28 = 287.86
Subtotal ADB		96.77 + 338.71 + 64.52 = 500.00	954.84 + 1,076.79 + 287.86 = 2,319.49

CURRENT CYCLE

Statement For	January 31 Days 12/11/94 - 1/10/95	February 31 Days 1/11/95 - 2/10/95	March 28 Days 2/11/95 - 3/10/95
ADB Current Purchases			
Subtotal ADB		500.00	2,319.49
TOTAL ADB	0.00		
Finance Charge	0.00	500.00 x 0.015 = 7.50	2,319.49 x 0.015 = 34.79
Balance Due	500.00	500.00 - 300.00 + 1,300.00 + 7.50 = 1,507.50	1,507.50 - 500 + 400 + 34.79 = 1,442.29

Figure 143

Solving Your Financial Puzzle

SUMMARY

The summary of finance charges using the same parameters, information, and data for each of the four basic methods are compared in figure 144 below.

SUMMARY OF FINANCE CHARGES CHART

	FINANCE CHARGES			
	ADB Excluding New Purchases	ADB Including New Purchases	2 - Cycle ADB Excluding New Purchases	2 - Cycle ADB Including New Purchases
January Statement	0.00	0.00	0.00	0.00
February Statement	6.05	20.37	7.50	21.82
March Statement	20.45	25.81	34.79	40.15
Total Charges	26.50	46.18	42.29	61.97

Figure 144

CONCLUSION

If you find the calculations to be unimportant or frustrating, it still is advantageous to review each of the monthly statements to become aware of the various types of information presented on a typical bankcard statement. In addition, it is important for you to know which of the methods your credit card company is using to calculate finance charges. Understanding your finance charges which result from large monthly balances will enable you to become more informed of significant costs.

APPENDIX C

FORMS AND WORKSHEETS

INSURANCE AND MEDICAL RECORDS

SAVINGS AND INVESTMENTS

NETWORTH AND BUDGETING

CHECKBOOK INFORMATION

FINANCIAL OBLIGATIONS, CREDIT CARDS, AND DEBT RETIREMENT

LIFE VALUES

- ❏ Adventure/Excitement
- ❏ Authority/Power
- ❏ Close Family Relationships
     (Spouse/Children/Parents)
- ❏ Freedom
- ❏ Friendships
- ❏ Good Health
- ❏ Happiness
- ❏ Independence
- ❏ Inner Peace
- ❏ Integrity
- ❏ _____
- ❏ _____
- ❏ _____

- ❏ Intimacy/Mature Love
- ❏ Knowledge/Education
- ❏ Pleasure
- ❏ Recognition/Fame
- ❏ Respect (Self/From Others)
- ❏ Security (Family/Financial)
- ❏ Sense of Achievement
- ❏ Spiritual Growth/Salvation
- ❏ Wealth
- ❏ Wisdom
- ❏ _____
- ❏ _____
- ❏ _____
- ❏ _____

VALUES CLARIFICATION WORKSHEET

1. Select - ☑ - up to five fundamental values from the above list that determine your current life style. Add any that do not appear on the list provided.

2. Rank the items in order, 1 being the most important and 5 the least important. (Read the "/" symbol as "or;" that is, Adventure or Excitement.)

◯ 1. _____

◯ 2. _____

◯ 3. _____

◯ 4. _____

◯ 5. _____

3. Place a "$" in the "◯" by the value(s) you selected that either require money or affect the use of money.

4. Set the remaining values aside for possible future use.

GOALS CLARIFICATION WORKSHEET

Goal: _____

1. **Positive Statement:** _____

2. **Specific and Well Defined:**

   Location _____   Make _____

   Model _____   Color _____

3. **Measurable:**

   Dollars _____   Amount _____

4. **Stated With Specific Starting and Completion Dates:**

   Starting Date _____   Completion Date _____

5. **A Plan of Action:**

   Strategy _____

   _____

   People or Organizations _____

   _____

   Potential Obstacles _____

   _____

   Financing _____

   _____

6. **Stated With Results or Benefits:**

   _____

   _____

7. **Prioritized:**

   _____

   _____

8. **Periodically Reviewed:**

   _____

   _____

                                    Form 2

FAMILY - INDIVIDUAL GOALS WORKSHEET

Goal	Importance	Length Of Time	Beginning Date	Completion Date
Increase Annual Income Increase Income At Retirement Early Retirement Eliminate/Reduce Debt	_____ _____ _____ _____	_____ _____ _____ _____	_____ _____ _____ _____	_____ _____ _____ _____
Purchase A Home Make Capital Home Improvements Purchase Vacation Home (Or Property) Purchase Car (Other Vehicle) Purchase Motor Home (Or Camper) Major Financial Purchase	_____ _____ _____ _____ _____ _____	_____ _____ _____ _____ _____ _____	_____ _____ _____ _____ _____ _____	_____ _____ _____ _____ _____ _____
Take Expensive Vacation Or Trip Purchase Or Begin A Business Fund Children's Education Evaluate/Update Insurance Programs (Life, Auto, Home, Health, Disability, Liability, etc.)	_____ _____ _____ _____	_____ _____ _____ _____	_____ _____ _____ _____	_____ _____ _____ _____
Preparation Of A Will Or Trust Evaluate/Update Current Will Or Trust	_____ _____	_____ _____	_____ _____	_____ _____
Evaluate Current Financial Situation Prepare Inventory Of Personal Net Worth Prepare Family (Individual) Budget Establish Cash Reserve (Emergency Fund) Review Investment Portfolio Evaluate Current Investment Strategy Adult Education Class in Money Management Or Investments	_____ _____ _____ _____ _____ _____ _____	_____ _____ _____ _____ _____ _____ _____	_____ _____ _____ _____ _____ _____ _____	_____ _____ _____ _____ _____ _____ _____
ADDITIONAL GOALS _____ _____ _____ _____	 _____ _____ _____ _____	 _____ _____ _____ _____	 _____ _____ _____ _____	 _____ _____ _____ _____

MONTHLY SAVINGS WORKSHEET

1	2	3	4	5	6	7	8	9	10
GOAL	Present Cost or Value	When Needed (In Years)	Inflation Rate	Cost of Living Adjustment Factor	Future Cost or Value (Cols. 2 x 5)	Annual Savings Investment Earnings	Annual Savings Factor	Annual Savings Needed (Cols. 6 x 8)	Monthly Savings Required (Col. 9) ÷ 12

Form 4

FINANCIAL PRIORITIES WORKSHEET

Financial Goals Ranked By Priority	Number Years To Accomplish Goal	Dollar Amount Needed	Amount Accumulated To Date	Current Savings Per Month	Remaining Amount Needed	Willing To Commit Dollars/Month

Form 5

CURRENT FINANCIAL OBLIGATIONS WORKSHEET

Financial Obligation (Exclude Home)	Total Years To Pay Off Obligation	Total Payment Amount	Amount Paid To Date	Current Monthly Payment	Remaining Dollar Amount Needed	Commit Extra Dollars/Month

Form 6

FAMILY INFORMATION

I. Family Name _____

II. Personal Information

Family Member	First Name	Social Security Number	Date of Birth	Birth Place (City, State)
Husband:		__ __ __ - __ __ - __ __ __ __		
Wife:		__ __ __ - __ __ - __ __ __ __		
Children:		__ __ __ - __ __ - __ __ __ __		
		__ __ __ - __ __ - __ __ __ __		
		__ __ __ - __ __ - __ __ __ __		
		__ __ __ - __ __ - __ __ __ __		

III. Key - Documents And Asset Location List

Column	Location	Address	Information
A			
B			
C			
D			
E			
F			
G			

Form 7

ADVISORS

Title	Individual Or Firm Name Address	Telephone Number(s)
Accountant		
Attorney		
Bank, S & L, Credit Union		
Business Partner(s) or Associates		
Dentist		
Employer(s)		
Executor(s) Of Will		
Financial Planner		
Insurance Agent(s)		
Physician(s)		
Religious Affiliation		
Stock Broker		
_____		
_____		

Form 8

DOCUMENTS AND ASSET LOCATION LIST

	A	B	C	D	E	F	G

BANK

1. Cancelled Checks .... ☐ ☐ ☐ ☐ ☐ ☐ ☐
2. Certificates of Deposit .... ☐ ☐ ☐ ☐ ☐ ☐ ☐
3. Checkbooks .... ☐ ☐ ☐ ☐ ☐ ☐ ☐
4. Checkbook Register(s) .... ☐ ☐ ☐ ☐ ☐ ☐ ☐
5. Checking/Savings Account Statements .... ☐ ☐ ☐ ☐ ☐ ☐ ☐
6. Investment Securities .... ☐ ☐ ☐ ☐ ☐ ☐ ☐
7. List of Checking/Savings Account Numbers .... ☐ ☐ ☐ ☐ ☐ ☐ ☐
8. List of Contents in Safe Deposit Box .... ☐ ☐ ☐ ☐ ☐ ☐ ☐
9. Money Market Accounts .... ☐ ☐ ☐ ☐ ☐ ☐ ☐
10. Savings Passbook .... ☐ ☐ ☐ ☐ ☐ ☐ ☐
11. Signature Card(s) .... ☐ ☐ ☐ ☐ ☐ ☐ ☐

CASH RECEIPTS

1. Clothing .... ☐ ☐ ☐ ☐ ☐ ☐ ☐
2. Jewelry .... ☐ ☐ ☐ ☐ ☐ ☐ ☐
3. Major Appliances .... ☐ ☐ ☐ ☐ ☐ ☐ ☐
4. Major Purchases .... ☐ ☐ ☐ ☐ ☐ ☐ ☐
5. Valuables .... ☐ ☐ ☐ ☐ ☐ ☐ ☐

CHILDREN'S FILE

1. Awards & Certificates .... ☐ ☐ ☐ ☐ ☐ ☐ ☐
2. Christmas & Birthday Cards .... ☐ ☐ ☐ ☐ ☐ ☐ ☐
3. Diplomas .... ☐ ☐ ☐ ☐ ☐ ☐ ☐
4. School Papers .... ☐ ☐ ☐ ☐ ☐ ☐ ☐

CURRENT BILLS & CREDIT RECORDS

1. Charge Card Account Slips .... ☐ ☐ ☐ ☐ ☐ ☐ ☐
2. Credit Bureau Report .... ☐ ☐ ☐ ☐ ☐ ☐ ☐
3. Creditor's Address & Phone Number .... ☐ ☐ ☐ ☐ ☐ ☐ ☐
4. Installment Contracts .... ☐ ☐ ☐ ☐ ☐ ☐ ☐
5. List of Credit Card Account Numbers .... ☐ ☐ ☐ ☐ ☐ ☐ ☐
6. Monthly Credit Card Statements .... ☐ ☐ ☐ ☐ ☐ ☐ ☐
7. Unpaid Bills .... ☐ ☐ ☐ ☐ ☐ ☐ ☐

EDUCATION

1. College Official Transcripts .... ☐ ☐ ☐ ☐ ☐ ☐ ☐
2. Correspondence Courses .... ☐ ☐ ☐ ☐ ☐ ☐ ☐
3. High School/Technical School Official Transcripts .... ☐ ☐ ☐ ☐ ☐ ☐ ☐
4. Night School Classes .... ☐ ☐ ☐ ☐ ☐ ☐ ☐
5. Professional Related Courses .... ☐ ☐ ☐ ☐ ☐ ☐ ☐

DOCUMENTS AND ASSET LOCATION LIST
Page 2

EMPLOYMENT INFORMATION   A B C D E F G
   1. Employee Benefits Information .... ☐ ☐ ☐ ☐ ☐ ☐ ☐
   2. Employee Handbook .... ☐ ☐ ☐ ☐ ☐ ☐ ☐
   3. Employee Retirement Information .... ☐ ☐ ☐ ☐ ☐ ☐ ☐
   4. Employment Contracts .... ☐ ☐ ☐ ☐ ☐ ☐ ☐
   5. Retirement/Pension Records From Previous Employer ... ☐ ☐ ☐ ☐ ☐ ☐ ☐

ESTATE PLANNING DOCUMENTS
   1. Anatomical Gift Declaration (Authorized Organ Donation) .. ☐ ☐ ☐ ☐ ☐ ☐ ☐
   2. Burial/Funeral Instructions .... ☐ ☐ ☐ ☐ ☐ ☐ ☐
   3. Cemetery Plot Deed .... ☐ ☐ ☐ ☐ ☐ ☐ ☐
   4. Document Appointing Children's Guardian .... ☐ ☐ ☐ ☐ ☐ ☐ ☐
   5. Executor of Will .... ☐ ☐ ☐ ☐ ☐ ☐ ☐
   6. Letter of Last Instruction (List of Special Bequests) .... ☐ ☐ ☐ ☐ ☐ ☐ ☐
   7. Living Will .... ☐ ☐ ☐ ☐ ☐ ☐ ☐
   8. Power of Attorney (General) .... ☐ ☐ ☐ ☐ ☐ ☐ ☐
   9. Power of Attorney (Health) .... ☐ ☐ ☐ ☐ ☐ ☐ ☐
  10. Will - Changes & Codicils .... ☐ ☐ ☐ ☐ ☐ ☐ ☐
  11. Will/Trust - Original .... ☐ ☐ ☐ ☐ ☐ ☐ ☐
  12. Will/Trust - Copies .... ☐ ☐ ☐ ☐ ☐ ☐ ☐

FINANCIAL PLANNING
   1. Budget .... ☐ ☐ ☐ ☐ ☐ ☐ ☐
   2. Financial Goals: Short-Term & Long-Term .... ☐ ☐ ☐ ☐ ☐ ☐ ☐
   3. Financial Plan (Financial Analysis) .... ☐ ☐ ☐ ☐ ☐ ☐ ☐

HOME RESIDENCE
   1. Cancelled Checks .... ☐ ☐ ☐ ☐ ☐ ☐ ☐
   2. Capital - Improvement Receipts .... ☐ ☐ ☐ ☐ ☐ ☐ ☐
   3. Closing Statement(s) & Selling Costs .... ☐ ☐ ☐ ☐ ☐ ☐ ☐
   4. Deed (Warranty Deed) .... ☐ ☐ ☐ ☐ ☐ ☐ ☐
   5. Home Inventory .... ☐ ☐ ☐ ☐ ☐ ☐ ☐
   6. Homeowners Insurance .... ☐ ☐ ☐ ☐ ☐ ☐ ☐
   7. Map - Subsurface Sprinkling System .... ☐ ☐ ☐ ☐ ☐ ☐ ☐
   8. Mortgage Papers (Include Mortgage Release) .... ☐ ☐ ☐ ☐ ☐ ☐ ☐
   9. Payment Book .... ☐ ☐ ☐ ☐ ☐ ☐ ☐
  10. Photographs/Videos -- Home Contents & Interior ...... ☐ ☐ ☐ ☐ ☐ ☐ ☐
  11. Purchase Contract .... ☐ ☐ ☐ ☐ ☐ ☐ ☐
  12. Record of Land Transfer Taxes .... ☐ ☐ ☐ ☐ ☐ ☐ ☐
  13. Surveys .... ☐ ☐ ☐ ☐ ☐ ☐ ☐
  14. Tax Records & Receipts .... ☐ ☐ ☐ ☐ ☐ ☐ ☐
  15. Title Abstract .... ☐ ☐ ☐ ☐ ☐ ☐ ☐
  16. Title Insurance Policy .... ☐ ☐ ☐ ☐ ☐ ☐ ☐
  17. Utilities - Electricity, Gas, Water, Sanitation .... ☐ ☐ ☐ ☐ ☐ ☐ ☐

Form 10

DOCUMENTS AND ASSET LOCATION LIST
Page 3

HOUSING - RENTED

		A	B	C	D	E	F	G
1.	Copy of "Owners" Liability Coverage	☐	☐	☐	☐	☐	☐	☐
2.	Copy of Release Rental Agreement	☐	☐	☐	☐	☐	☐	☐
3.	Photographs/Videos Showing Condition of Rental Property When Moving In	☐	☐	☐	☐	☐	☐	☐
4.	Renter's (Tenant's) Insurance Policy	☐	☐	☐	☐	☐	☐	☐

INSURANCE

Include (A) Policy Numbers (B) Name of Insured Person(s) (C) Beneficiaries (D) Insuring Company (E) Type & Amount of Coverage (F) Representative or Agent (G) Complete Address (H) Telephone Number

1.	Airplane/Boat Insurance Policy	☐	☐	☐	☐	☐	☐	☐
2.	Business Insurance	☐	☐	☐	☐	☐	☐	☐
3.	Dental Insurance	☐	☐	☐	☐	☐	☐	☐
4.	Disability Income	☐	☐	☐	☐	☐	☐	☐
5.	Health (Medical) Insurance	☐	☐	☐	☐	☐	☐	☐
6.	Homeowners/Renters Insurance	☐	☐	☐	☐	☐	☐	☐
7.	Hospital Insurance	☐	☐	☐	☐	☐	☐	☐
8.	Property & Casualty Insurance	☐	☐	☐	☐	☐	☐	☐
9.	Life Insurance - Individual & Family	☐	☐	☐	☐	☐	☐	☐
10.	Life Insurance - Group Coverage	☐	☐	☐	☐	☐	☐	☐
11.	Title Insurance	☐	☐	☐	☐	☐	☐	☐
12.	Umbrella Liability Insurance	☐	☐	☐	☐	☐	☐	☐
13.	Vehicle(s) Insurance	☐	☐	☐	☐	☐	☐	☐

INVESTMENTS

1.	Annuity Certificates or Policies	☐	☐	☐	☐	☐	☐	☐
2.	Bonds	☐	☐	☐	☐	☐	☐	☐
3.	Brokerage Account Records	☐	☐	☐	☐	☐	☐	☐
4.	Limited Partnership & Private Placement Documents	☐	☐	☐	☐	☐	☐	☐
5.	Money Market Funds	☐	☐	☐	☐	☐	☐	☐
6.	Mutual Fund Account Statements	☐	☐	☐	☐	☐	☐	☐
7.	Mutual Fund Certificates	☐	☐	☐	☐	☐	☐	☐
8.	Real Estate Investment Property - Records, Titles, Deeds	☐	☐	☐	☐	☐	☐	☐
9.	Record of Investment Securities	☐	☐	☐	☐	☐	☐	☐
10.	Stock Certificates	☐	☐	☐	☐	☐	☐	☐

DOCUMENTS AND ASSET LOCATION LIST
Page 4

PAPERS, RECORDS, CERTIFICATES, LISTS

		A	B	C	D	E	F	G
1.	Adoption/Foster Child Papers	☐	☐	☐	☐	☐	☐	☐
2.	Birth Certificates	☐	☐	☐	☐	☐	☐	☐
3.	Certified Death Certificate of Family Member or Relative	☐	☐	☐	☐	☐	☐	☐
4.	Citizenship Papers	☐	☐	☐	☐	☐	☐	☐
5.	Diploma/Graduation Certificate(s)	☐	☐	☐	☐	☐	☐	☐
6.	Divorce/Separation Records	☐	☐	☐	☐	☐	☐	☐
7.	Frequent Flyer Certificates	☐	☐	☐	☐	☐	☐	☐
8.	Gift Certificates	☐	☐	☐	☐	☐	☐	☐
9.	Immunization & Health Records	☐	☐	☐	☐	☐	☐	☐
10.	Keys	☐	☐	☐	☐	☐	☐	☐
11.	List of Credit Cards	☐	☐	☐	☐	☐	☐	☐
12.	List of Loaned Possessions	☐	☐	☐	☐	☐	☐	☐
13.	List of Memberships In Fraternal or Professional Organizations	☐	☐	☐	☐	☐	☐	☐
14.	List of Relatives & Friends - Name, Address, Telephone Number	☐	☐	☐	☐	☐	☐	☐
15.	List of Stored Possessions	☐	☐	☐	☐	☐	☐	☐
16.	List of Valuable Possessions	☐	☐	☐	☐	☐	☐	☐
17.	Marriage Certificate	☐	☐	☐	☐	☐	☐	☐
18.	Military Papers - Current & Discharge Records	☐	☐	☐	☐	☐	☐	☐
19.	Passport/Visa	☐	☐	☐	☐	☐	☐	☐
20.	Resume	☐	☐	☐	☐	☐	☐	☐
21.	Safe Combination - Business	☐	☐	☐	☐	☐	☐	☐
22.	Safe Combination - Home	☐	☐	☐	☐	☐	☐	☐
23.	Social Security Card - Copy	☐	☐	☐	☐	☐	☐	☐
24.	Veterinarian Records	☐	☐	☐	☐	☐	☐	☐

PERSONAL PROPERTY

Include (A) Original Purchase Price (B) Description (C) Photographs/Videos of Valuable or Unusual Possessions

1.	Antiques	☐	☐	☐	☐	☐	☐	☐
2.	Appraisals	☐	☐	☐	☐	☐	☐	☐
3.	Collectibles	☐	☐	☐	☐	☐	☐	☐

RETIREMENT PROGRAMS/PLANS

1.	Annuity Contracts	☐	☐	☐	☐	☐	☐	☐
2.	Corporate Retirement Plan	☐	☐	☐	☐	☐	☐	☐
3.	IRA/TSA Accounts	☐	☐	☐	☐	☐	☐	☐
4.	Keogh, Simplified Pension, "457" Plan	☐	☐	☐	☐	☐	☐	☐
5.	Profit Sharing Plan	☐	☐	☐	☐	☐	☐	☐
6.	Stock Option/Stock Purchase Plan	☐	☐	☐	☐	☐	☐	☐

                    Form 12

DOCUMENTS AND ASSET LOCATION LIST
Page 5

TAX INFORMATION   A   B   C   D   E   F   G

1. Annual Federal/State Tax Returns &
   Supporting Information .... ☐ ☐ ☐ ☐ ☐ ☐ ☐
2. Business/Corporation Tax Returns .... ☐ ☐ ☐ ☐ ☐ ☐ ☐
3. Business Related Expenses .... ☐ ☐ ☐ ☐ ☐ ☐ ☐
4. Gift Tax Returns .... ☐ ☐ ☐ ☐ ☐ ☐ ☐
5. Inheritance Tax Return (Tax Waiver) .... ☐ ☐ ☐ ☐ ☐ ☐ ☐
6. Medical Reimbursement Claims .... ☐ ☐ ☐ ☐ ☐ ☐ ☐
7. Receipts For Taxable Items - Interest,
   Dividends, K-1's, etc. .... ☐ ☐ ☐ ☐ ☐ ☐ ☐
8. Police Theft Reports & Insurance Claims .... ☐ ☐ ☐ ☐ ☐ ☐ ☐
9. Receipts For Tax-Deductible Items - Child
   Care, Interest, Charitable Gifts, etc. .... ☐ ☐ ☐ ☐ ☐ ☐ ☐
10. Tax Forms
   Form 2119 (Sale of a Home) .... ☐ ☐ ☐ ☐ ☐ ☐ ☐
   Form 8606 (Non Deduct. IRA Contributions) .... ☐ ☐ ☐ ☐ ☐ ☐ ☐
   Form 8582 (Passive Activity Loss Limitations) .... ☐ ☐ ☐ ☐ ☐ ☐ ☐
   Form 942 (Paying FICA Expenses For
   Household Employees) .... ☐ ☐ ☐ ☐ ☐ ☐ ☐
   Form 5498 (Annual IRA Trustee Form) .... ☐ ☐ ☐ ☐ ☐ ☐ ☐
   Form 1099R or W-2P (Distribution Form) .... ☐ ☐ ☐ ☐ ☐ ☐ ☐

VEHICLE(S)

1. Boat/Plane Ownership Records .... ☐ ☐ ☐ ☐ ☐ ☐ ☐
2. Driver's License Information .... ☐ ☐ ☐ ☐ ☐ ☐ ☐
3. Ownership Manuals .... ☐ ☐ ☐ ☐ ☐ ☐ ☐
4. Payment Book(s) .... ☐ ☐ ☐ ☐ ☐ ☐ ☐
5. Record of Traffic Violations/Accidents .... ☐ ☐ ☐ ☐ ☐ ☐ ☐
6. Registration Card(s) .... ☐ ☐ ☐ ☐ ☐ ☐ ☐
7. Repair/Maintenance Records .... ☐ ☐ ☐ ☐ ☐ ☐ ☐
8. Vehicle Ownership Records .... ☐ ☐ ☐ ☐ ☐ ☐ ☐

WARRANTIES & GUARANTEES

1. Instruction Manuals .... ☐ ☐ ☐ ☐ ☐ ☐ ☐
2. Warranties (eg. Carpet, Major appliances, Tires) .... ☐ ☐ ☐ ☐ ☐ ☐ ☐

ADDITIONAL ITEMS

1. _____ .... ☐ ☐ ☐ ☐ ☐ ☐ ☐

2. _____ .... ☐ ☐ ☐ ☐ ☐ ☐ ☐

3. _____ .... ☐ ☐ ☐ ☐ ☐ ☐ ☐

HOUSEHOLD INVENTORY

Check each of the boxes - ❑ - for those Rooms and Special Inventory items that apply in your situation. Make multiple copies of the Rooms and Special Inventory sheets (pages 241 - 242) and use separate sheets for each item checked below, ☑. The Special Inventory items can be placed on a single form. Finally, place the <u>totals</u> of each form on the appropriate line of the Inventory Summary.

ROOMS

❑ Living Room
❑ Dining Room
❑ Kitchen, Breakfast, Pantry
❑ Master Bedroom
❑ Bedroom 2, 3, etc., Nursery
❑ Master Bathroom
❑ Bathrooms 2, 3, etc.
❑ Den, Study, Library
❑ Shop

❑ Recreation, Family Room
❑ Garage
❑ Basement
❑ Mudroom, Laundry
❑ Attic
❑ Halls
❑ Storage Room
❑ Outdoor Storage Shed

SPECIAL INVENTORY

❑ Patio
❑ Books
❑ China, Glassware
❑ Silverware
❑ Personal Effects - Clothing -
    Men's, Women's, Children's
❑ Jewelry, Furs
❑ Camcorder, Camera Equipment
❑ Tools

❑ Swimming Pool, Tennis Court
❑ Musical Instruments
❑ Sports & Hobby Equipment, Guns
❑ Television, VCR(s), CD Player(s)
❑ Antiques, Works of Art
    Rare Coins, Collectibles
❑ Stereo/Tape Equipment, Records
❑ Carpet
❑ Outdoor Equipment & Machinery

 Form 14

ROOMS

_____

Number of Items	Item	Year Purchased	Original Cost	Estimated Present Value
		Totals		

SPECIAL INVENTORY

Number of Articles	Article	Year Purchased	Original Cost	Estimated Present Value
		Totals		

                         Form 16

INVENTORY SUMMARY

Number of Items	Room or Special Inventory	Original Cost	Estimated Present or Replacement Value
	Living Room		
	Dining Room		
	Kitchen, Breakfast, Pantry		
	Master Bedroom		
	Additional Bedrooms		
	Bathroom(s)		
	Books		
	China, Glassware		
	Silverware		
	Personal Effects - Clothing		
	Jewelry, Furs		
	Television, VCR, CD		
Final Group Totals			
Total Amount of Insurance Covering Personal Property			
Additional Insurance, if Any, Required			

Form 17

SAFE DEPOSIT BOX INVENTORY

Owner	Description	Current Value	Original Cost	Comments

                                    Form 18

ANTIQUES & COLLECTIBLES INVENTORY

Owner	Description	Current Value	Original Cost	Comments

Form 19

MONTHLY GAS & ELECTRIC UTILITIES

Account Number _____

Month	Dates	Number Of Days	Number CCF Gas Units	Base Energy Charge	Number KWH Electric Units	Base Energy Charge	Total Amount Billed	Comments
Jan								
Feb								
Mar								
Apr								
May								
June								
July								
Aug								
Sept								
Oct								
Nov								
Dec								
Total								
Ave								

Form 20

MONTHLY CITY UTILITIES

Account Number _____

Month	Dates	Number Of Days	Number Of Cubic Feet Water Used	Sewer Expense	Refuse Expense	Other City Expenses	Total Amount Billed	Comments
Jan								
Feb								
Mar								
Apr								
May								
June								
July								
Aug								
Sept								
Oct								
Nov								
Dec								
Total								
Ave								

Form 21

MONTHLY TELEPHONE EXPENSES

Account Number _____

Month	Base Service Charge	Regular Long Distance Charge	Selected Long Distance Carrier	Charge By Long Distance Carrier	Total Amount Billed	Comments
Jan						
Feb						
Mar						
Apr						
May						
June						
July						
Aug						
Sept						
Oct						
Nov						
Dec						
Total						
Ave						

Form 22

ANNUAL HOME IMPROVEMENTS
PROJECT RECORD SHEET

Month	Date	Project Task	Cost	Notes Comments
Jan				
Feb				
Mar				
Apr				
May				
June				
July				
Aug				
Sept				
Oct				
Nov				
Dec				
Total				
Ave				

ANNUAL LAWN & GARDEN CARE
RECORD SHEET

Month	Date	Objective Task	Cost	Notes Comments
Jan				
Feb				
Mar				
Apr				
May				
June				
July				
Aug				
Sept				
Oct				
Nov				
Dec				
Total				
Ave				

Form 24

AUTOMOBILE SERVICE RECORD
GENERAL INFORMATION

Model	Make	ID Number	Purchase Price	Date Purchased

REPAIR & REPLACEMENT

Engine Area	Date	Mileage	Date	Mileage
	Repair/Service Completed		Repair/Service Completed	
Oil Change/Lube				
Electrical Tune Up				
Carburetor Over Haul				
Air Filter				
Fuel Pump				
Water Pump				
Battery				
Heater				
Air Conditioner				
Radiator/Coolant				
Belts				
Hoses				
_____				
_____				
_____				

Form 25

AUTOMOBILE SERVICE RECORD
Page 2

Transmission	Date	Mileage	Date	Mileage
	Repair/Service Completed		Repair/Service Completed	
Filter, Oil, etc.				
_____				
_____				

Exhaust System	Date	Mileage	Date	Mileage
	Repair/Service Completed		Repair/Service Completed	
Muffler				
Tail Pipe				
Exhaust Pipe				
Catalytic Converter				
_____				
_____				
_____				

Differential	Date	Mileage	Date	Mileage
	Repair/Service Completed		Repair/Service Completed	
Fluid, Check, etc.				
_____				
_____				

   Form 26

AUTOMOBILE SERVICE RECORD
Page 3

Suspension System	Date	Mileage	Date	Mileage
	Repair/Service Completed		Repair/Service Completed	
Front Shock Absorbers				
Rear Shock Absorbers				
Alignment				
_____				
_____				

Wheels/Brakes	Date	Mileage	Date	Mileage
	Repair/Service Completed		Repair/Service Completed	
Tires				
Rotation				
Disc Brakes				
Drum Rotor				
Front Brake Lining				
Rear Brake Lining				
Repack Wheel Bearings				
_____				
_____				
_____				

AUTOMOBILE SERVICE RECORD
Page 4

Windshield/Windows	Date	Mileage	Date	Mileage
	Repair/Service Completed		Repair/Service Completed	
Wiper Blades				
Repair Windshield				
Replace Windshield				
Side/Rear Windows				
_____				
_____				
_____				

General/Body Work	Date	Mileage	Date	Mileage
	Repair/Service Completed		Repair/Service Completed	
Undercoat				
_____				
_____				
_____				
_____				
_____				

 Form 28

AUTOMOBILE SERVICE RECORD
Page 5

OIL CHANGE - LUBE RECORD SHEET

Oil Change - Lube	Date	Date	Date	Date
	Mileage	Mileage	Mileage	Mileage

MOVING PREPARATION PLANNING GUIDE
ORGANIZATION TIMETABLE

Planning Duty	Notes & Information
One Month Before Moving	1. _____
☐ 1. Confirm arrangements with a moving company or make truck rental reservations.	2. _____
☐ 2. Purchase moving supplies: boxes, strapping tape, bubble wrap, styrofoam fill, marking pens or labels and tape measure.	3. _____
☐ 3. Plan your travel itinerary if moving out-of-state; make reservations for lodging, car rental, and airplane if necessary.	4. _____
☐ 4. Save each of your moving receipts as expenses may be tax deductible.	5. _____
☐ 5. Pack your financial, medical, legal, and insurance records in a safe and accessible place; you may want to take such records with you if driving.	6. _____
☐ 6. Give new home a thorough cleaning; paint interior where necessary.	7. _____
☐ 7. Check out local schools in your area.	8. _____
☐ 8. Obtain the appropriate forms from the post office, then notify the following persons, businesses, or institutions of your new address:	
☐ Your local post office and mail carrier.	
☐ Family members, relatives, and friends.	
☐ Banks and businesses.	
☐ Credit card and finance companies.	
☐ Professional service providers: doctors, dentists, and hospitals.	
☐ Government agencies: local, state, and federal tax authorities.	

 Form 30

MOVING PREPARATION PLANNING GUIDE
ORGANIZATION TIMETABLE
Page 2

Planning Duty	Notes & Information
Two Weeks Before Moving	1. _____
☐ 1. Inform public utilities of your move: public service (gas and electricity), water and sewer, and cable television.	2. _____
☐ 2. Sign up for the above services at your new location.	3. _____
☐ 3. Notify your local telephone company and long-distance carrier of your new address.	4. _____
☐ 4. Begin packing:	5. _____
☐ Number each box and keep a list of its contents.	6. _____
☐ Write on each box the room where it's to be delivered.	7. _____
☐ 5. Arrange for help on moving day.	8. _____
☐ 6. Confirm rental truck or moving company reservations.	
☐ 7. Confirm lodging, airplane ticket, and/or rental car reservations.	
☐ 8. Make arrangements with your financial institutions to close or transfer any accounts.	

Planning Duty	Notes & Information
The Day Before Moving	1. _____
☐ 1. Put away and organize the following moving supplies: extra boxes, tape, bubble wrap or styrofoam, tape measure, etc.	2. _____
☐ 2. Pick up rental truck if you are moving yourself.	3. _____
☐ 3. Get your car serviced or carefully check it over yourself for the trip.	4. _____
☐ 4. Be sure that you have your plane ticket(s) and rental car confirmation as well as credit cards and traveler's checks.	5. _____
☐ 5. Get maps organized for your trip.	

MOVING PREPARATION PLANNING GUIDE

ORGANIZATION TIMETABLE

Page 3

Planning Duty	Notes & Information
One - Two Days Prior To Your Arrival	1. _____
☐ 1. Arrange with public utilities to resume service: gas and electricity, water and sewer, trash and recycle removal, and cable television.	2. _____
☐ 2. Contact your local telephone and long-distance carrier to install service at your new location.	

Planning Duty	Notes & Information
Immediately After Arriving At Your New Home	1. _____
☐ 1. Notify each sender of your new address for mail forwarded by the post office.	2. _____
☐ 2. If you have moved from another state, contact the State Department of Motor Vehicles regarding a new driver's license.	3. _____
☐ 3. Exchange your automobile license plates at your County (or State) Motor Vehicles' Department.	4. _____
☐ 4. Contact your county (or city) auditor's office and register to vote.	5. _____
☐ 5. Set up an account (or accounts) at a local bank, credit union, or other financial institution.	6. _____
☐ 6. Select all appropriate doctors and dentist in your area.	7. _____
☐ 7. Contact your local Chamber of Commerce regarding civic organizations, churches, etc.	8. _____
☐ 8. Locate your nearest area hospital, police department, and fire station.	9. _____
☐ 9. List emergency phone numbers and post on or near all telephones.	

Form 32

TRAVEL PLANNING AND PACKING GUIDE
NECESSITIES

- ❏ Extra pair of prescription eyeglasses/sunglasses/contacts.
- ❏ Secured (pick-pocket proof) pouch for carrying extra money, passport, visa, and credit, charge, or ATM cards. In addition:
  - ❏ Ladies fanny pack, shoulder bag, or handbag which is difficult to gain entry (not zipped).
  - ❏ Mens wallet or billfold inside jacket or suit coat instead of back or side pockets.
- ❏ Prescription drugs (one set in carry on and one set in regular luggage).
- ❏ Legible copy of prescription drugs from your doctor for emergency refills.
- ❏ Comfort medications that you require (aspirin, cough drops/medicine, motion sickness wrist bands/medicine, cold medications, medication for pain relief, upset stomach, flu symptoms, sleeping aids, etc.).
- ❏ Two pairs of comfortable walking shoes with rubber soles and appropriate socks.
- ❏ Light weight raincoat or poncho and travel umbrella.
- ❏ First aid supplies such as bandaids, disinfectant, etc.
- ❏ Appropriate converter with adopter(s) for razor, hair dryer, curler, etc.
- ❏ Reliable travel alarm clock.
- ❏ Small flash light for night use or power outages.
- ❏ Pint size plastic bottle for drinking water or other beverages.
- ❏ Maps, information, and guidebook(s) for the specific areas, countries and major cities you plan to visit.
- ❏ Fluorescent high lighter for map use.
- ❏ Sunburn cream or lotion.
- ❏ Comfortable backpack for food, water, extra clothes, jackets, shoes, maps, etc.
- ❏ Gloves for cooler/cold weather.
- ❏ A dozen large safety pins.
- ❏ Envelopes for receipts of purchases and/or credit, charge, and ATM cards.
- ❏ One 3" x 5" card carried in wallet listing essential phone numbers: doctors, relatives, neighbors, pharmacy, etc.
- ❏ Toiletries, cosmetics, lotions, personal supplies.
- ❏ Address book.

CONVENIENCE ITEMS

- ❏ Face cloth and bath towel (beach towel if necessary).
- ❏ Camera, extra lenses, film, and extra batteries.
- ❏ Instant tea, tea bags and/or decaf coffee packages (artificial sweeteners and creamers).
- ❏ Kleenex, toilet tissue, and moist towelettes.
- ❏ Drain plug (or stop) for wash basin.
- ❏ Plastic hangers, ("clothes-pin" hangers are available), soap, and clothes line for hand laundry.
- ❏ Body soap, laundry detergent (handwash and machine).
- ❏ Ziplock plastic bags for damp clothes and towels.
- ❏ Small calculator or currency converter.
- ❏ Small, hand held mirror.
- ❏ Compact manicure kit.
- ❏ Cap or sun visor.
- ❏ Post card stamps.
- ❏ Jewelry/case.
- ❏ Sewing kit for mending.
- ❏ Extra shoe laces.
- ❏ Rubber bands.
- ❏ Stationery.
- ❏ Pill boxes.

WEDDING PREPARATION PLANNING GUIDE
BRIDE'S ORGANIZATION TIMETABLE

Planning Duty	Notes & Information
Six - Twelve Months Before Your Wedding	
☐ 1. Purchase a wedding planning book or memory album.	1. ___
☐ 2. Discuss your wedding budget; include sharing of expenses.	2. ___
☐ 3. Decide on type of wedding: ☐ Formal ☐ Informal	3. ___
☐ 4. Select wedding attendants.	4. ___
☐ 5. Select ceremony location.	5. ___
☐ 6. Select and reserve reception location; plan details for reception.	6. ___
☐ 7. Compile invitation lists with addresses and zip codes for bride and groom.	7. ___
☐ 8. Select and order wedding gown, veil, and accessories.	8. ___
☐ 9. Schedule dates for wedding gown fittings and delivery.	9. ___
☐ 10. Plan the theme and color scheme for your wedding ceremony and reception.	10. ___
☐ 11. Shop with your groom for engagement ring.	11. ___
☐ 12. Visit a clergy or other officiating authority with your groom.	12. ___
☐ 13. Decide on the date and time for the wedding rehearsal.	13. ___
☐ 14. Select florist or floral designer.	14. ___
☐ 15. Choose musicians and select music for the wedding ceremony.	15. ___
☐ 16. Select musicians or disk jockey for the reception.	16. ___
☐ 17. Select decorations, center pieces, menu, etc. for reception.	17. ___
☐ 18. Select and book photographer for the ceremony and reception.	18. ___
☐ 19. Select and book videographer.	19. ___
☐ 20. Select a caterer.	20. ___
☐ 21. Select and register silver, china, crystal, etc.	21. ___
☐ 22. Organize a list or master file of all service people, businesses, etc.	22. ___

Form 34

WEDDING PREPARATION PLANNING GUIDE
BRIDE'S ORGANIZATION TIMETABLE
Page 2

Planning Duty	Notes & Information
Six - Twelve Months Before Your Wedding (Continued)	
☐ 23. Discuss plans with your groom (and travel agent) regarding your honeymoon. (If traveling outside the U.S., check on passports, visas, and inoculations).	23. _____
☐ 24. Submit engagement announcement with release date to the newspaper(s).	24. _____
☐ 25. Begin looking for house or apartment.	23. _____
Four - Six Months Before Your Wedding	
☐ 1. Shop with your groom for wedding rings; order engraving.	1. _____
☐ 2. Select and order attendants' dresses and headpieces; make appointments for fittings.	2. _____
☐ 3. Select men's formal attire.	3. _____
☐ 4. Finalize your guest list; check it with your groom's list to avoid possible duplication.	4. _____
☐ 5. Order your invitations, announcements, and wedding programs; proof them before the final printing.	5. _____
☐ 6. Pick up invitation envelopes in advance; begin addressing them.	6. _____
☐ 7. Order thank-you notes (with and without married name.)	7. _____
☐ 8. Set appointment for complete physical exam; update immunizations.	8. _____
☐ 9. Set appointment for blood test.	9. _____
☐ 10. Complete honeymoon plans with your groom.	10. _____
☐ 11. Shop for your personal trousseau.	11. _____
☐ 12. Begin shopping for household furnishings.	12. _____

Form 35

WEDDING PREPARATION PLANNING GUIDE
BRIDE'S ORGANIZATION TIMETABLE
Page 3

Planning Duty	Notes & Information
Two - Four Months Before Your Wedding	1. _____
☐ 1. Reserve transportation for wedding party.	2. _____
☐ 2. Discuss color scheme with your mother in order that she can choose her dress and attire; then confirm with the groom's mother on selecting her dress.	3. _____
☐ 3. Confirm delivery date for your wedding gown.	4. _____
☐ 4. Order wedding cake and groom's cake.	5. _____
☐ 5. Confirm details with hired professionals: caterer, photographer, florist, musicians, organist, soloist, etc.	6. _____
☐ 6. Arrange accommodations for out-of-town relatives and guests. (Make arrangements at least 9 - 12 months in advance IF the wedding takes place in a university community at commencement time.)	7. _____
☐ 7. Arrange with a photographer for your bridal portrait.	8. _____
☐ 8. Select date with your groom to get the marriage license.	9. _____
☐ 9. Complete your guest list.	10. _____
☐ 10. Purchase accessories: candles, toasting goblets, garter, ring pillow, etc.	

Form 36

WEDDING PREPARATION PLANNING GUIDE
BRIDE'S ORGANIZATION TIMETABLE
Page 4

Planning Duty

One - Two Months Before Your Wedding

☐ 1. Have final gown and headpiece fitting.

☐ 2. Pick up wedding rings; check engraving.

☐ 3. Mail invitations; include maps and pew cards if necessary. (Record acceptances and regrets as they arrive.)

☐ 4. Obtain an insurance "floater" policy to cover wedding gifts.

☐ 5. Remind bridesmaids of final dress fitting date.

☐ 6. Arrange for wedding announcement in the newspaper(s); check for the proper procedures and announcement deadline.

☐ 7. Record wedding gifts and write thank-you notes as the gifts arrive.

☐ 8. Plan and make reservations for the bridesmaids' party or luncheon.

☐ 9. Make rehearsal dinner reservations; finalize details with host and groom.

☐ 10. Pick up, and check for fit, your wedding gown and accessories.

☐ 11. Have formal bridal portrait taken.

☐ 12. Be sure all legal, medical, and religious documents are in order.

☐ 13. Purchase your groom's wedding gift.

☐ 14. Select and order gifts for wedding attendants and favors for guests.

☐ 15. Test any new hairstyles you have been considering.

☐ 16. Complete shopping for wedding trousseau.

☐ 17. Acquire appropriate attire for honeymoon.

☐ 18. Confirm honeymoon reservations; buy luggage if necessary.

Notes & Information

1. _____
2. _____
3. _____
4. _____
5. _____
6. _____
7. _____
8. _____
9. _____
10. _____
11. _____
12. _____
13. _____
14. _____
15. _____
16. _____
17. _____
18. _____

Form 37

WEDDING PREPARATION PLANNING GUIDE
BRIDE'S ORGANIZATION TIMETABLE
Page 5

Planning Duty

Two Weeks Before Your Wedding

☐ 1. Complete addressing announcements.

☐ 2. If you are acquiring the groom's name, arrange for name and address changes on insurance policies, bank account(s), credit cards, drivers license, employee forms, social security documents, and utilities.

☐ 3. Go with your groom to get the marriage license.

☐ 4. Make a date for early in the week of your wedding to obtain hair, manicure, pedicure appointments.

☐ 5. Check on wedding cake.

☐ 6. Remind each of the members of your wedding party of the date, time, and location of the wedding rehearsal and dinner.

☐ 7. Confirm, for each member of the wedding party, their attire and accessories.

☐ 8. Continue to record wedding gifts as they arrive; write thank-you notes immediately.

☐ 9. Review reception seating arrangements with your groom to determine whether seating preferences or place cards are necessary.

☐ 10. Confirm honeymoon reservations; pick up tickets if required.

☐ 11. Arrange to move your wedding gifts and personal belongings to your new home.

Notes & Information

1. _____
2. _____
3. _____
4. _____
5. _____
6. _____
7. _____
8. _____
9. _____
10. _____
11. _____

 Form 38

WEDDING PREPARATION PLANNING GUIDE
BRIDE'S ORGANIZATION TIMETABLE
Page 6

Planning Duty	Notes & Information
One Week Before Your Wedding ☐ 1. Give a final guest count to the caterer. ☐ 2. Confirm final details with the florist, musicians, organist, soloist, photographers, etc. ☐ 3. Began packing for your honeymoon; purchase traveler's checks. ☐ 4. Go to or give a party or luncheon for your bridesmaids. ☐ 5. Rehearse wedding ceremony. ☐ 6. Present gifts to attendants at the bridesmaids' party or rehearsal dinner.	1. _____ 2. _____ 3. _____ 4. _____ 5. _____ 6. _____
On Your Wedding Day ☐ 1. Get a good rest the night before your wedding day. ☐ 2. Appointment with hair dresser ☐ 3. Mail wedding announcement to the newspaper(s). ☐ 4. Bring your marriage license and your groom's wedding ring to the ceremony. ☐ 5. Relax and enjoy your wedding day!	1. _____ 2. _____ 3. _____ 4. _____ 5. _____

Form 39

© 1996 by John M. Orth, Iowa City, IA.   265

WEDDING BUDGET WORKSHEET

	Bride's or Bride's Family Responsibility - Traditional Wedding		
Item Description	**Budgeted Expense**	**Actual Cost**	**Notes & Reminders**
☐ 1. Bridal gown, veil, & accessories	$_____	$_____	1._____
★☐ 2. Matron/maid of honor's dress and accessories	_____	_____	2._____
★☐ 3. Bridesmaids' dresses & headpieces	_____	_____	3._____
☐ 4. Bouquets or corsages for attendants & flower girl(s)	_____	_____	4._____
☐ 5. Groom's wedding ring	_____	_____	5._____
☐ 6. Invitations & announcements	_____	_____	6._____
☐ 7. Bride's personal stationery	_____	_____	7._____
☐ 8. Reception	_____	_____	8._____
☐ 9. Caterer	_____	_____	9._____
☐ 10. Music & entertainment	_____	_____	10._____
☐ 11. Wedding cake and/or groom's cake	_____	_____	11._____
☐ 12. Flowers for ceremony & reception	_____	_____	12._____
☐ 13. Photography and/or videography	_____	_____	13._____
☐ 14. Bride's wedding portrait	_____	_____	14._____
☐ 15. Transportation for wedding party to the ceremony & reception	_____	_____	15._____
☐ 16. Parents' gift(s) to the newlyweds	_____	_____	16._____
☐ 17. Attendants' gifts	_____	_____	17._____
☐ 18. Church sanctuary or chapel rental fee	_____	_____	18._____
☐ 19. Fees for organist & soloist	_____	_____	19._____
☐ 20. Bride's gift to the groom	_____	_____	20._____
★☐ 21. Lodging arrangements for out-of-town relatives and guests	_____	_____	21._____
★☐ 22. "Floater" insurance policy to cover wedding gifts	_____	_____	22._____
☐ 23. Announcement in newspaper(s)	_____	_____	23._____
★☐ 24. Party or luncheon for attendants	_____	_____	24._____
☐ 25. _____	_____	_____	25._____
☐ 26. _____	_____	_____	26._____
Totals	$_____	$_____	

★ An optional responsibility

 Form 40

WEDDING PREPARATION PLANNING GUIDE
GROOM'S ORGANIZATION TIMETABLE

Planning Duty	Notes & Information

Planning Duty

Six Months Before Your Wedding

☐ 1. Discuss and decide upon the sharing of wedding expenses with your bride and/or the bride's family.

☐ 2. Discuss general finances with your bride and set a budget.

☐ 3. Order your bride's engagement ring.

☐ 4. Begin preparing your guest list.

☐ 5. Schedule an appointment with a clergy or person performing the wedding.

☐ 6. Choose your best man and groomsmen.

☐ 7. Select your ushers (approximately one for every 50 guests)

☐ 8. Plan your honeymoon with your bride and travel agent.

☐ 9. Update passports, arrange for visas, and check on inoculations if traveling outside of the U.S.

Three - Four Months Before Your Wedding

☐ 1. Purchase wedding rings and order engraving.

☐ 2. Draw up a will and update the beneficiary on your life insurance policies.

☐ 3. Get complete physical and dental exams, and update your immunizations.

☐ 4. Set an appointment for your blood test.

☐ 5. Make your honeymoon reservations and purchase necessary travel tickets.

☐ 6. Make arrangements for "get-away" car.

Notes & Information

1. _____
2. _____
3. _____
4. _____
5. _____
6. _____
7. _____
8. _____
9. _____

1. _____
2. _____
3. _____
4. _____
5. _____
6. _____

Form 41

267

WEDDING PREPARATION PLANNING GUIDE
GROOM'S ORGANIZATION TIMETABLE
Page 2

Planning Duty	Notes & Information

Three - Four Months Before Your Wedding (Continued)

- ☐ 7. Consult with your bride regarding appropriate formal wear; then order attire for yourself and all men in the wedding party.
- ☐ 8. Finalize your family's guest list; be sure that addresses and zip codes are current, then give list to your bride.
- ☐ 9. Make financial arrangements and find a place in which to live.
- ☐ 10. Arrange special transportation for the bridal couple and wedding party.
- ☐ 11. Purchase clothing for your wedding trip.

Notes & Information

7. _____
8. _____
9. _____
10. _____
11. _____

One - Two Months Before Your Wedding

- ☐ 1. Be sure that all necessary legal, medical, and religious documents are in order.
- ☐ 2. Select a date with your bride to get the marriage license.
- ☐ 3. Arrange lodging for out-of-town relatives and guests. (See comment for item #6, page 3 of Bride's Organization Timetable).
- ☐ 4. Select a gift for your bride.
- ☐ 5. Choose gifts for your attendants and ushers.
- ☐ 6. Help plan and make reservations for the rehearsal dinner.
- ☐ 7. Be sure that ushers have ordered their attire.
- ☐ 8. Assist your bride in the writing of thank-you notes.
- ☐ 9. Confirm all honeymoon reservations.
- ☐ 10. Acquire appropriate attire for honeymoon.

1. _____
2. _____
3. _____
4. _____
5. _____
6. _____
7. _____
8. _____
9. _____
10. _____

Form 42

WEDDING PREPARATION PLANNING GUIDE
GROOM'S ORGANIZATION TIMETABLE
Page 3

Planning Duty	Notes & Information

Two - Four Weeks Before Your Wedding

☐ 1. Make arrangements to move belongings to your new home.

☐ 2. Arrange for a bachelor party or dinner.

☐ 3. Arrange transportation with your best man from the reception site to "wherever" you are planning to leave for your honeymoon.

1. _____
2. _____
3. _____

One Week Before Your Wedding

☐ 1. Pick up the wedding rings; check engraving.

☐ 2. Confirm final guest count of rehearsal party to restaurant.

☐ 3. Verify time and location of wedding rehearsal and rehearsal dinner with your best man, groomsmen, and ushers.

☐ 4. Pick up wedding attire for yourself and attendants.

☐ 5. Get your hair styled.

☐ 6. If special seating arrangements are necessary for the ceremony, discuss them with the head usher.

☐ 7. Present gifts to your attendants (at rehearsal dinner).

☐ 8. Give the clergy's or officiant's fee in a sealed envelop to the best man for delivery following the ceremony.

☐ 9. Arrange going-away clothes so that you can conveniently change following the reception.

☐ 10. Pack for your honeymoon; purchase traveler's checks.

☐ 11. Try to get a good night's rest before your wedding day.

☐ 12. Arrange for the cleaning and storage of the "get-away" car before the wedding and delivery to the wedding location.

1. _____
2. _____
3. _____
4. _____
5. _____
6. _____
7. _____
8. _____
9. _____
10. _____
11. _____
12. _____

WEDDING BUDGET WORKSHEET

Groom's or Groom's Family Responsibility - Traditional Wedding			
Item Description	**Budgeted Expense**	**Actual Cost**	**Notes & Reminders**
❏ 1. Bride's engagement ring	$_____	$_____	1._____
❏ 2. Bride's wedding ring	_____	_____	2._____
❏ 3. Groom's wedding attire	_____	_____	3._____
❏ 4. Bride's bouquet & going-away corsage	_____	_____	4._____
❏ 5. Gift for your bride	_____	_____	5._____
❏ 6. Marriage license	_____	_____	6._____
❏ 7. Boutonnieres for the groom & his attendants	_____	_____	7._____
❏ 8. Corsages for mothers & grand-mothers	_____	_____	8._____
★ ❏ 9. Rental of formal wear for men in the wedding party	_____	_____	9._____
❏ 10. Gifts for best man, groomsmen, and ushers	_____	_____	10._____
❏ 11. Clergy or officiant's fee	_____	_____	11._____
❏ 12. All honeymoon expenses	_____	_____	12._____
★ ❏ 13. Cocktail party & rehearsal dinner	_____	_____	13._____
★ ❏ 14. Rehearsal hall or site rental	_____	_____	14._____
★ ❏ 15. Bachelor party or dinner	_____	_____	15._____
❏ 16. Parents' gift(s) to the newlyweds	_____	_____	16._____
❏ 17. Transportation for bridal couple and wedding party	_____	_____	17._____
★ ❏ 18. Lodging arrangements for out-of-town relatives and guests	_____	_____	18._____
❏ 19. _____	_____	_____	19._____
❏ 20. _____	_____	_____	20._____
❏ 21. _____	_____	_____	21._____
❏ 22. _____	_____	_____	22._____
Totals	$_____	$_____	

★ An optional responsibility

 Form 44

FUNERAL ARRANGEMENTS PLANNING SHEET
FOR _____

GENERAL INFORMATION

Birth Date	Birth Place
Parents	
Schools, Colleges, or Universities Attended	
Occupation(s) or Profession(s)	
Married to	on	at
Residence(s)	
Church Affiliation(s)	

SERVICE ARRANGEMENTS

Cremation or Burial	Funeral Home
Place of Service (Church/Funeral Home/Other)	
Name of Minister, Priest, or Rabbi	
Participating Organizations	
Veteran	Flag (Folded, Draped, Placement)
War	Branch of Service
Rank or Rating	Serial Number
Date Entered Service	Date of Discharge
Fraternal	Civic Organizations
Casket (Type, Material, & Color)	
Vault/Outer Enclosure	
Wardrobe	Jewelry
Wedding Ring or Other Jewelry Stays or is Returned to	
Organist	Selections
Soloist	Selections
Flowers	

FUNERAL ARRANGEMENTS PLANNING SHEET
Page 2

SERVICE ARRANGEMENTS (Continued)

Favorite Bible Passage(s) or Other Literature _____

_____

Anecdotes/Things to be Remembered by _____

_____

Special Requests _____

_____

Memorial Contributions

Pallbearers & Alternates

_____ | _____
_____ | _____
_____ | _____
_____ | _____

CEMETERY DECISIONS

Cemetery Name & Location		
Address		
City	State	Zip
Exchange Privileges (Yes or No)		
Mausoleum Entombment Name	Crypt	Tier
Cemetery Interment Name	Number of Graves Lot Number	Space Number
Memorial Marker/Headstone Material _____ Inscription _____ Emblem _____		
Flower Container Description		
Cremation: ☐ Yes ☐ No	Location:	Time:
Distribution of Ashes: ☐ Yes ☐ No	Location:	Time:

                                        Form 46

IMMEDIATE FUNERAL ARRANGEMENTS
PLANNING SHEET FOR
_____

Funeral Home in Charge of Arrangements	
Name of Deceased	Age
Level of Education Attained	
Current Address	City
County	State/Zip
Length of Residence	Formerly of
Name for Newspaper	Social Security Number

Name of Newspaper(s) for Announcement			
Place of Death	Time	Day	Date ˜
Cause of Death			
Doctor	Length of Illness		
Occupation or Place of Business			
Date Last Worked			
Memberships			
He/She is Survived by (Name of Spouse)			
He/She is Predeceased by (Name of Spouse)			
He/She is Predeceased by Family Members			
Father's Name	Father's Birth Place		
Mother's Maiden Name	Mother's Birth Place		

IMMEDIATE FUNERAL ARRANGEMENTS
PLANNING SHEET
Page 2

Names of Surviving Sons, Daughters, Brothers, Sisters, Grandparents

Name	Relation	City, State
_____	_____	_____
_____	_____	_____
_____	_____	_____
_____	_____	_____
_____	_____	_____
_____	_____	_____
_____	_____	_____
_____	_____	_____
_____	_____	_____
_____	_____	_____
_____	_____	_____
_____	_____	_____

Number of Grandchildren	Great Grandchildren	Great Great Grandchildren

Funeral services will be held (time)   at (Place)

with   Officiating

Burial will be in the   Cemetery

in (City)   (State)

Location of reception following the service

Special services provided by (name of group)

Friends may call at   Time(s)   Day(s)

Memorial donations may be made to_____

    or to _____

                    Form 48

INSURANCE RECORD

Property, Casualty, Automobile, Liability, Fire, Business Insurance Policies

Name of Insured	Name of Insurer	Policy Number	Policy Date	Coverage Amount	Coverage Deductible	Annual Premium	Item(s) Insured

Form 49

INSURANCE RECORD

Life Insurance Policies

Name of Insured	Name of Insurer	Policy Owner	Policy Number	Policy Date	Type of Policy	Face Amount	Annual Premium	Name of Beneficiary

Form 50

INSURANCE RECORD

Health, Accident, Major Medical, Disability Insurance Policies

Name of Insured	Name of Insurer	Policy Number	Group Number	Policy Date	Coverage Amount	Deductible	Annual Premium	Name of Beneficiary

Form 51

MEDICAL PAYMENTS RECORD

Date of Record _____

Name of Patient _____

Date of Service	Provider or Hospital	Charged Amount	Amount Approved By Medicare	Date Paid / Amount Paid By Medicare	Date Paid / Amount Paid By Supplemental Insurance	Date Paid / Amount Paid By Patient	Date Received / Benefit or Reimbursed Amount	Diagnosis, Problem, or Comments & Information

Form 52

PERSONAL HEALTH RECORD
IMMUNIZATIONS, ILLNESSES, ALLERGIES, & SURGERIES

Date of Record _____

Name of Individual _____

Immunization Vaccination (Inoculation)	Booster		Surgery	Hospital		Major Illness (Description)	Doctor(s)		Dental Surgery (Description)	Dentist(s)		Shots (Description)	Allergies or Adverse Reactions
Date	Date		Date	Doctor		Date(s)	Hospital		Date	Hospital		Date(s)	Date(s)

Form 53

279

CERTIFICATES OF DEPOSIT AND SAVINGS BONDS

Date of Record _____

Certificate or ID Number	Owner	Amount of Investment	Issue Date	Length of Term	Maturity Date	Interest Rate or Value at Maturity	Name of Institution

    Form 54

RECORD OF MUTUAL FUND INVESTMENTS

Date of Record _____

Owner of Investment	Fund Group or Sponsor	Name of Fund	Listed Newspaper Symbol	Fund Objectives	Account & Fund Number	Date Account Opened or Purchase Date	Initial Dollar Amount Invested	Opening Share Balance	Initial Price per Share

Form 55

ANNUAL ACCOUNT HISTORY
INDIVIDUAL MUTUAL FUND INVESTMENTS

Date of Record _____

Owner of Investment _____

Name of Fund Group/Sponsor _____

Date Account Opened _____

Name of Fund _____

Listed Newspaper Symbol _____

Account & Fund Number _____

Investment Firm _____

Current Year	Dec. 31 Selling Price	Dollar Purchases Year To Date	Dollar Amount Sold/Redeemed Year To Date	Cumulative Dollars Invested	Cumulative Share Purchases	Cumulative Fund Shares	Dec 31 Market Value	Cumulative Profit or Loss

Form 56

INVESTMENT RECORD OF STOCKS, BONDS, AND ANNUITIES

Date of Record _____

Owner of Investment or Annuity	Name of Company	Type of Investment or Annuity	Account Number	Certificate Number	Date Account Opened or Purchase Date	Unit Price or Price Per Share	Number of Shares or Units Purchased	Dollar Amount Invested

ACCOUNT HISTORY OF INDIVIDUAL
STOCK, BOND, AND ANNUITY INVESTMENTS

Date of Record _____

Owner of Investment _____

Company _____

Date Account Opened _____

Name of Investment _____

Account Number _____

Certificate Number _____

Listed Newspaper Symbol _____

Date of Transaction	Dollar Amount This Transaction	Purchase Price Per Share	Number of Shares Purchased or Sold	Dollar Amount Received Or Reinvested Dividends/ Cap Gains	Shares Obtained By Reinvested Dividends/ Cap Gains	Cumulative Dollars Invested To Date	Cumulative Shares Owned To Date	Selling Price Per Share	Market Value of Account

 Form 58

TAX-FAVORED INVESTMENTS

Date of Record _____

Owner of Investment	Investment Description	Year Purchased	Dollar Amount Invested	Expected Annual Deductions or Depreciation	Present Value (If Known)	Annual Income Expected

Form 59

285

REAL ESTATE INVESTMENTS

Date of Record _____

Owner of Investment	Description of Property (General/Legal)	Cost Basis	Remaining Mortgage	Current Market Value	Purpose or Use of Property	Annual Expenses & Depreciation	Annual Income Produced	Notes/Comments Regarding Property

PERSONAL NETWORTH STATEMENT WORKSHEET

Liquid Assets

Cash $ _____

Checking Accounts   _____

Savings Accounts   _____

Money Market Funds   _____

Credit Union Accounts   _____

_____   _____

_____   _____

_____   _____

Total Liquid Assets $ _____

Investment Assets

Stocks, Bonds $ _____

Institution Securities   _____

Mutual Funds   _____

Government Securities   _____

Real Estate   _____

Business Interests   _____

Limited Partnerships   _____

_____   _____

_____   _____

Total Investment Assets $ _____

Property Assets

Home $ _____

Other Real Estate   _____

Vehicles   _____

Furniture   _____

Personal Items   _____

Antiques, Collectibles   _____

_____   _____

_____   _____

Total Property Assets $ _____

PERSONAL NETWORTH STATEMENT WORKSHEET
(Continued)

Other Assets
IRA $ _____
Keogh   _____
Pension Plans   _____
Profit Sharing Plans   _____
Other Retirement Plans   _____
Trust Assets   _____

_____   _____
_____   _____

Total 'Other' Assets $ _____

TOTAL ASSETS $ _____

Liabilities
Home Mortgage $ _____
Other Mortgages   _____
Credit Card Debt   _____
Charge Accounts   _____
Life Insurance Loans   _____
Auto Loans   _____
Other Personal Loans   _____
Outstanding Bills   _____
Tax Liabilities   _____

_____   _____
_____   _____

TOTAL LIABILITIES $ _____

PERSONAL NETWORTH $ _____
   (Total Assets - Total Liabilities)

Date information is updated. _____

                     Form 62

CASH-FLOW STATEMENT WORKSHEET

Sources of Income	(_____)	(_____)	(_____)
Salary, Commissions	$ _____	$ _____	$ _____
_____	_____	_____	_____
_____	_____	_____	_____
TOTAL GROSS INCOME	$ _____	$ _____	$ _____
Less Deductions			
Federal Taxes	$ _____	$ _____	$ _____
State, Local Taxes	_____	_____	_____
FICA	_____	_____	_____
Retirement, Pension	_____	_____	_____
_____	_____	_____	_____
_____	_____	_____	_____
_____	_____	_____	_____
TOTAL DEDUCTIONS	$ _____	$ _____	$ _____
NET SPENDABLE INCOME (Gross Income - Deductions)	$ _____	$ _____	$ _____

	Current Money Spent	**Current Money Spent**	**Current Money Spent**
Housing			
Mortgage, Rent	$ _____	$ _____	$ _____
House Insurance	_____	_____	_____
Gas, Electric Utilities	_____	_____	_____
Water, Sanitation, Trash	_____	_____	_____
Telephone	_____	_____	_____
Property Taxes	_____	_____	_____
_____	_____	_____	_____
_____	_____	_____	_____
_____	_____	_____	_____
_____	_____	_____	_____
_____	_____	_____	_____
Total Housing	$ _____	$ _____	$ _____

Form 63

CASH-FLOW STATEMENT WORKSHEET
Page 2

	Current Money Spent	Current Money Spent	Current Money Spent
Food			
Food, Groceries	$ _____	$ _____	$ _____
Household Supplies	_____	_____	_____
Total Food	$ _____	$ _____	$ _____
Transportation			
Vehicle(s) Payments	$ _____	$ _____	$ _____
Vehicle(s) Insurance	_____	_____	_____
Gas	_____	_____	_____
Oil, Lube	_____	_____	_____
_____	_____	_____	_____
_____	_____	_____	_____
_____			
Total Transportation	$ _____	$ _____	$ _____
Installment Debt			
Credit Card(s)	$ _____	$ _____	$ _____
Loan(s) Payments	_____	_____	_____
_____	_____	_____	_____
Total Installment Debt	$ _____	$ _____	$ _____
Insurance			
Medical, Health	$ _____	$ _____	$ _____
Dental Insurance	_____	_____	_____
Life Insurance	_____	_____	_____
Disability Income Insurance	_____	_____	_____
_____	_____	_____	_____
_____	_____	_____	_____
Total Insurance	$ _____	$ _____	$ _____

                    Form 64

CASH-FLOW STATEMENT WORKSHEET
Page 3

	Current Money Spent	Current Money Spent	Current Money Spent
Health Care			
Doctor	$ _____	$ _____	$ _____
Dentist, Orthodontist	_____	_____	_____
Medicine, Prescriptions	_____	_____	_____
_____	_____	_____	_____
_____	_____	_____	_____
Total Health Care	$ _____	$ _____	$ _____
Clothing			
Purchases	$ _____	$ _____	$ _____
_____	_____	_____	_____
Total Clothing	$ _____	$ _____	$ _____
Entertainment			
Eating Out	$ _____	$ _____	$ _____
Sports, Concerts, Movies	_____	_____	_____
Family Recreation	_____	_____	_____
Travel, Vacation	_____	_____	_____
_____	_____	_____	_____
_____	_____	_____	_____
_____	_____	_____	_____
Total Entertainment	$ _____	$ _____	$ _____
Children Expenses			
Allowances	$ _____	$ _____	$ _____
_____	_____	_____	_____
_____	_____	_____	_____
_____	_____	_____	_____
Total Child. Expenses	$ _____	$ _____	$ _____

CASH-FLOW STATEMENT WORKSHEET

Page 4

	Current Money Spent	Current Money Spent	Current Money Spent
Personal Care			
Allowance (Wife)	$ _____	$ _____	$ _____
Allowance (Husband)	_____	_____	_____
Personal Growth	_____	_____	_____
Newspapers, Subscriptions	_____	_____	_____
_____	_____	_____	_____
_____	_____	_____	_____
_____	_____	_____	_____
Total Personal Care	$ _____	$ _____	$ _____
Professional Services			
Attorney	$ _____	$ _____	$ _____
Accountant	_____	_____	_____
_____	_____	_____	_____
Total Prof. Services	$ _____	$ _____	$ _____
Education Expenses			
Tuition, Fees	$ _____	$ _____	$ _____
_____	_____	_____	_____
Total Educ. Expenses	$ _____	$ _____	$ _____
Gifts			
Christmas	$ _____	$ _____	$ _____
Birthdays	_____	_____	_____
_____	_____	_____	_____
Total Gifts	$ _____	$ _____	$ _____

Form 66

CASH-FLOW STATEMENT WORKSHEET
Page 5

	Current Money Spent	Current Money Spent	Current Money Spent
Replacement Accounts			
Medical, Dental	$ _____	$ _____	$ _____
Periodic Payments	_____	_____	_____
Automobile	_____	_____	_____
_____	_____	_____	_____
_____	_____	_____	_____
Total Replace. Acc'ts.	$ _____	$ _____	$ _____
Miscellaneous			
Toiletries, Cosmetics	$ _____	$ _____	$ _____
Hairdresser, Barber	_____	_____	_____
Charity, Contributions	_____	_____	_____
_____	_____	_____	_____
_____	_____	_____	_____
Total Miscellaneous	$ _____	$ _____	$ _____
Savings			
Cash Reserves	$ _____	$ _____	$ _____
Emergency Funds	_____	_____	_____
_____	_____	_____	_____
_____	_____	_____	_____
Total Savings	$ _____	$ _____	$ _____
Investments			
Short-Term	$ _____	$ _____	$ _____
Medium-Term	_____	_____	_____
Long-Term	_____	_____	_____
Total Investments	$ _____	$ _____	$ _____
TOTAL LIVING EXPENSES, SAVINGS, & INVESTMENTS	$ _____	$ _____	$ _____

CASH-FLOW SUPPLEMENT
Suggested Additions To Pages 289 - 293

Sources Of Income

Alimony
Annuity
Bonuses
Child support
Consultant fees, charges
Dividend, interest income
Government retirement benefits
Home employment (music lessons,
    arts, crafts, tutoring, etc.)
Income from investments

Insurance benefits
    (disability income, etc.)
Proceeds from the sale of a property
    or a business
Proceeds from the sale of securities
Rental income
Retirement plan distributions
Royalties
Social security
Unemployment Compensation

Less Deductions

Alimony
Business loans
Child support
Church, charity

Insurance benefits
Savings plans
Union, professional dues

Housing

Additional real estate
Appliance replacement
Furniture, home furnishings
Home improvements
Kitchen utensils, necessities
Landscaping

Maintenance
Major appliances
Repairs
Supplies
Umbrella liability insurance coverage

Food

Maintenance and general supplies

Transportation

License and taxes
Parking fees, tolls
Public transportation (bus, taxi,
    train fares, etc.)

Vehicle maintenance
Vehicle repairs
Vehicle replacement
Umbrella liability coverage

Insurance

Accident protection insurance
Business insurance

Credit card insurance
Medicare supplement insurance

                                    Form 68

CASH-FLOW SUPPLEMENT
Page 2

Insurance (Continued)
Mortgage insurance
Nursing home care insurance

Property, casualty insurance
(homeowners, vehicle)
Umbrella liability insurance

Installment Debt
Notes

Health Care
Hospital
Medical specialists

Medical supplies
Unexpected bills

Clothing
Cleaning

Specialty, uniforms

Entertainment
Boat, camper, airplane, etc.
Cable TV
Child care
Clubs (social, athletic, etc.)

Hobbies
Lottery, gambling, races, etc.
Special activities

Children
Camps, lessons, activities (music
dance, sports, church, summer,
scout, winter, etc.)
College savings programs

Day care (child care) service
Private, church schools
School lunches
Tuition, books, fees

Personal Care
Church, charity
Computer
Education, correspondence classes

Magazines, books
Music lessons, enrichment classes
Support, church groups

Professional Services
Book keeper
Financial planner (or consultant)

Estate planning attorney
Home, live-in assistance

Form 69

295

CASH-FLOW STATEMENT
Page 3

Education Expenses
    Miscellaneous expenses   Textbooks
    Room, board

Gifts
    Donations and charity   Special family holidays
    Organizations   Weddings, anniversaries
    Religious groups

Replacement Accounts
    Medical (prescriptions)

    Periodic payment accounts
        College tuition   School expenses
        Estimated taxes   Vacations
        Property taxes

    Automobile replacement

    Major appliance replacement
        Air conditioner   Stove
        Clothes dryer   Television
        Dishwasher   VCR, camcorder, camera
        Garbage disposal   Washer
        Refrigerator   Water softener

    Unusually high utility bills

Miscellaneous
    Pet, animal care   Petty cash

Savings
    Regular, day-to-day account   Retirement supplement
    Replacement accounts

Investments
    Short-term investments   Long-term investments
        (usually 1 year or less)   (usually 7 years or longer)

    Medium-term investments
        (usually 1 to 6 or 7 years)

                                  Form 70

MONTHLY INCOME
PIE CHART

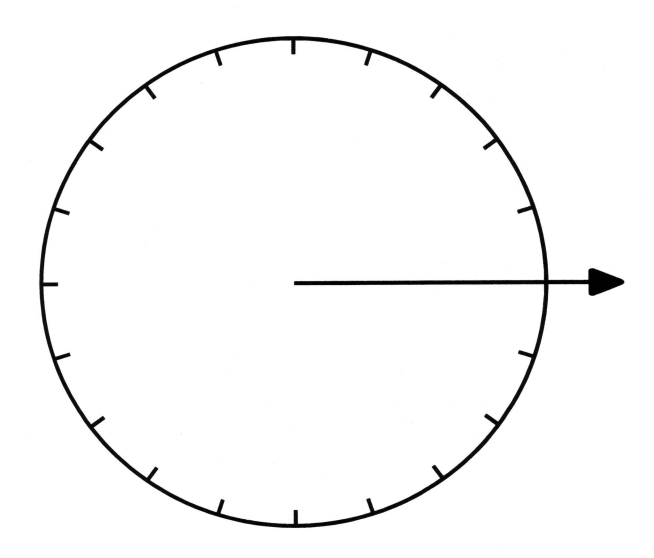

MONTHLY EXPENSES
PIE CHART

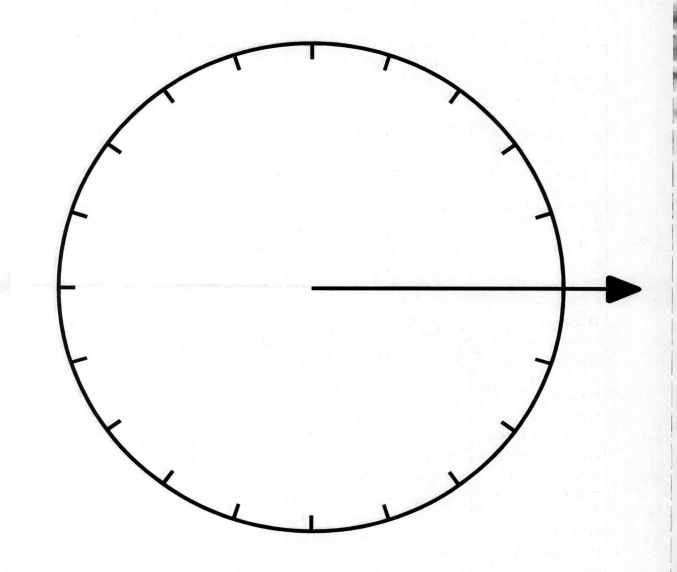

                                    Form 72

BUDGET PLANNING WORKSHEET

				Current Budget	
Monthly Payment Category	**Current Budget (Dollars)**	**Current Budget (Percent)**	**Proposed Monthly Budget**	**Minus Proposed Budget**	**Revised Monthly Budget**

1 Monthly Income	$ _____				
Deductions					
2 Federal Taxes	$ _____	_____ %	$ _____	$ _____	$ _____
3 State/Local Taxes	_____	_____	_____	_____	_____
4 FICA	_____	_____	_____	_____	_____
5 Retirement/Pension	_____	_____	_____	_____	_____
6 _____	_____	_____	_____	_____	_____
7 **Total Deductions**	$ _____	_____ %	$ _____	$ _____	$ _____
8 **Net Spendable Income** (per month)	$ _____	_____ %	$ _____	$ _____	$ _____
9 Housing	$ _____	_____ %	$ _____	$ _____	$ _____
10 Food	_____	_____	_____	_____	_____
11 Transportation	_____	_____	_____	_____	_____
12 Installment Debt	_____	_____	_____	_____	_____
13 Insurance	_____	_____	_____	_____	_____
14 Health Care	_____	_____	_____	_____	_____
15 Clothing	_____	_____	_____	_____	_____
16 Entertainment	_____	_____	_____	_____	_____
17 Children	_____	_____	_____	_____	_____
18 Personal Care	_____	_____	_____	_____	_____
19 Professional Services	_____	_____	_____	_____	_____
20 Education Expenses	_____	_____	_____	_____	_____
21 Gifts	_____	_____	_____	_____	_____
22 Replacement Accounts	_____	_____	_____	_____	_____
23 Miscellaneous	_____	_____	_____	_____	_____
24 Savings	_____	_____	_____	_____	_____
25 Investments	_____	_____	_____	_____	_____
26 _____	_____	_____	_____	_____	_____
27 _____	_____	_____	_____	_____	_____
28 **Total Expenses**	$ _____	_____ %	$ _____	$ _____	$ _____
29 **Net Spendable Income**	$ _____	_____ %	$ _____	$ _____	$ _____
30 **Monthly Profit or Loss**	$ _____	_____ %	$ _____	$ _____	$ _____

Form 73

INCOME ALLOCATION WORKSHEET

		MONTHLY OR WEEKLY PAY PERIOD			
		Week 1	Week 2	Week 3	Week 4
1 Monthly Income	$ _____	$ _____	$ _____	$ _____	$ _____
Category	**Allocation Amount**	**Week 1**	**Week 2**	**Week 3**	**Week 4**
Deductions					
2 Federal Taxes	$ _____	$ _____	$ _____	$ _____	$ _____
3 State/Local Taxes	_____	_____	_____	_____	_____
4 FICA	_____	_____	_____	_____	_____
5 Retirement/Pension	_____	_____	_____	_____	_____
6 _____	_____	_____	_____	_____	_____
7 Total Deductions	$ _____	$ _____	$ _____	$ _____	$ _____
8 Net Spendable Income (per month)	$ _____	$ _____	$ _____	$ _____	$ _____
9 Housing	$ _____	$ _____	$ _____	$ _____	$ _____
10 Food	_____	_____	_____	_____	_____
11 Transportation	_____	_____	_____	_____	_____
12 Installment Debt	_____	_____	_____	_____	_____
13 Insurance	_____	_____	_____	_____	_____
14 Health Care	_____	_____	_____	_____	_____
15 Clothing	_____	_____	_____	_____	_____
16 Entertainment	_____	_____	_____	_____	_____
17 Children	_____	_____	_____	_____	_____
18 Personal Care	_____	_____	_____	_____	_____
19 Professional Services	_____	_____	_____	_____	_____
20 Education Expenses	_____	_____	_____	_____	_____
21 Gifts	_____	_____	_____	_____	_____
22 Replacement Accounts	_____	_____	_____	_____	_____
23 Miscellaneous	_____	_____	_____	_____	_____
24 Savings	_____	_____	_____	_____	_____
25 Investments	_____	_____	_____	_____	_____
26 _____	_____	_____	_____	_____	_____
27 _____	_____	_____	_____	_____	_____
28 Total Expenses	$ _____	$ _____	$ _____	$ _____	$ _____
29 Net Spendable Income	$ _____	$ _____	$ _____	$ _____	$ _____
30 Monthly Profit or Loss	$ _____	$ _____	$ _____	$ _____	$ _____

Form 74

ACCOUNT SUMMARY

ACCOUNT CATEGORY		MONTHLY ALLOCATED AMOUNT $

Date	Transaction Item	Payment/ Withdrawal (-)	Deposit/ Credit (+)	Account Balance
——	————	———	———	———	——	———	——	———	——
——	————	———	———	———	——	———	——	———	——
——	————	———	———	———	——	———	——	———	——
——	————	———	———	———	——	———	——	———	——
——	————	———	———	———	——	———	——	———	——
——	————	———	———	———	——	———	——	———	——
——	————	———	———	———	——	———	——	———	——
——	————	———	———	———	——	———	——	———	——
——	————	———	———	———	——	———	——	———	——
——	————	———	———	———	——	———	——	———	——
——	————	———	———	———	——	———	——	———	——
——	————	———	———	———	——	———	——	———	——
——	————	———	———	———	——	———	——	———	——
——	————	———	———	———	——	———	——	———	——
——	————	———	———	———	——	———	——	———	——
——	————	———	———	———	——	———	——	———	——
——	————	———	———	———	——	———	——	———	——
——	————	———	———	———	——	———	——	———	——
——	————	———	———	———	——	———	——	———	——
——	————	———	———	———	——	———	——	———	——
——	————	———	———	———	——	———	——	———	——
——	————	———	———	———	——	———	——	———	——
——	————	———	———	———	——	———	——	———	——

Form 75

ALLOCATED SAVINGS ACCOUNT

Page 1

Date	Balance	Housing	Food	Transportation	Install. Debt	Insurance	Health Care	Clothing

                    Form 76

ALLOCATED SAVINGS ACCOUNT
Page 2

Entertainment	Personal Care	Replacement				

CHECKBOOK REGISTER

RECORD ALL CHARGES OR CREDITS THAT AFFECT YOUR ACCOUNT

CHECK NUMBER	DATE	TRANSACTION DESCRIPTION	PAYMENT/ WITHDRAWAL (-)	✓ T	BUD-GET CODE	DEPOSIT/ CREDIT (+)	$	BALANCE

          Form 78

CHECKBOOK SAVINGS RECORD

	PERSONAL SAVINGS ACCOUNT RECORD				BALANCE
DATE	EXPLANATION	WITHDRAWAL (-)	DEPOSIT (+)	INTEREST (+)	$
		$	$	$	

Form 79

1996 by John M. Orth, Iowa City, IA. 305

AUTOMATIC PAYMENT/DEPOSIT REMINDER

	Remember to add to your account balance any automatic deposits on the date the deposit is made.			Remember to deduct from your account balance each month any automatic transfer payments you have authorized.	
DATE	AUTOMATIC DEPOSIT	AMOUNT	DATE	AUTOMATIC PAYMENT	AMOUNT
		$			$

  Form 80

CREDIT CARD INVENTORY

Date of Record _____

Name(s) of Card Holder	Name of Company	Card Number	Date Card Obtained	Credit Limit	Type/Amount Fee	Company Address	Telephone Number

CREDIT CARD OBLIGATIONS

Date of Record _____

Name of Finance Company	Telephone Number	Budget Category & Description	Remaining Payoff Amount	Number Remaining Payments	Current Monthly Payment	Date Payment Made

Form 82

CREDIT CARD ACCOUNT FORM

Date of Record _____

Name of Finance Company _____

Date	Item or Expense Charged	Budget Code	Monthly Payment	Charged Amount	Principal Applied	Finance Charge	Credit Balance
	Totals						

CREDIT CARD ACCOUNT WORKSHEET

Date of Record _____

Name of Finance Company _____

Date	Previous Remaining Balance		Finance Charge (%)	Monthly Payment		Finance Charge Amount		Principal Applied Amount		New Remaining Balance
		x			= .		= .		=	
		x			= .		= .		=	
		x			= .		= .		=	
		x			= .		= .		=	
		x			= .		= .		=	
		x			= .		= .		=	

Form 84

CREDIT AND LOAN SUMMARY WORKSHEET

Name of Creditor or Finance Company	Date of Last Payment	Annual Finance Rate	Monthly Payment Amount	Remaining Card Balance
Total Monthly Payments			$	
Total Of Outstanding Loans				$
Monthly Family Take-Home (Net) Pay			$	
Percent Of Debt Obligation				%

STEPS TO IDENTIFY FINANCIAL PROBLEMS

1. Define the problem as you <u>now</u> perceive it. Be specific and list only one problem at a time.

   _____

   _____

   _____

2. List ways you believe the problem can be solved. Write down all possible solutions that come to mind. Do not make a value judgment at this time.

   _____

   _____

   _____

3. Evaluate each of the solutions you listed in step 2.

   _____

   _____

   _____

   Are the solutions workable, practical, and agreeable to everyone involved? Can you combine alternatives?

   _____

   _____

4. Now, select <u>one</u> desired solution. Outline the steps.

   _____

   _____

   _____

5. List any obstacles that might prevent you from solving the problem. What sacrifices are you willing to make in order to reach a solution that will be agreed to by each person involved? What outside support do you need to reach a final consensus?

   _____

   _____

   _____

                    Form 86

FINANCIAL DEBTS WORKSHEET

Item or Service	Debt Amount	Debt + Interest (Finance Charge)	Interest (Finance) Rate

DEBT REDUCTION WORKSHEET
ROLL-OVER METHOD

Date Month/Year	Debt 1 ______ ($______)	Debt 2 ______ ($______)	Debt 3 ______ ($______)	Debt 4 ______ ($______)	Debt 5 ______ ($______)	Debt 6 ______ ($______)	Total Monthly Payment
______	______	______	______	______	______	______	______
______	______	______	______	______	______	______	______
______	______	______	______	______	______	______	______
______	______	______	______	______	______	______	______
______	______	______	______	______	______	______	______
______	______	______	______	______	______	______	______
______	______	______	______	______	______	______	______
______	______	______	______	______	______	______	______
______	______	______	______	______	______	______	______
______	______	______	______	______	______	______	______
______	______	______	______	______	______	______	______
______	______	______	______	______	______	______	______
______	______	______	______	______	______	______	______
______	______	______	______	______	______	______	______
______	______	______	______	______	______	______	______
______	______	______	______	______	______	______	______
______	______	______	______	______	______	______	______
______	______	______	______	______	______	______	______
______	______	______	______	______	______	______	______
______	______	______	______	______	______	______	______
______	______	______	______	______	______	______	______
______	______	______	______	______	______	______	______
______	______	______	______	______	______	______	______
______	______	______	______	______	______	______	______
______	______	______	______	______	______	______	______
______	______	______	______	______	______	______	______
______	______	______	______	______	______	______	______
______	______	______	______	______	______	______	______
______	______	______	______	______	______	______	______
______	______	______	______	______	______	______	______
______	______	______	______	______	______	______	______
______	______	______	______	______	______	______	______
______	______	______	______	______	______	______	______
______	______	______	______	______	______	______	______
______	______	______	______	______	______	______	______
______	______	______	______	______	______	______	______

DEBT PAYMENT OPTIONS
PERCENT OF TOTAL DEBT

Debt	Individual Debt	Percent of Total Debt	Original Monthly Payment	Adjusted Payment

DEBT PAYMENT OPTIONS
PRO-RATED PERCENT

Debt	Individual Debt	Original Monthly Payment	Pro-rated Share	Adjusted Payment	Number of Adjusted Payments

Form 90

DEBT PAYMENT OPTIONS
ADJUSTED PER NUMBER OF CREDITORS

Debt	Individual Debt	Original Monthly Payment	Adjusted Monthly Payment	Number of Adjusted Payments

Form 91

INSURANCE NEEDS ANALYSIS

Insurance Needs For	Age	Date
_____	_____	_____

1. **Capital Needs**
   A. Death Expenses
   1. Funeral, burial costs .... $ _____
   2. Medical expenses not covered by insurance .... _____
   3. Estate, inheritance taxes .... _____
   4. Attorney, court fees .... _____
   Total Death Expenses .... $ _____
   (1)

   B. Liabilities
   1. Home mortgage balance .... $ _____
   2. Installment debt .... _____
   3. Personal loans .... _____
   Total Liabilities .... $ _____
   (2)

   C. Future Obligations
   1. Children's education fund .... $ _____
   2. Emergency fund .... _____
   3. Short-term income (6 months) .... _____
   4. Other _____ .... _____
   Total Future Obligations .... $ _____
   (3)

   Total Capital Needs .... $ _____
   (Add lines 1, 2, & 3)   (4)

                    Form 92

INSURANCE NEEDS ANALYSIS

Page 2

2. Available Capital	
A. Liquid Assets	
1. Checking account(s)	$ _____
2. Savings, money market account(s)	_____
3. Certificates of deposit	_____
4. Other _____	_____
Total Liquid Assets	$ _____
	(5)
B. Investible Assets	
1. Stocks	$ _____
2. Bonds	_____
3. Mutual funds	_____
4. Other _____	_____
Total Investible Assets	$ _____
	(6)
C. Employee Benefit Proceeds	
(Include "lump sum" payments only)	
1. Company insurance	$ _____
2. Retirement program death benefit	_____
Total Employee Benefit Proceeds	$ _____
	(7)
D. Other Assets	
(Include "lump sum" payments only)	
1. IRA, TSA, 401(k), Keogh, etc.	$ _____
2. Current personal insurance	_____
3. Other _____	_____
Total 'Other' Assets	$ _____
	(8)
Total Available Capital	$ _____
(Add lines 5, 6, 7, & 8)	(9)

INSURANCE NEEDS ANALYSIS
Page 3

3. **Care Of Survivors**
   A. **Annual Income Needs**
      (General rule: Approximately 75% of take home pay)
      1. Spouse $ _____
      2. Children   _____
      3. Parent(s)   _____
      Total Annual Survivor Needs $ _____
                                                                     (10)

   B. **Annual Income of Survivors**
      1. Spouse's income $ _____
      2. Social security survivors' benefits   _____
      3. Current investment income   _____
      4. Survivors' benefit from retirement programs
         (Include payments in "installments" only)   _____
      5. Other income _____
      Total Annual Survivors' Income $ _____
                                                                     (11)

4. **Calculations To Determine Life Insurance Needs**
   A. **Net Capital Required** $ _____
      (Line 4 - line 9)   (12)

   B. **Net Annual Income Needs** $ _____
      (Line 10 - line 11)   (13)

   C. **Rate Of Investment Return You Expect After
      Taxes**   _____ %
                                                                     (14)

   D. **Additional Capital Required** $ _____
      (Divide line 13 by the rate of investment return   (15)
      on line 14)

   E. **Estimated Insurance Needs** $ _____
      (Add line 12 + line 15)   (16)

                                    Form 94

EDUCATION NEEDS ANALYSIS

Education Needs For	Age	Date
_____	_____	_____

1.	Number of years before child enters college	_____
2.	Current annual cost of selected college	$ _____
3.	Annual inflation rate for selected college	_____ %
4.	Inflation factor from the Cost of Living Adjustment table (Use Cost of Living Adjustment (COLA) table on page 351)	_____ %
5.	Approximate cost for child's first year of college (Multiply line 2 x line 4)	$ _____
6.	Multiplication factor for annual college cost increases (See explanation on page 195)	_____
7.	Approximate cost for child's second year of college (Multiply line 5 x line 6)	$ _____
8.	Approximate cost for child's third year of college (Multiply line 7 x line 6)	$ _____
9.	Approximate cost for child's fourth year of college (Multiply line 8 x line 6)	$ _____
10.	Approximate cost for each additional year of college (Continue as in line 9)	$ _____
11.	Approximate cost for child's education (Add lines 5, 7, 8, 9, & 10)	$ _____
12.	Current value of education savings and investments	$ _____
13.	Remaining education funds required (Line 11 - line 12)	$ _____
14.	Number of years to complete college investments (See explanation on page 196)	_____
15.	Investment rate of return you expect after taxes	_____ %
16.	Savings factor necessary to produce the required capital (Use the Annual Savings Accumulation table on page 352)	_____
17.	Annual savings required to achieve college funding (Multiply line 13 x line 16)	$ _____
18.	Monthly savings required to achieve college funding (Divide line 17 by 12)	$ _____

Form 95

321

RETIREMENT INCOME NEEDS ANALYSIS

Retirement Income Needs For	Age	Date
_____	_____	_____

1. **General Retirement Information**
   A. Current family salary(ies) $ _____
   B. Desired annual income at retirement $ _____
      (Usually 70 - 80% of current take-home pay)
   C. Number of years until retirement   _____
   D. Age to which retirement income must continue <u>before</u>
      beginning to consume assets   _____
   E. Number of years to age on line 1D   _____
   F. Projected annual increase in the cost of living (inflation)
      until retirement   _____ %
   G. Inflation factor from the Cost of Living Adjustment
      (COLA) table   _____
      (See explanation on pages 13 - 14)
   H. Future annual needs in today's dollars $ _____
      (Multiply line 1B x line 1G)

2. **Projected Annual Retirement Benefits**
   A. Estimated annual social security benefits $ _____
      (Contact the Social Security Administration for an
      "Earnings and Benefit Estimate Statement")
   B. Estimated annual company pension or retirement plan
      in today's dollars $ _____
      (Contact employee benefits office or human relations
      department for this information)
   C. Total projected <u>annual</u> retirement benefits $ _____
      (Add lines 2A + 2B)
   D. Annual income required from savings, investments, and
      other sources at retirement $ _____
      (Subtract line 1H - line 2C)

      Form 96

RETIREMENT INCOME NEEDS ANALYSIS
Page 2

3. Investment Capital Necessary For Desired Income At Retirement	
A. Projected "average" rate of annual return on retirement investments (Investments include: IRA's, TSA's, 401(k's), SEP's, etc.)	_____ %
B. Capital sum in today's dollars required to produce the annual income desired on line 2D (Divide line 2D by line 3A)	$ _____
C. Estimated value in today's dollars employee pension (or retirement) fund to be received as a <u>lump</u> <u>sum</u> distribution at retirement (Contact employee benefit's office for this information)	$ _____
D. Current value of investments and savings designated for retirement	$ _____
E. Current value of IRA's	$ _____
F. Current value of employee supplemental retirement plans	$ _____
G. Total current value of investment programs for retirement funding (Add lines 3D, 3E, & 3F)	$ _____
H. Investment growth factor from the Cost of Living Adjustment (COLA) table (Use line for 1C and column for 3A)	_____
I. Future value of investment capital (line 3G) in today's dollars (Multiply line 3G x line 3H)	$ _____
J. Additional capital to be accumulated during the next _____ (line 1C) years until retirement (Line 3B - line 3C - line 3I)	$ _____

Form 97

RETIREMENT INCOME NEEDS ANALYSIS
Page 3

<table>
<tr>
<td>

4. Savings Program To Accumulate Necessary Capital

  A. Savings factor from the Annual Savings Accumulation table to produce the required capital
(Use the Annual Savings Accumulation table on page 352. See explanation on pages 14 - 15)

★ B. Capital to be invested annually for _____ (line 1C) years until retirement
(Multiply line 3J x line 4A)

  C. Monthly investment required to reach desired goal
(Divide line 4B by 12)

  D. Weekly investment required to reach desired goal
(Divide line 4B by 52)

</td>
<td>

_____

$ _____

$ _____

$ _____

</td>
</tr>
</table>

★ The value on this line is the **projected** annual investment necessary to produce the desired retirement income until the indicated age on line 1D without the consumption of capital assets **provided** the other values in this analysis are accurate.

                                      Form 98

INCOME TAX RECORD FORM
W-2 WAGE AND TAX STATEMENT

Employer _____

Employer's Tax Identification Number _____

Employee's Social Security Number _____

Pay Period _____ (Weekly, Bi-Weekly, Monthly)

(1) Wages, Tips, etc.	(2) Federal Income Tax Withheld	(3) Social Security Wages	(4) Social Security Tax Withheld	(5) Medicare Wages	(6) Medicare Tax Withheld	(10) Dependent Care Benefits	(11) Non-Qualified Plans	(12) Benefits Included In Box 1	(17) State Wages	(18) State Income Tax Withheld	(21) Local Income Tax Withheld

Form 99

325

INCOME TAX RECORD FORM
1099 - MISCELLANEOUS EARNINGS

Payer _____

Recipient's Identification Number _____

Payer's Tax Identification Number _____

Pay Period _____ (Weekly, BiWeekly, Monthly)

(1) Rents	(2) Royalties	(3) Other Income	(4) Federal Income Tax Withheld	(5) Fishing Boat Proceeds	(6) Medical Health Care Payments	(7) Non-Employee Compensation	(8) Substitute Payments	(10) Crop Insurance Proceeds	(11) State Income Tax Withheld

Form 100

INCOME TAX RECORD FORM
REPORTING OF INTEREST

★ Type of interest key. Use one of the letters below for identifying each of your reported interest income amounts.

R - Regular interest
E - Nontaxable interest (Both Federal and State)
F - Taxable: Federal, Tax-Free: State
(Examples: US Savings Bonds, Federal Obligations)
T - Tax-Free: Federal, Taxable: State
S - Seller financed mortgage
N - Nominee
O - Original issue discount
K - K-1 investment interest

Name of Individual	Payer's Name	★ Type of Interest	Total Interest Amount	OID/ US Savings Adjustment

Form 101

INCOME TAX RECORD FORM
REPORTING OF DIVIDENDS

Name Of Individual	Name Of Fund Or Security	(1a) Gross Dividends & Other Distributions On Stock	(1b) Ordinary Dividends	(1c) Capital Gain Distributions	(1d) Nontaxable Distributions	(2) Federal Income Tax Withheld	(3) Foreign Tax Paid

Form 102

INCOME TAX RECORD FORM
EXPENSE WORKSHEET

TAXES PAID				LICENSE FEES			
Name of Payor	Date Paid	Type of Tax	Amount Paid	Name of Payor	Date Paid	Type of Fee	Amount Paid

Form 103

INCOME TAX RECORD FORM
EXPENSE WORKSHEET

CONTRIBUTIONS				HOME MORTGAGE INTEREST & POINTS			
Name of Donor	Date Paid	To Whom	Amount Paid	Name of Payor	Date Paid	Interest or Points	Amount Paid

                                                                                          Form 104

INCOME TAX RECORD FORM
EXPENSE WORKSHEET

UNREIMBURSED EMPLOYEE EXPENSES				REIMBURSED INSURANCE BENEFITS			
Name	Date Paid	Type of Expense	Amount Paid	Name	Date Received	Type of Benefit	Amount Received

Form 105

331

INCOME TAX RECORD FORM
EXPENSE WORKSHEET

Name	Date Paid	Description	Amount Paid	Name	Date Paid	Description	Amount Paid

Form 106

INCOME TAX RECORD FORM
MEDICAL EXPENSE WORKSHEET

PHYSICIANS, DENTISTS, CHIROPRACTORS, ETC.

Patient Name	Date of Service	Clinic or Physician	Service or Diagnosis	Amount Charged to Patient	Patient Expense	Date Patient Paid	Amount of Insurance Benefit	Date Benefit Received

Form 107

333

INCOME TAX RECORD FORM
MEDICAL EXPENSE WORKSHEET

HOSPITAL OR CLINIC

Patient Name	Date of Service	Hospital or Clinic	Service or Diagnosis	Amount Charged to Patient	Patient Expense	Date Patient Paid	Amount of Insurance Benefit	Date Benefit Received

Form 108

INCOME TAX RECORD FORM
MEDICAL EXPENSE WORKSHEET

LABORATORY AND X-RAYS

Patient Name	Date of Service	Hospital or Clinic	Service or Diagnosis	Amount Charged to Patient	Patient Expense	Date Patient Paid	Amount of Insurance Benefit	Date Benefit Received

Form 109

335

INCOME TAX RECORD FORM
MEDICAL EXPENSE WORKSHEET

MEDICAL SUPPLIES AND EQUIPMENT

Patient Name	Date of Purchase	Supply Company	Type of Equipment	Amount Charged to Patient	Patient Expense	Date Patient Paid	Amount of Insurance Benefit	Date Benefit Received

Form 110

INCOME TAX RECORD FORM
MEDICAL EXPENSE WORKSHEET

PRESCRIPTION DRUGS - MEDICINE

Patient Name	Date of Service	Name of Pharmacy	Item Purchased	Amount Charged to Patient	Patient Expense	Date Patient Paid	Amount of Insurance Benefit	Date Benefit Received

Form 111

INCOME TAX RECORD FORM
MEDICAL EXPENSE WORKSHEET

MEDICAL & DENTAL INSURANCE PREMIUMS				
Premium Payor	Name of Company	Person(s) Covered	Premium Amount	Date Paid

                   Form 112

FARM CROP REPORT

Farm Size _____

Date of Record _____

CROP PLANTED _____

Landlord _____

Tenant _____

Crop Year	Acres Planted		Production - Bushels		Yield Bu./Acre	Landlord's Share				
	Farm Total	Landlord's	Farm Total	Landlord's		Average Bu./Acre	Sold ($)	Stored	Gov't Program	Insurance Payments

FARM EXPENSES

Farm Size _____

Date of Record _____

Landlord _____

Tenant _____

Item	Variety	Number Units	Unit Price	Total Cost	Landlord's Share	Tenant's Share	Dealer/ Supplier	Statement Date	Paid Date

    Form 114

INCOME TAX RECORD FORM
4835 - FARM RENTAL INCOME & EXPENSES

INCOME

Item	Amount	Item	Amount
Livestock		Commodity Credit Corp. Payments	
Produce		Dairy Products	
Grain		Deferred Payments (Prior Year)	
Crop Insurance/Disaster Payments		_____	
_____		Total Income	

EXPENSES

Item	Amount	Item	Amount
Car & Truck Expenses		Labor Hired	
Check Off Expenses		Management Fees	
Chemicals		Pension & Profit Sharing Plans	
Conservation Expenses		Rent Or Lease	
Custom Hire		Repairs & Maintenance	
Depreciation/Section 179		Seeds & Plants Purchased	
Drainage & Tile Assessments		Storage & Warehousing	
Drying Charges		Supplies Purchased	
Employee Benefit Programs		Taxes	
Feed Purchased		Test Weight Charges	
Fertilizers & Lime		Travel Mileage	
Freight & Trucking		Utilities	
Gasoline, Fuel, & Oil		Veterinary, Breeding, & Medicine	
Insurance (Other Than Health)		_____	
Interest		_____	
Column Expense Total		Column Expense Total	
Total Expenses			

MONTHLY RETIREMENT INCOME

Month	Husband ------- Wife	Employee Pension Payment	Social Security Payment	IRA, TSA, Keogh, etc. Distribution	_____	_____	Total Taxes Paid Or Withheld	Net Monthly Income
Jan								
Feb								
Mar								
Apr								
May								
June								
July								
Aug								
Sept								
Oct								
Nov								
Dec								
Total								

          Form 116

INCOME TAX RECORD FORM
1099 - R DISTRIBUTIONS FROM PENSIONS,
ANNUITIES, RETIREMENT, PROFIT SHARING PLANS, IRA'S, etc.

Name of Payer _____

Payer's Federal Identification Number _____

Recipient's Identification Number _____

Distribution Code _____

Distribution Period _____

IRA/SEP _____

(1) Gross Distribution	(2) Taxable Amount	(4) Federal Income Tax Withheld	(10) State Income Tax Withheld	(12) Local Income Tax Withheld

Form 117

343

_____

_____

Form 119

© 1996 by John M. Orth, Iowa City, IA. 345

Form 120

DAILY SCHEDULE

_____

TIME

TO CALL			

TO DO			

TO DO LIST

_____

Done ✔

1. _____ ☐

2. _____ ☐

3. _____ ☐

4. _____ ☐

5. _____ ☐

6. _____ ☐

7. _____ ☐

8. _____ ☐

9. _____ ☐

10. _____ ☐

11. _____ ☐

12. _____ ☐

                    Form 122

APPENDIX D

TABLES

FINANCIAL TABLES

COST OF LIVING ADJUSTMENT (COLA) TABLE

Years	3%	4%	5%	6%	7%	8%	9%	10%	12%	14%
2	1.061	1.082	1.103	1.124	1.145	1.166	1.188	1.210	1.254	1.300
3	1.093	1.125	1.158	1.191	1.225	1.260	1.295	1.331	1.405	1.482
4	1.126	1.170	1.216	1.262	1.311	1.360	1.412	1.464	1.574	1.689
5	1.159	1.217	1.276	1.338	1.403	1.469	1.539	1.611	1.762	1.925
6	1.194	1.265	1.340	1.419	1.501	1.587	1.677	1.772	1.974	2.195
7	1.230	1.316	1.407	1.504	1.606	1.714	1.828	1.949	2.211	2.502
8	1.267	1.369	1.477	1.594	1.718	1.851	1.993	2.144	2.476	2.853
9	1.305	1.423	1.551	1.689	1.838	1.999	2.172	2.358	2.773	3.252
10	1.344	1.480	1.629	1.791	1.967	2.159	2.367	2.594	3.106	3.707
11	1.384	1.539	1.710	1.898	2.105	2.332	2.580	2.853	3.479	4.226
12	1.426	1.601	1.796	2.012	2.252	2.518	2.813	3.138	3.896	4.818
13	1.469	1.665	1.886	2.133	2.410	2.720	3.066	3.452	4.363	5.492
14	1.513	1.732	1.980	2.261	2.579	2.937	3.342	3.797	4.887	6.261
15	1.558	1.801	2.079	2.397	2.759	3.172	3.642	4.177	5.474	7.138
16	1.605	1.873	2.183	2.540	2.952	3.426	3.970	4.595	6.130	8.137
17	1.653	1.948	2.292	2.693	3.159	3.700	4.328	5.054	6.866	9.276
18	1.702	2.026	2.407	2.854	3.380	3.996	4.717	5.560	7.690	10.575
19	1.754	2.107	2.527	3.026	3.617	4.316	5.142	6.116	8.613	12.056
20	1.806	2.191	2.653	3.207	3.870	4.661	5.604	6.727	9.646	13.743
25	2.094	2.666	3.386	4.292	5.427	6.848	8.623	10.835	17.000	26.462
30	2.427	3.243	4.322	5.743	7.612	10.063	13.268	17.449	29.960	50.950
35	2.814	3.946	5.516	7.686	10.677	14.785	20.414	28.102	52.800	98.100
40	3.262	4.801	7.040	10.286	14.974	21.725	31.409	45.259	93.051	188.884
45	3.782	5.841	8.985	13.765	21.002	31.920	48.327	72.890	163.988	363.679

Table 1

ANNUAL SAVINGS ACCUMULATION TABLE

Years	5%	6%	7%	8%	9%	10%	11%	12%	13%	14%	15%
2	0.488	0.485	0.483	0.481	0.478	0.476	0.474	0.472	0.469	0.467	0.465
3	0.317	0.314	0.311	0.308	0.305	0.302	0.299	0.296	0.294	0.291	0.288
4	0.232	0.229	0.225	0.222	0.219	0.215	0.212	0.209	0.206	0.203	0.200
5	0.181	0.177	0.174	0.170	0.167	0.164	0.161	0.157	0.154	0.151	0.148
6	0.147	0.143	0.140	0.136	0.133	0.130	0.126	0.123	0.120	0.117	0.114
7	0.123	0.119	0.116	0.112	0.109	0.105	0.102	0.099	0.096	0.093	0.090
8	0.105	0.101	0.097	0.094	0.091	0.087	0.084	0.081	0.078	0.076	0.073
9	0.091	0.087	0.083	0.080	0.077	0.074	0.071	0.068	0.065	0.062	0.060
10	0.080	0.076	0.072	0.069	0.066	0.063	0.060	0.057	0.054	0.052	0.049
11	0.070	0.067	0.063	0.060	0.057	0.054	0.051	0.048	0.046	0.043	0.041
12	0.063	0.059	0.056	0.053	0.050	0.047	0.044	0.041	0.039	0.037	0.034
13	0.056	0.053	0.050	0.047	0.044	0.041	0.038	0.036	0.033	0.0331	0.029
14	0.051	0.048	0.044	0.041	0.038	0.036	0.033	0.031	0.029	0.027	0.025
15	0.046	0.043	0.040	0.037	0.034	0.031	0.029	0.027	0.025	0.023	0.021
16	0.042	0.039	0.036	0.033	0.030	0.028	0.026	0.023	0.021	0.020	0.018
17	0.039	0.035	0.032	0.030	0.027	0.025	0.022	0.020	0.019	0.017	0.015
18	0.036	0.032	0.029	0.027	0.024	0.022	0.020	0.018	0.016	0.015	0.013
19	0.033	0.030	0.027	0.024	0.022	0.020	0.018	0.016	0.014	0.013	0.011
20	0.030	0.027	0.024	0.022	0.020	0.017	0.016	0.014	0.012	0.011	0.010
25	0.021	0.018	0.016	0.014	0.012	0.010	0.009	0.007	0.006	0.005	0.005
30	0.015	0.013	0.011	0.009	0.007	0.006	0.005	0.004	0.003	0.003	0.002
35	0.011	0.009	0.007	0.006	0.005	0.004	0.003	0.002	0.002	0.001	0.001
40	0.008	0.006	0.005	0.004	0.003	0.002	0.002	0.001	0.001	0.001	0.001
45	0.006	0.005	0.003	0.003	0.002	0.001	0.001	0.001	0.001	0.000	0.000

Table 2

DEBT RETIREMENT TABLE

Outstanding Debt	Annual Finance Rate	Approximate Monthly Payment Necessary To Retire Outstanding Debt In:									
		1 Year	2 Years	3 Years	4 Years	5 Years	6 Years	7 Years	8 Years	9 Years	10 Years
$ 500	10%	$ 43.96	$ 23.07	$ 16.13	$ 12.68	$ 10.62	$ 9.26	$ 8.30	$ 7.59	$ 7.04	$ 6.61
	12	44.42	23.54	16.61	13.17	11.12	9.78	8.83	8.13	7.59	7.17
	14	44.89	24.01	17.09	13.66	11.63	10.30	9.37	8.69	8.17	7.76
	16	45.37	24.48	17.58	14.17	12.16	10.85	9.93	9.26	8.76	8.38
	18	45.84	24.96	18.08	14.69	12.70	11.40	10.51	9.86	9.38	9.01
$ 1,000	10%	$ 87.92	$ 46.14	$ 32.27	$ 25.36	$ 21.25	$ 18.53	$ 16.60	$ 15.17	$ 14.08	$ 13.22
	12	88.85	47.07	33.21	26.33	22.24	19.55	17.65	16.25	15.18	14.35
	14	89.79	48.01	34.18	27.33	23.27	20.61	18.74	17.37	16.33	15.53
	16	90.73	48.96	35.16	28.34	24.32	21.69	19.86	18.53	17.53	16.75
	18	91.68	49.92	36.15	29.37	25.39	22.81	21.02	19.72	18.76	18.02
$ 3,000	10%	$ 263.75	$ 138.43	$ 96.80	$ 76.09	$ 63.74	$ 55.58	$ 49.80	$ 45.52	$ 42.24	$ 39.65
	12	266.55	141.22	99.64	79.00	66.73	58.65	52.96	48.76	45.55	43.04
	14	269.36	144.04	102.53	81.98	69.80	61.82	56.22	52.11	49.00	46.58
	16	272.19	146.89	105.47	85.02	72.95	65.08	59.59	55.59	52.58	50.25
	18	275.04	149.77	108.46	88.12	76.18	68.42	63.05	59.17	56.27	54.06
$ 5,000	10%	$ 439.58	$ 230.72	$ 161.34	$ 126.81	$ 106.24	$ 92.63	$ 83.01	$ 75.87	$ 70.39	$ 66.08
	12	444.24	235.37	166.07	131.67	111.22	97.75	88.26	81.26	75.92	71.74
	14	448.94	240.06	170.89	136.63	116.34	103.03	93.70	86.86	81.67	77.63
	16	453.65	244.82	175.79	141.70	121.59	108.46	99.31	92.64	87.63	83.76
	18	458.40	249.62	180.76	146.87	126.97	114.04	105.09	98.62	93.78	90.09
$ 7,500	10%	$ 659.37	$ 346.09	$ 242.00	$ 190.22	$ 159.35	$ 138.94	$ 124.51	$ 113.81	$ 105.59	$ 99.11
	12	666.37	353.05	249.11	197.50	166.83	146.63	132.40	121.90	113.88	107.60
	14	673.40	360.10	256.33	204.95	174.51	154.54	140.55	130.29	122.50	116.45
	16	680.48	367.22	263.68	212.55	182.39	162.69	148.97	138.97	131.44	125.63
	18	687.60	374.43	271.14	220.31	190.45	171.06	157.63	147.92	140.68	135.14

Table 3

APPENDIX E

ADDITIONAL RESOURCES

Applegarth, Virginia. How To Protect Your Family With Insurance. Boston: Houghton Mifflin Company, 1990.

Blue, Ronald W. Master Your Money: A Step-By-Step Plan For Financial Freedom. Nashville, Tennessee: Thomas Nelson, Inc., 1986.

Blue, Ronald W. And Judith W. Money Matters For Parents And Their Kids. Nashville, Tennessee: Thomas Nelson, Inc., 1988.

Burkett, Larry. The Complete Financial Guide For Single Parents. Wheaton, Illinois: Victor Books, 1991.

Burkett, Larry. The Complete Financial Guide For Young Couples. Wheaton, Illinois: Victor Books, 1989.

Dominguez, Joe And Vicki Robin. Your Money Or Your Life: Transforming Your Relationship With Money And Achieving Financial Independence. New York: Viking Penguin Books, Ltd., 1992.

Mason, Jerald W. The Easy Family Budget. Boston: Houghton Mifflin Company, 1990.

Tillman, Fred And Susan G. Parker. Your Will And Estate Planning. Boston: Houghton Company, 1990.

VanCaspel, Venita. Money Dynamics For The 1990s. New York: Simon And Schuster, Inc., 1988.

APPENDIX F

GLOSSARY

Annual	Occurring on a yearly basis.
Annual Percentage Rate (APR)	Yearly rate of interest paid by consumers; must be clearly disclosed to consumers in all loan agreements according to the Federal Truth In Lending Act.
Annuitant	A person who receives an annuity.
Annuitize	To begin receiving payments from your annuity; payments can be for a stated number of years or for the lifetime of the annuitant depending upon the option(s) selected.
Annuity	An investment contract, usually with an insurance company, that offers future payments to the holder of the contract at a future time.
Appreciation	The increase in value of an investment or asset.
Asset	All properties; total value of things we own.
Audit	An official examination and verification of financial records and accounts.
Automatic Teller Machines (ATM)	Also known as an instant access machine in which cash can be immediately withdrawn by using an appropriate bank card.
Average Daily Balance (ADB)	The method by which finance companies charge their customers interest; the average amount of money kept in a bank account on a monthly basis.
Balance Sheet	Systematic method of keeping a record showing an individual/company assets and liabilities posted at a definite time of the month.
Bank	A financial institution which loans, invests, saves, and exchanges money.
Bank Account	Money kept in a bank that can be deposited and withdrawn by the account holder.
Bankbook	A bank customer's book containing his/her deposits and withdrawals.
Bankcard	A credit card distributed by a bank.

Bankruptcy	Situation when an individual or business is unable to pay their debts.
Beneficiary	The individual, institution, or organization that receives assets from a will or insurance policy.
Billing Cycle	Specific timely intervals at which bills (or statements) are calculated and distributed.
Bond	A certificate that guarantees the payment of principal plus a specified amount of interest by a certain time.
Broker	An individual who sells investments for a commission or fee.
Budget	A written plan indicating the amount of income and expenses for a given period of time.
Capital Gain	Amount of money made from the sale of assets.
Capital Loss	Amount of money lost from the sale of assets.
Cash Flow	The amount of money remaining after taxes and expenses.
Cash Flow Statement	A written record showing income and expenses over a given period of time; see income statement.
Cash Surrender Value	The money that a person receives when he voluntarily terminates a cash value life insurance policy or an annuity before the maturity date.
Cash Value Insurance	Term insurance with a built in savings plan.
Certificate	A legal document showing ownership or endorsement to perform professional services.
Certificate of Deposit (CD)	A bank document for a specified amount and guaranteed interest rate.
Certified Public Accountant (CPA)	A person that has meet the states legal requirements for preparing taxes.
Certified Financial Planner (CFP)	A person that has met requirements from the Institute of Certified Financial Planners for preparing a program involving a client's investments, insurance programs, and taxes.
Charge Account	An arrangement between a business and a customer in which a customer receives goods or services before payment.

Check	A document written by an individual or institution for the payment of services or goods debited to a checking account.
Checkbook	A book containing a number of blank checks issued to a depositor by a bank.
Checkbook Register	A book for recording formal or official entries (numbers, dates, amounts) for bank transactions.
Checking Account	An account that allows checks to be written against funds on deposit in a bank.
Codicil	A written document amending a will by adding, striking, or otherwise changing the terms or provisions of that will previously drawn by the same individual.[1]
Compounding	The process of paying interest on principal plus interest on accrued interest for prior periods of time; interest may be compounded daily, monthly, quarterly, semi-annually, annually, etc.
Consumer Price Index (CPI)	A statistical method to evaluate the change in the cost of living for consumers as measured by the US Bureau of Labor Statistics.
Cost of Living Adjustment (COLA)	An adjustment of income that corresponds to the cost of living based upon the consumer price index.
Coverage	The extent of protection provided by an insurance policy.
Credit	Trust in a customer's ability to pay for goods or services; funds deposited in a client's bank account.
Credit Bureau	An agency that has access to credit information on perspective customers.
Credit Card	A card allowing the holder full or partial payments from month to month and charges interest on the balance owed.
Credit Line/ Credit Limit	The maximum limit of credit available to a customer; also known as Line of Credit.
Creditor	A person or institution who lends money.
Credit Rating	A record of a consumer's credit history.
Credit Worthy	A person or business having an acceptable credit rating.
Dead Storage	An area where records or documents that are no longer current are kept.

Making Ends Meet Plus More   ©1996 by John M. Orth, Iowa City, IA.   359

Debt	The amount owned by a consumer.
Debtor	A person or business who owes money.
Deduction	An amount that is subtracted from the total.
Deferred Payment	An agreement to receive goods or services in exchange for the borrower's promise to pay at a future date.
Delinquency Assessment	A fee charged an individual or business for a late payment.
Depreciation	Writing off the cost of an asset over a given time period.
Discretionary Income	The amount of money remaining after essential budget expenses (housing, food, transportation, insurance, etc.) have been paid.
Disposable Income	The amount of money remaining after taxes, social security, and retirement expenses have been paid; also known as net spendable income.
Diversification	To reduce risk by investing in several different companies or securities.
Dividend	A timely payment made to shareholders reflecting the profits of a company.
Dollar Cost Averaging	A system of accumulating wealth by investing specific and equal amounts of money at fixed intervals of time.
Durable Power of Attorney	A legal document authorizing one person to act on behalf of another; the document becomes or remains in effect should the individual later become disabled or incompetent.
Equity	The amount of money accumulated in assets (houses) after all mortgages and liabilities have been paid.
Estate	The entire assets and liabilities of a deceased person.
Estate Plan/ Estate Planning	A system of organizing and providing for the transfer of assets upon a person's death with limited tax assessment and court involvement.
Estate Tax	A tax assessed against the estate of a decedent, rather than again the share of one who has inherited property.[*1]
Executor/ Executrix	The person or institution assigned to carry out the intent of a will.

★From <u>Your Worldly Possessions</u>, The McGraw-Hill Companies, ● 1992. Used by permission.

360   Solving Your Financial Puzzle

Family of Funds	A group of mutual funds managed by the same investment company that allows you to change from one investments type to another within the company with no or little cost.
Family Trust	A trust that provides income to a spouse; upon his/her death the assets are automatically distributed to the children.
Federal Deposit Insurance Corporation (FDIC)	A federal agency that insures customer deposits up to $100,000 in member banks.
Federal Estate Tax	The death tax that may be assessed by the federal government against an estate of the decedent at the time of his or her death.[*1]
Federal Insurance Contribution Act (FICA)	Federal legislation that requires employers to withhold a tax for social security from the wages of each employee.
Fiduciary	A person, company, or organization who holds a position of trust for another.
Finance Charge	An amount of money owed to a creditor which includes the initial cost, interest, and service changes; the Truth in Lending Act mandates that this be disclosed to the customer in advance.
Finance Company	A company that makes loans to individuals or businesses.
Financial Plan	A written analysis of an individual's or business's current financial status and a plan of action to meet immediate and future financial needs, objectives, and goals.
Financial Planner	A professional who analyzes the current financial status and plans a course of action to meet immediate and future financial needs of a customer.
Financial Statement	A summary record showing the financial status of an individual or business.
Fixed Expenses	Budget expenditures that remain constant.
Fixed Value	An asset that cannot grow or decrease in value; for example, a certificate of deposit.
Grace Period	The period of time to make payments without incurring finance charges with loans or cancellation when referring to insurance policies.

Making Ends Meet Plus More

Heir	An individual or institution who receives assets or benefits from a deceased person as provided by will or law.
Household Inventory	An accurate record of all contents and possessions of a home with current value and original costs for individual items.
Illiquid	Assets or possessions that are not readily converted into cash.
Income Statement	A summary record of an individual's or company's income and expenses for a specific period of time; see cash-flow statement.
Individual Retirement Account	A retirement provision established by law that allows an individual to deduct from his/her income up to $2,000 annually for future retirement; also known as an Individual Retirement Arrangement.
Inflation	The increase of price levels in relation to the supply of goods and services.
Inheritance Tax	A state death tax assessed against one who inherits property from another who died either with or without a will.[1]
Insurance	A legal binding contract sustained by premium payments to guarantee protection against loss.
Interest	Money charged for the use of money at a percentage rate of the initial loan amount.
Intestate	The estate of a person who dies without a will.[1]
Inventory	A record of assets; (see Household Inventory).
Investment	Money, property or other assets necessary for future well-being and financial security.
Investment Company	A business or corporation that professionally manages stocks, bonds, etc. for individuals; it provides a wide variety of services and management opportunities.
Investment Income	Money received from indirect income (interest, royalties, dividends, etc.).
Investment Program	A plan of action for financial investments to meet future needs.
Investor	Anyone who dedicates money in investments for future gains.
Joint Tenancy	Two or more persons holding title to property jointly with equal rights; the survivor(s) is/are to receive the entire property upon the death of the first joint tenant.

★From Your Worldly Possessions, The McGraw-Hill Companies, © 1992. Used by permission.
Solving Your Financial Puzzle

Letters of Administration	A short, usually one-page document issued under seal by the clerk or officer of the court showing the appointment and qualification of a fiduciary to act as executor, administrator, conservator, guardian, personal representative, or trustee of an estate proceeding; also known as Letters of Appointment and Letters Testamentary.[*1]
Letter of (last) Instruction	A letter, which is not a legal or binding document, that is usually placed with a will and contains the testator's personal requests and final comments as well as specific information regarding such things as funeral arrangement provisions, location of assets and documents, list of advisors and other significant people, and the like.
Liabilities	A financial debt or obligations.
Lien	The right of a creditor to place a claim against a property as security for debt.
Limited Partner	A passive investor who has limited personal liability in a partnership; usually limited to the amount of his/her investment.
Limited Partnership	A form of business in which investors participate with limited liability for losses incurred by the partnership.
Liquidity	An individual's or company's assets that are easily converted into cash.
Marginal Tax	The amount of tax paid on the last dollar of taxable income.
Market Value	The value at which goods and services are sold on the open market.
Maturity	The date at which a bond, note, certificate of deposit, etc. is due and payable.
Money Market Account	A savings account, that can have check writing capabilities, with a depository institution that pays a money market rate of interest.
Money Market Fund	A mutual fund that invests in short term securities such as Treasury Bills, U.S. Government Issues, etc.
Mortgage	A promise of property to a creditor as collateral for the payment of a loan.
Mortgagee	The lender of money for a mortgage.
Mortgagor	The borrower of money for a mortgage.
Mutual Fund	A investment company that raises money by selling shares and invests in a diversified portfolio of stocks, bonds, commodities, etc.

Net Spendable Income	See disposable income.
Networth	The total amount of all assets minus liabilities.
Nonliquid	See illiquid.
Obligation	A financial debt to repay goods or services.
Periodic Expenses	Expenses paid regularly at specific times of the year (quarterly, semi-annual, annual, etc.).
Portfolio	A diversified holding of securities (stocks, bonds, mutual funds, etc.) by an individual or institution.
Post	Transferring financial information from a journal entry into a permanent record book.
Power of Attorney	A legal document authorizing someone to act in the best interest of another.
Premium	The amount paid to an insurance company for the purpose of securing a policy.
Present Value	The value of a future asset in today's dollars (example: the present value of $1000 to be received 10 years from now is approximately $247.18, using a discount rate equal to 15% compounded annually).
Prime Rate	The lowest rate of interest that banks charge their most credit worthy customers.
Principal	Money owed on a loan excluding interest; face value of a bond.
Probate	The legal action through the judicial system to establish that a deceased person's will is valid and to appoint an administrator to carry out the instructions stated in the will.
Property and Casualty Insurance	Insurance covering loss, damage, or replacement of property such as homes, automobiles, recreational vehicles, etc.
Qualified Retirement Plan	An individual retirement plan that complies with the rules and regulations of the Internal Revenue Code; in most cases contributions are tax-deductible and earnings accumulate tax-deferred until withdrawn at retirement or termination of employment.
Revolving Credit	The situation whereby the loan is not paid in full and finance charges accumulate on the remaining balance.

Rule of 72	A simple financial formula for calculating the period of time it takes an investment to double at a given rate of return (example: an investment earning 8% will double in nine years since 72 ÷ 8 = 9).
Speculator	A person who engages in high risk investments and is willing to assume a loss for the opportunity of achieving greater financial rewards.
Stock	A certificate which indicates ownership in a corporation through a defined number of shares.
Stockbroker	A person who buys, sells, and trades stocks, bonds, mutual funds, etc. on the behalf of clients and receives a commission for the transactions.
Stock Certificate	A legal document that defines the number of shares of stock owned.
Stockholder	An individual, business, or organization that owns shares of stock in a corporation; also called a shareholder or shareowner.
Tax Deferral	Delaying the payment of tax on investments until action is taken at a later time.
Tax Shelter	A means of investing to legally reduce or avoid the payment of taxes.
Tenancy by the Entirety	A form of holding title to real property by husband and wife whereby, upon the death of the first tenant, title to the property automatically passes to the surviving spouse to the exclusion of other heirs or beneficiaries.[*1]
Tenancy in Common	A form of holding title to property by two or more persons in such an arrangement that upon the death of the first tenant, title to the property passes, not to the surviving tenant(s), but instead to the heirs or beneficiaries of the deceased tenant.[*1]
Term Insurance	Insurance without an attached savings program and is in force for a defined period of time.
Testate	The estate of a person who dies leaving a will.[*1]
Testator	One who makes a will or one who dies leaving a will.[*1]
Trust	A legal document that places ownership of property in the name of another party (individual or institution) called the trustee for the use and benefit of some other party (beneficiary).

Unified Credit	One of the items (credits) deductible from the gross federal estate tax in order to arrive at the net federal estate tax. The unified credit for the year 1987 and thereafter (unless the law is hereafter changed) is $192,800. This sum is equivalent to the federal estate tax exemption of $600,000.[1]
Variable Assets	Assets that have the potential to appreciate and depreciate in value; examples include: stocks, mutual funds, real estate, commodities, etc.
Variable Expenses	Expenses capable of changing in periods of time and also in amount (holiday gifting, vacations, major emergencies, etc.); sometimes referred to as "periodic" expenses.
Variable Rate Loan	A debt that changes with changes in the index rate.
Vested	The gradual increase of employee ownership rights to receive employer contributed benefits from a profit-sharing, pension, or other qualified retirement plan.
Warranty	A guarantee on a product by the seller to cover workmanship, parts, and service for a stated period of time; the insured's written guarantee that all statements are true and complete when applying for an insurance policy and that the insured will fulfill all conditions as stated.
Will	A legal document that states the last testament of an individual for the purpose of disposing of all assets upon his/her death.
Yield	Investment income received as interest or dividends and expressed as a percentage of the current market (selling) price.

---

[1]Reproduced with the permission of The McGraw-Hill Companies from Your Worldly Possessions - A Complete Guide To Preserving, Passing On, And Inheriting Property by Theodore L. Kubicek. The McGraw-Hill Companies (New York, 1992) 297-309.

APPENDIX G

INDEX

Solving Your Financial Puzzle

ACKNOWLEDGEMENTS

Adult Financial Management Matrix (no longer in print), © late 1970's by the American Council of Life Insurance and the U.S. Department of Agriculture Extension Service, Washington, D.C. Adapted by Permission.

Jackson, Michael. The MacMillian Book of Business & Economic Quotations (pages 51 and 59), © 1984 by MacMillian Publishing Company. Reprinted by permission from Simon & Schuster.

Kubicek, Theodore L. Your Worldly Possessions (pages 297 - 309), © 1992 by The McGraw-Hill Companies. Reprinted by permission.